lonely planet

Pocket

LONDON

TOP SIGHTS • LOCAL LIFE • MADE EASY

Damian Harper

In This Book

QuickStart Guide

Your keys to understanding the city – we help you decide what to do and how to do it

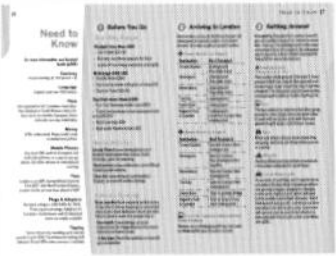

Need to Know
Tips for a smooth trip

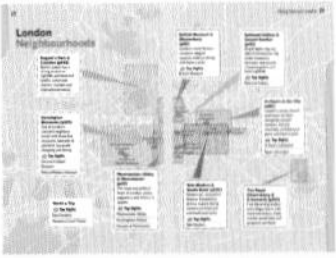

Neighbourhoods
What's where

Explore London

The best things to see and do, neighbourhood by neighbourhood

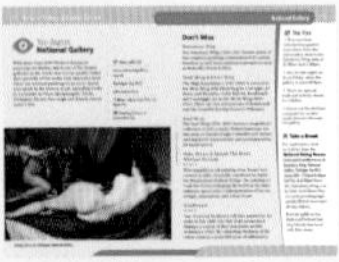

Top Sights
Make the most of your visit

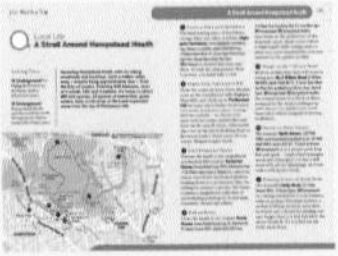

Local Life
The insider's city

The Best of London

The city's highlights in handy lists to help you plan

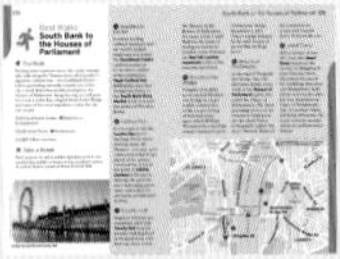

Best Walks
See the city on foot

London's Best...
The best experiences

Survival Guide

Tips and tricks for a seamless, hassle-free city experience

Getting Around
Travel like a local

Essential Information
Including where to stay

Our selection of the city's best places to eat, drink and experience:

◉ Sights

✖ Eating

◯ Drinking

✪ Entertainment

🏠 Shopping

These symbols give you the vital information for each listing:

📞 Telephone Numbers	👪 Family-Friendly
🕐 Opening Hours	🐾 Pet-Friendly
🅿 Parking	🚌 Bus
🚭 Nonsmoking	⛴ Ferry
@ Internet Access	Ⓜ Metro
📶 Wi-Fi Access	Ⓢ Subway
🍴 Vegetarian Selection	⊖ London Tube
📖 English-Language Menu	🚋 Tram
	🚆 Train

Find each listing quickly on maps for each neighbourhood:

Bar Hemingway
16 ◯ Map p233, B2

Legend has it that Hem
self, wielding a machine
rate this timber-pan
ered bar during
showpiece is a
en by Papa ar
town. Dress
s.com; Hôtel Rit
🕐6.30pm-2a

6 ◉ Plac

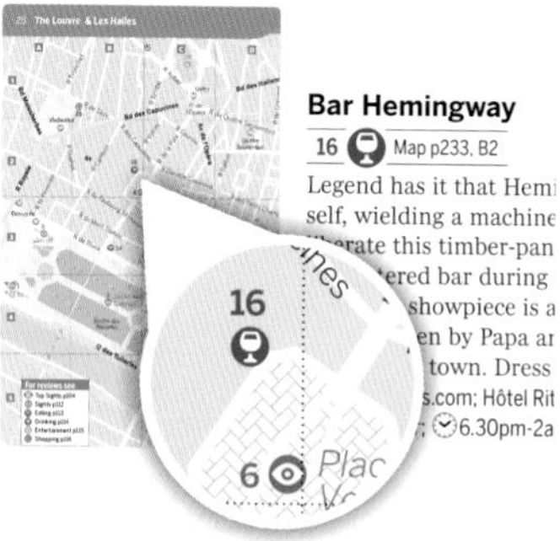

Lonely Planet's London

Lonely Planet Pocket Guides are designed to get you straight to the heart of the city.

Inside you'll find all the must-see sights, plus tips to make your visit to each one really memorable. We've split the city into easy-to-navigate neighbourhoods and provided clear maps so you'll find your way around with ease. Our expert authors have searched out the best of the city: walks, food, nightlife and shopping, to name a few. Because you want to explore, our 'Local Life' pages will take you to some of the most exciting areas to experience the real London.

And of course you'll find all the practical tips you need for a smooth trip: itineraries for short visits, how to get around, and how much to tip the guy who serves you a drink at the end of a long day's exploration.

It's your guarantee of a really great experience.

Our Promise

You can trust our travel information because Lonely Planet authors visit the places we write about, each and every edition. We never accept freebies for positive coverage, so you can rely on us to tell it like it is.

QuickStart Guide 7

Explore London 21

Worth a Trip:

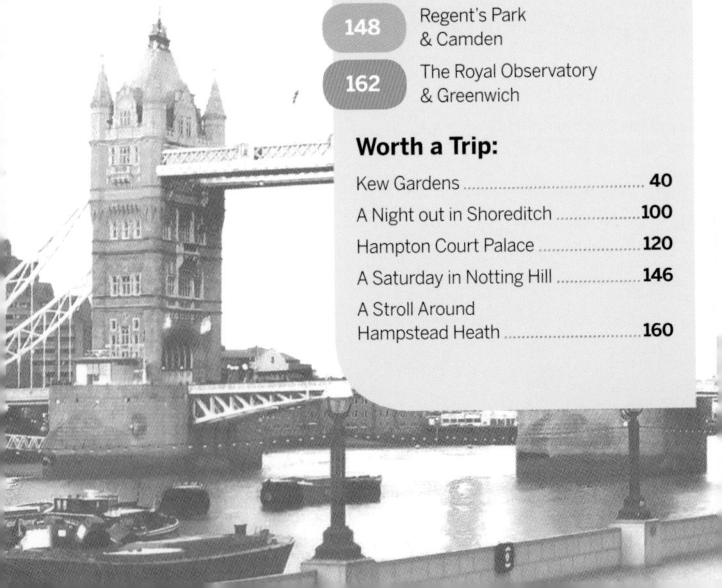

The Best of London 173

Londons Best Walks

Londons Best...

Survival Guide 209

QuickStart Guide

Welcome to London

London has something for everyone, from art to grand museums, dazzling architecture, royalty, diversity, glorious parks and irrepressible pizazz. It's immersed in history, but London is also a tireless innovator of culture and creative talent, while a cosmopolitan dynamism makes it quite possibly the world's most international city, yet one that remains somehow intrinsically British.

Millennium Bridge (p111) designed by architect Sir Norman Foster and sculptor Sir Anthony Caro and St Paul's Cathedral (p82)
KIMBERLEY COOLE/LONELY PLANET IMAGES ©

London Top Sights

British Museum (p64)

With five million visitors annually, the British Museum is London's most popular tourist attraction – a vast and hallowed collection of artefacts, art and antiquity. You could spend a lifetime here and still make discoveries.

National Gallery (p44)

This superlative collection of (largely pre-modern) art is one of the world's largest; with some of the most outstanding artistic talent, including Leonardo da Vinci, Michelangelo, Turner, Monet, Renoir, Van Gogh and more.

Tower of London (p86)

With a palpable sense of ancient history at every turn, few parts of the UK are as steeped in myth or as impregnated with legend and superstition as the titanic stonework of this fabulous fortress.

Tate Modern (p104)

Housed in a former power station, this modern art collection enjoys a triumphant position right on the Thames. The Tate Modern is a vigorous statement of modernity and architectural renewal.

Victoria & Albert Museum (p126)

You could virtually spend your entire trip in this magnificent South Kensington museum dedicated to the decorative arts and still be astounded by its variety and depth.

Natural History Museum (p130)

With its animatronic *T. rex*, towering diplodocus skeleton, Wildlife Garden and Gothic fairy tale architecture, this museum is a work of great curatorial imagination.

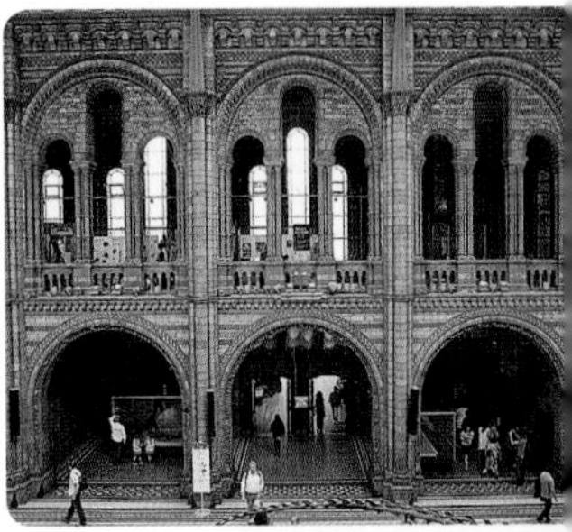

Westminster Abbey (p24)

Adorers of medieval ecclesiastic architecture will be in seventh heaven at this sublime abbey and sacred place of coronation for England's sovereigns. Get in the queue early.

Houses of Parliament (p30)

There's nothing as magnificent or more London than the sublime view of Big Ben and the Houses of Parliament from the River Thames, especially when the sun is shining on its fabulous facade.

St Paul's Cathedral (p82)

This astonishing church is renowned, but a visit to its consecrated ground promises a full appreciation. The climb up into the dome is rewarded with some truly majestic views at the top.

Buckingham Palace (p28)

That the hoi polloi is able to breach this imperious, blue-blooded bastion is remarkable enough in itself. For royal enthusiasts, the palace is a superlative highlight of London.

JANE SWEENEY/LONELY PLANET IMAGES ©

SIMON GREENWOOD/LONELY PLANET IMAGES ©

Kew Gardens (p40)

Where else in London can you size up an 18th-century ten-storey Chinese pagoda and a Japanese gateway while finding yourself among one of the world's most outstanding botanical collections?

Hampton Court Palace (p120)

Henry VIII's well-preserved Tudor palace, gardens and maze by the River Thames makes for a stunning escape from urban London, but put aside a day to do it justice.

London Local Life

Insider tips to help you find the real cit

After ticking off the top sights, get a more intimate sense of London and what make it tick – explore the city's hip nightlife, its literary quarters, epic heathland, riverside charms, individual and striking shops as well as its boho heritage.

A Stroll Around Soho (p46)

- Historic squares
- Creative vitality

At the heart of the West End, Soho's web of streets compresses culture, vitality, charm, shopping and diversity into a fascinating neighbourhood. Start in Chinatown and thread your way through historic squares, unique shops, back streets and markets to a drink in a celebrated Soho bar.

A Literary Walk Around Bloomsbury (p68)

- Georgian squares
- Literary heritage

Luminaries of the written word – Virginia Woolf, TS Eliot, Ted Hughes *et al* – have all left their mark on this part of London indelibly associated with literary circles. Spend a day discovering the bookish charms of this elegant part of town, concluding with a drink in a historic pub.

A Night out in Shoreditch (p100)

- Pubs and clubs
- Late night snacking

Put sightseeing on hold as the sun sinks over Shoreditch for a fun and exuberant night out. This part of town fully comes alive at evening, with gastropubs, clubs and converted Victorian drinking holes welcoming gregarious crowds and night owls looking for excitement on either side of the witching hour.

Shopping Around Chelsea & Knightsbridge (p134)

- Unique shops
- Art and architecture

The well-heeled streets of Chelsea and Knightsbridge harbour a select choice of shops for every one, from the bibliophile to those on the hunt for painfully stylish fashion accessories. Explore Harrods, pass some gorgeous architecture then relax at one the city's most characteristic pubs.

A Saturday in Notting Hill (p146)

- Market life
- Stylish street life

Save a visit to Notting Hill for the weekend and

Soho Square (p47)

ıtch the area at its best. verything revolves :ound the lively hub f Portobello Market › make browsing and ıopping your calling for ıe day, interlaced with ›me fine dining and a ass at one of the neigh- ›urhood's best pubs.

Stroll Around ampstead Heath ›160)

Panoramic views
Hampstead style

esert the urban density central London for e town's most famous eath. Start your jour- y in London's most ıblime cemetery before ımbing to wide-angle ews over town and ossing Hampstead Heath. Conclude your stroll discovering local architectural gems and relaxing with a meal and a drink.

A Taste of Greenwich (p164)

▶ Snacking, dining and drinking
▶ Savouring local culture

The good-looking streets and architecture of Greenwich were designed to be explored. Go beyond the big-ticket sights to sample more of the unique flavours of this riverside neighbourhood, going under the Thames, browsing Greenwich Market, dining in a brewery and enjoying drinks by the river.

Other great places to experience the city like a local:

Afternoon Tea in Bloomsbury (p75)

Speakers' Corner (p140)

Walking along Regent's Canal (p155)

Portrait (p55)

North London Sounds (p156)

Pie & Mash (p113)

Greenwich Comedy Festival (p171)

High Street Kensington (p144)

Free View (p98)

London Day Planner

Day One

First stop, **Trafalgar Square** (p50) for its architectural grandeur and photo-op views down Whitehall to Big Ben. Art lovers will head for the **National Gallery** (p44) while the **Houses of Parliament** (p30), **Westminster Abbey** (p24) and **Buckingham Palace** (p28) can all be reached on foot. If the sun's out, seize a sandwich and race to leafy **St James's Park** (p34).

Cross **Westminster Bridge** (p179) to Waterloo and, with your pre-booked ticket for the **London Eye** (p110), enjoy a revolution in the city skies and astronomical views. Sashay along the South Bank and head down into the depths of the **Tate Modern** (p104) for some grade-A art. Aim your camera at **St Paul's Cathedral** (p82) on the far side of the elegant **Millennium Bridge** (p111) and don't forget **Shakespeare's Globe** (p110).

Southwark Cathedral (p110) is well worth a gander and if **Borough Market's** (p118) open, follow your nostrils to some fine snacking on the move. Sink a drink in the historic **George Inn** (p116) off Borough High St or have theatre tickets booked for the **Globe** (p117), the **National Theatre** (p117) or the **Old Vic** (p118).

Day Two

London's finance-driven Square Mile is home to the must-see sights of **St Paul's Cathedral** (p82) and the **Tower of London** (p86). This is the oldest part of town, so there are plentiful churches and historic buildings, while innovative chunks of modern architecture also pierce the sky. Don't overlook the **Museum of London** (p92) if there's time and, of course, views of iconic **Tower Bridge** (p92).

Stand amid the swirling traffic at **Piccadilly Circus** (p50) before exploring bustling **Chinatown** (p46) and historic **Soho** (p46), then head to **Covent Garden Piazza** (p51) to watch the street performers and shop. Alternatively, save some calories for the immensity of the **British Museum** (p64) or embark on a tour of the literary heritage of the area (see p68).

Relax on the grass of **Green Park** (p35) or **St James's Park** (p34) as lights prepare to sparkle across the West End. Squeeze into **French House** (p47) for a quick drink, aim for one of the neighbourhood's outstanding dining options and have theatre tickets booked way ahead for a hit musical in London's 'theatreland'.

Short on time?

We've arranged London's must-sees into these day-by-day itineraries to make sure you see the very best of the city in the time you have available.

Day Three

Explore the **Victoria & Albert Museum** (p126) or the **Natural History Museum** (p130), before roaming around **Hyde Park** (p138) and **Kensington Gardens** (p138). For full-on historic grandeur, earmark **Apsley House** (p139), **Wellington Arch** (p139), **Royal Albert Hall** (p144), **Albert Memorial** (p139) and **Kensington Palace** (p138) for exploration. **Notting Hill** (p146) is well worth a small detour, or alternatively head to **Knightsbridge** (p134) to join the crowds in **Harrods** (p135). Have a table booked at **Zuma** (p141) or **Launceston Place** (p140).

Greenwich's (p162) architectural and maritime sights are world-renowned, along with lovely village charms and some tremendous pubs. Sights such as the **Royal Observatory** (p167), **National Maritime Museum** (p167) and **Old Royal Naval College** (p168) are near each other, so sightseeing can easily be done on foot.

In the evening, head out to **Shoreditch** (p100) for a taste of its quirky bars and throbbing nightlife options.

Day Four

Devote a morning of sightseeing to **Kew Gardens** (p40): check out its magnificent Victorian glasshouse architecture, unusual 18th-century Chinese pagoda and the astonishing variety of trees, shrubs and plants. Don't forget to clamber up into the treetop walkway for fabulous views. Enjoy lunch at the **Orangery** (p41).

Continue southwest for an afternoon's discovery of the glories of **Hampton Court Palace** (p120). You'll need an entire afternoon to fully explore this magnificent Tudor creation by the Thames, but don't forget to enjoy the grounds before becoming totally lost in the famous maze. Consider returning to central London by boat along the river.

For mouth-watering international dining, buzzing nightlife, live music and outstanding pubs, head north to pulsing **Camden** (p148) – weekends, especially, are hopping. An excellent choice of gastropubs, restaurants, pubs, bars and DJ-bars right across the neighbourhood concocts all the ingredients for a fun and eventful evening.

Need to Know

For more information, see Survival Guide (p209)

Currency
Pound sterling (£). 100 pence = £1

Language
English (and over 300 others)

Visas
Not required for US, Canadian, Australian, New Zealand or South African visitors for stays up to six months. European Union nationals can stay indefinitely.

Money
ATMs widespread. Major credit cards accepted everywhere.

Mobile Phones
Buy local SIM cards for European and Australian phones, or a pay-as-you-go phone. Set other phones to international roaming.

Time
London is on GMT; during British Summer Time (BST; late March to late October), London clocks are one hour ahead of GMT.

Plugs & Adaptors
Standard voltage is 230/240V AC, 50Hz. Three square pin plugs. Adaptors for European, Australasian and US electrical items are widely available.

Tipping
Tip taxi drivers by rounding up to nearest pound or up to 10%. Tip restaurant waiting staff between 10 and 15% unless service is included.

1 Before You Go

Your Daily Budget

Budget less than £60

- Dorm beds £10-30
- Markets, lunchtime specials for food
- Loads of free/cheap museums and sights

Midrange £60-150

- Double Room £100
- Two-course dinner with glass of wine £30
- Theatre Ticket £10-50

Top End more than £150

- Four-star/boutique hotel room £200
- Three-course dinner in top restaurant with wine £80-100
- Black cab trips £30
- Best-seats theatre tickets £65

Useful Websites

Lonely Planet (www.lonelyplanet.com/london) Destination information, hotel bookings, great for planning.

Visit London (www.visitlondon.com) Official London guide website.

Time Out (www.timeout.com/london) Snappy, au courant London listings.

Advance Planning

Three months Book weekend performance of top shows; dinner bookings at renowned restaurants; book tickets for must-see exhibitions; book a room at a popular hotel.

One month Check listings on www.timeout.com for fringe theatre, live music, festivals and book tickets.

A few days Check the weather on www.tfl.gov.uk/weather.

2 Arriving in London

Most visitors arrive at Heathrow Airport, 15 miles west of central London, or Gatwick Airport, 30 miles south of central London.

From Heathrow Airport

Destination	Best Transport
Covent Garden	Underground (Piccadilly Line)
Kensington	Underground (Piccadilly Line)
Bloomsbury	Underground (Piccadilly Line)
The City	Underground
South Bank	Underground
Regent's Park & Camden	Underground, Heathrow Express then Underground

From Gatwick Airport

Destination	Best Transport
Covent Garden	Gatwick Express then Underground
Kensington	Gatwick Express then Underground or easyBus
Bloomsbury	Gatwick Express then Underground
The City	Gatwick Express then Underground
South Bank	Train to London Bridge
Regent's Park & Camden	Train to King's Cross, then Underground

From St Pancras International Train Station

Station on six Underground lines; taxi rank on Midland Rd near Eurostar arrivals.

3 Getting Around

Managed by Transport for London (www.tfl.gov.uk), public transport in London is excellent, if pricey. The Underground is the most convenient form of transport; the cheapest way to travel is with an Oyster Card (p214). See p213 for more information.

Underground, Overground & DLR

The London Underground ('the tube'), Overground & DLR are, overall, the quickest and easiest ways to get about the city, if not the cheapest. The cheapest way to travel on the Underground is with an Oyster Card (p214).

Bus

The bus network is extensive but slow-going except for short hops; fares are good value if used with an Oyster card and there are plentiful night buses and 24-hour routes.

Taxi

Black cab drivers always know where they are going, but fares are steep unless you're in a group.

Bicycle

Barclays Bikes are everywhere around central London and great for short hops.

Car & Motorcycle

As a visitor, it's unlikely you'll need to drive in London. Disincentives include extortionate parking charges, congestion charges, traffic jams, high price of petrol, efficient traffic wardens and wheel clampers. But if that doesn't put you off, numerous car hire operations can be found across town from self-service, pay-as-you-drive vehicles to international firms (such as Avis and Hertz, see p215).

London Neighbourhoods

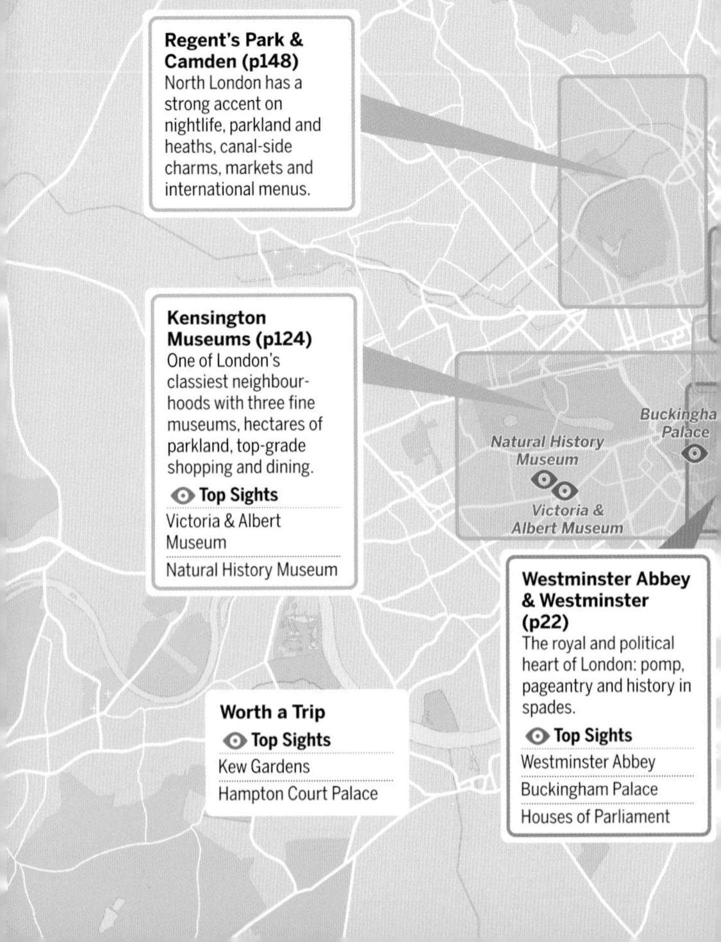

Regent's Park & Camden (p148)
North London has a strong accent on nightlife, parkland and heaths, canal-side charms, markets and international menus.

Kensington Museums (p124)
One of London's classiest neighbourhoods with three fine museums, hectares of parkland, top-grade shopping and dining.

Top Sights
- Victoria & Albert Museum
- Natural History Museum

Worth a Trip

Top Sights
- Kew Gardens
- Hampton Court Palace

Westminster Abbey & Westminster (p22)
The royal and political heart of London: pomp, pageantry and history in spades.

Top Sights
- Westminster Abbey
- Buckingham Palace
- Houses of Parliament

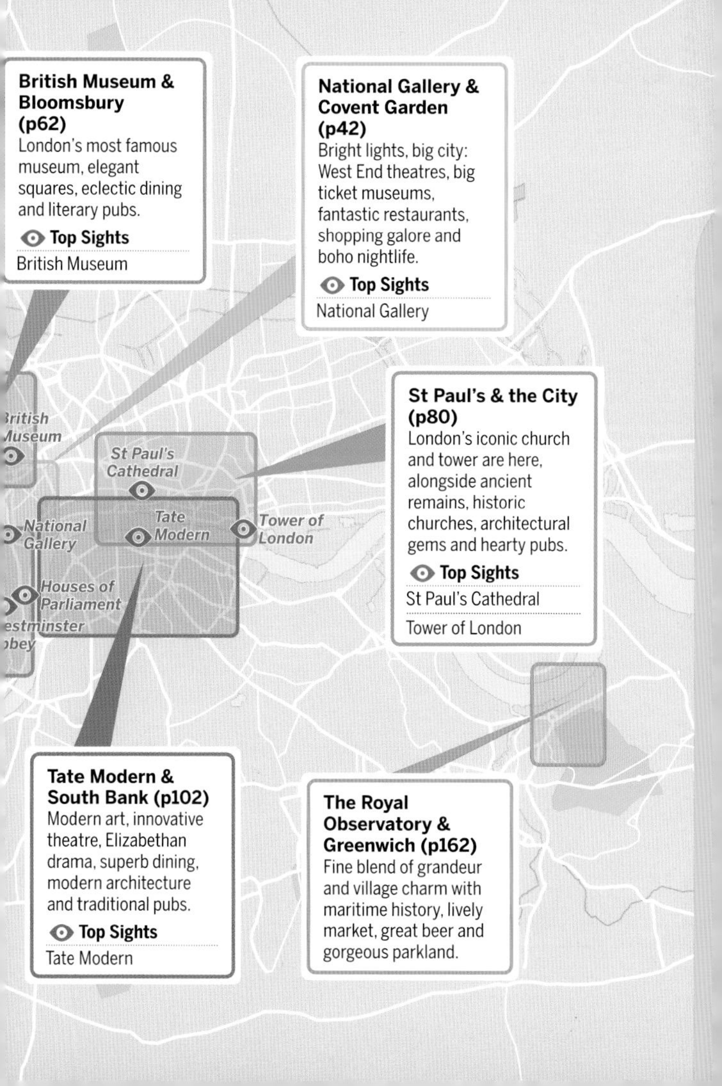

British Museum & Bloomsbury (p62)
London's most famous museum, elegant squares, eclectic dining and literary pubs.

Top Sights
British Museum

National Gallery & Covent Garden (p42)
Bright lights, big city: West End theatres, big ticket museums, fantastic restaurants, shopping galore and boho nightlife.

Top Sights
National Gallery

St Paul's & the City (p80)
London's iconic church and tower are here, alongside ancient remains, historic churches, architectural gems and hearty pubs.

Top Sights
St Paul's Cathedral
Tower of London

Tate Modern & South Bank (p102)
Modern art, innovative theatre, Elizabethan drama, superb dining, modern architecture and traditional pubs.

Top Sights
Tate Modern

The Royal Observatory & Greenwich (p162)
Fine blend of grandeur and village charm with maritime history, lively market, great beer and gorgeous parkland.

Explore London

City of London
ADINA TOVY AMSEL/LONELY PLANET IMAGES ©

Westminster Abbey & Westminster

Westminster is the political heart of London, and the level of pomp and circumstance here is astounding – state occasions are marked by convoys of gilded carriages, elaborate parades and, in the case of the opening of Parliament, by a man in a black coat banging on the front door with a jewelled sceptre. Tourists flock here to marvel at Buckingham Palace and the neo-Gothic Houses of Parliament.

The Sights in a Day

Get queuing at **Westminster Abbey** (p24) early in the day to thwart the crowds. You'll want to spend most of the morning here admiring its mighty stonework, exploring the cloisters and the Abbey's endless procession of historic grandeur but you'll also have your eye on the **Changing of the Guard** (p34) at 11.30am and the **Houses of Parliament** (p30) – either for a gander at its breathtaking brickwork, a tour or to catch a parliamentary debate; if a dose of art is high on your list, earmark the excellent **Tate Britain** (34). For lunch, dine at **Vincent Rooms** (p36) or **Cinnamon Club** (p37).

Walk north up Whitehall to take in its regal sights and if you didn't tie a visit in with the Changing of the Guard, amble west along The Mall to explore the lavish state rooms of **Buckingham Palace** (p28; open August to September). Relax afterwards in **St James's Park** (p34) before shopping around Piccadilly, including at **Fortnum & Mason** (p38) and **Burlington Arcade** (p38).

Dine at **Inn the Park** (p37) and catch an evening film at the **Institute of Contemporary Arts** (p37) or select from the astonishing palette of West End bars, pubs, theatres, cinemas and clubs in the contiguous National Gallery and Covent Garden chapter (p42).

Top Sights

Westminster Abbey (p24)
Buckingham Palace (p28)
Houses of Parliament (p30)

Best of London

Architecture

Westminster Abbey (p24)
Westminster Hall (p31)
Buckingham Palace (p28)
Houses of Parliament (p30)

Royal Events

Changing of the Guard (p34)
Changing of the Guard at the Horse Guards Parade (p35)

Eating

Vincent Rooms (p36)
Cinnamon Club (p37)

Getting There

Underground Westminster and St James's Park (both on Circle and District lines). The Jubilee line runs through Westminster.

Underground Embankment station (Circle, District, Northern and Bakerloo lines) or Charing Cross tube (Northern and Bakerloo lines). The Victoria line runs through Victoria station.

Top Sights
Westminster Abbey

Adorers of medieval, ecclesiastic architecture will be in seventh heaven at this sublime abbey and hallowed place of coronation for England's sovereigns. Within the Abbey, almost every nook and adorable cranny has a story attached to it, but few sights in London are as beautiful, or as well-preserved, as the Henry VII Lady Chapel. Elsewhere you will find the oldest door in the UK, Poet's Corner, the Coronation Chair, 14th-century cloisters, a 900-year-old garden, royal sarcophagi and much more.

Map p32, D4

www.westminster-abbey.org

adult/child £16/6

9.30am-4.30pm Mon-Fri, to 6pm Wed, to 2.30pm Sat

Westminster or St James's Park

The choir at Westminster Abbey

Don't Miss

North Transept, Sanctuarium & Quire

The north transept is often referred to as Statesmen's Aisle: politicians and eminent public figures are commemorated by staggeringly large marble statues and plaques. The Whig and Tory prime ministers who dominated late Victorian politics, Gladstone (who is buried here) and Disraeli (who is not), have their monuments uncomfortably close to one another.

Sanctuary

At the heart of the Abbey, is the sanctuary where coronations, royal weddings and funerals take place. George Gilbert Scott designed the ornate high altar in 1897. In front of the altar is a rare marble pavement dating back to 1268. It has intricate designs of small pieces of marble inlaid into plain marble.

Henry VII Lady Chapel

This spectacular chapel has a fan-vaulted ceiling, colourful heraldic banners and oak stalls. Behind the chapel's altar is the elaborate sarcophagus of Henry VII and his queen, Elizabeth of York. Opposite the entrance to the Lady Chapel is the Coronation Chair, seat of coronation for almost every monarch since the late 13th century.

Tomb of Mary Queen of Scots

There are two small chapels either side of Lady Chapel with the tombs of famous monarchs: on the left is where Elizabeth I and her half-sister 'Bloody Mary' rest. On the right is the tomb of Mary Queen of Scots, beheaded on the orders of her cousin Elizabeth and with the acquiescence of her son, the future James I.

Top Tips

- Crowds are almost as solid as the Abbey's unshakeable stonework, so get to the front of the queue first thing in the morning.
- Hop on one of the 90-minute tours (7654 4834; £3) led by vergers and departing from the north door.
- Grab an audio-guide, free with your individual entry tickets at the north door.

Take a Break

You can get drinks and snacks at the **Coffee Club** in the Abbey's Great Cloister; you're allowed to take them to the College Garden for quiet enjoyment but not inside the buildings.

Not far from the Abbey, the **Vincent Rooms** (p36) is the place to go for top-notch modern European cuisine at rock-bottom prices.

Shrine of St Edward the Confessor

The most sacred spot in the Abbey lies behind the high altar; access is generally restricted to protect the 13th-century floor. St Edward was the founder of the Abbey and the original building was consecrated a few weeks before his death. His tomb was slightly altered after the original was destroyed during the Reformation. Verger's tours access the shrine.

Poets Corner

The south transept contains Poet's Corner, where many of England's finest writers are buried and/or commemorated. The first poet to be buried here was Geoffrey Chaucer, joined later by Tennyson, Charles Dickens, Robert Browning, Rudyard Kipling and other great names. Admire the 700-year old frescoes on the wall.

Cloisters

Providing access to the monastic buildings, the quadrangular cloisters – dating largely from the 13th to 15th centuries – would have once been a very active part of the Abbey, busy with monks. The cloisters also afford access to the Chapter House, the Pyx Chamber and the Abbey Museum, situated in the vaulted undercroft.

Chapter House

The octagonal Chapter House has one of Europe's best-preserved medieval tile floors and retains traces of religious murals. Used as a meeting place by the House of Commons in the second half of the 14th century, it also boasts what is claimed to be the oldest door in the UK – it's been there 950 years.

Pyx Chamber

Next to the Chapter House and off the East Cloister, the Pyx Chamber is one of the few remaining relics of the original Abbey and contains the Abbey's treasures and liturgical objects. Note the enormous trunks, which were made inside the room and used to store valuables from the Exchequer.

Abbey Museum

Next door to the Pyx Chamber, this museum exhibits the death masks of generations of royalty, wax effigies representing Charles II and William III, as well as armour and stained glass.

College Garden

To reach the 900-year-old **College Garden** (⏲10am-6pm Tue-Thu Apr-Sep, to 4pm Tue-Thu Oct-Mar), enter Dean's Yard and the Little Cloisters off Great College St. It occupies the site of the Abbey's first infirmary garden for cultivating medicinal herbs, established in the 11th century.

Sir Isaac Newton's Tomb

On the western side of the cloister is Scientists' Corner, where you will find Sir Isaac Newton's tomb; a nearby section of the northern aisle of the nave is known as Musicians' Aisle, where Baroque composers Henry Purcell and John Blow are buried.

Understand

History of Westminster Abbey

Although a mixture of architectural styles, Westminster Abbey is considered the finest example of Early English Gothic (1180–1280). The original church was built in the 11th century by King (later St) Edward the Confessor, who is buried in the chapel behind the main altar. Henry III (r 1216–72) began work on the new building but didn't complete it; the French Gothic nave was finished in 1388. Henry VII's huge and magnificent chapel was added in 1519.

Benedictine Monastery & Dissolution

The Abbey was initially a monastery for Benedictine monks. Many of the building's features attest to this collegial past (the octagonal chapter room, the Quire and cloisters). In 1540, Henry VIII separated the Church of England from the Catholic Church and dissolved the monastery. The King became head of the Church of England and the Abbey acquired its 'royal peculiar' status (administered directly by the Crown and exempt from any ecclesiastical jurisdiction).

Site of Coronation

With the exception of Edward V and Edward VIII, every English sovereign has been crowned here since William the Conqueror in 1066, and most of the monarchs from Henry III (died 1272) to George II (died 1760) were also buried here.

The Quire

The Quire, a sublime structure of gold, blue and red Victorian Gothic by Edward Blore, dates back to the mid-19th century. It sits where the original choir for the monk's worship would have been but bears no resemblance to the original. It is still used for singing but its regular occupants are the Westminster Choir.

Royal Wedding

On 29 April 2011, Prince William married Catherine Middleton at Westminster Abbey. The couple had chosen the Abbey for the relatively intimate setting of the Sanctuary – because of the Quire, three-quarters of the 1900 or so guests couldn't see a thing!

Top Sights
Buckingham Palace

The official residence of Her Royal Highness Queen Elizabeth II – Lilibet to those who know her – is a stunning piece of Georgian architecture, crammed with the kind of gold- and gem-encrusted chintz that royals like to surround themselves with. Built in 1705 as Buckingham House for the duke of the same name, the palace has been the Royal Family's London lodgings since 1837, when Queen Victoria moved in.

Map p32, A4

www.royalcollection.org.uk

Buckingham Palace Rd

adult/child £18/10

9.30am-6.30pm late Jul-late Sep

St James's Park, Victoria or Green Park

Buckingham Palace

Don't Miss

State Rooms

The route starts in the Guard Room, takes in the State Dining Room (all red damask and Regency furnishings); then moves on to the Blue Drawing Room (with a gorgeous fluted ceiling by John Nash), the White Drawing Room, where foreign ambassadors are received, and the ballroom. The Throne Room displays his-and-hers pink chairs initialled 'ER' and 'P'.

Picture Gallery & Gardens

The 76.5m-long Picture Gallery features splendid works by such artists as Van Dyck, Rembrandt, Canaletto, Poussin, Canova and Vermeer. Wandering the gardens is another highlight: admire some of the 350 or so species of flowers and plants, get beautiful views of the palace and a peek at the lake.

Queen's Gallery

Over the past half millennium, the Royal Family has amassed paintings, sculpture, ceramics, furniture and jewellery. The splendid **Queen's Gallery** (adult/child £9/4.50; ⏲10am-5.30pm) showcases some of the palace's treasures on a rotating basis, through temporary exhibitions. Entrance to the gallery is through Buckingham Gate.

Royal Mews

A short walk southwest of Buckingham Palace, the **Royal Mews** (adult/child £8/5; ⏲10am-5pm Apr-Oct, to 4pm Mon-Sat Nov-Dec) started life as a falconry but is now a working stable looking after the royals' horses, along with the opulent vehicles the monarchy uses for transport. Highlights include the magnificent gold coach of 1762 and the 1910 Glass Coach.

Top Tips

- The Changing of the Guard is highly popular, so arrive early to grab a good spot.
- If bought direct from the palace ticket office, your ticket grants free re-admission to the palace for one year; simply get your ticket stamped on your first visit.
- Combined tickets for the Queen's Gallery with the Royal Mews cost £16/9 for adult/child.
- Audioguides are included in the ticket price for all tours.

Take a Break

Within the palace, the **Garden Café** (⏲9.45am-6.30pm) on the West Terrace overlooks the lawn and lake.

In nearby St James's Park, **Inn the Park** (p37) offers both terrific British cuisine and great views.

Top Sights
Houses of Parliament

The House of Commons and House of Lords are housed here in the sumptuous Palace of Westminster. The House of Commons is where Members of Parliament (MPs) meet to propose and discuss new legislation, and to grill the prime minister and other ministers. When Parliament is in session, visitors are allowed to attend the debates in the House of Commons and the House of Lords. Even if you can't get inside, marvel at Sir Charles Barry's stunning building and its iconic tower.

Map p32, E4

www.parliament.uk

St Stephen's Entrance, St Margaret St SW1

admission free

during Parliamentary sessions

Westminster

Houses of Parliament

Don't Miss

The Towers

The most famous feature of the Houses of Parliament is the Clock Tower, commonly known as **Big Ben**. Ben is the bell hanging inside and is named after Benjamin Hall, the commissioner of works when the tower was completed in 1858. Thirteen-tonne Ben has rung in the New Year since 1924.

Westminster Hall

One of the most stunning features of the Palace of Westminster, seat of the English monarchy from the 11th to the early 16th centuries, is Westminster Hall. The building was originally built in 1099; the roof was added between 1394 and 1401 and has been celebrated as 'the greatest surviving achievement of medieval English carpentry'.

House of Commons

The layout of the Commons Chamber is based on that of St Stephen's Chapel in the original Palace of Westminster. The current chamber, designed by Giles Gilbert Scott, replaced the one destroyed by a 1941 bomb.

House of Lords

The **House of Lords** (2.30-10pm Mon & Tue, 3-10pm Wed, 11am-7.30pm Thu, 10am to close of session Fri) can be visited via the 'Strangers' Gallery'. The intricate Gothic interior led its architect, Pugin (1812–52), to an early death from overwork.

Tours

On Saturdays and when Parliament is in recess, visitors can join a 75-minute **guided tour** (booking 0844 847 1672; adult/child £15/6) of both chambers, Westminster Hall and other historic buildings.

Top Tips

- The best time to watch a debate is during Prime Minister's Question Time on Wednesday, but it's also the busiest.
- To find out what's being debated on a particular day, check the noticeboard beside the entrance, or check online at www.parliament.uk.
- It's not unusual to have to wait up to two hours to access the chambers, so give yourself time.

Take a Break

The **Jubilee Café** (10am-5.30pm Mon-Fri, 10am-6pm Sat) near the north door of Westminster Hall serves hot drinks and snacks.

Elegant and inviting **Cinnamon Club** (p37) is within strolling distance for stunning Indian cuisine.

Strand
Trafalgar Square
Trafalgar Square
Charing Cross
Charing Cross
Villiers St
Craven St
Northumberland Ave
Great Scotland Yard
Whitehall Pl
Whitehall Ct
Horse Guards Ave
Victoria Embankment
Richmond Tce
Whitehall
Banqueting House
5
Horse Guards Parade
7
Spring Gdns
Whitehall
Cockspur St
Pall Mall
Suffolk St
Haymarket
St Alban's St
Regent St
Britain Visitor Centre
Charles II St
ST JAMES'S
Carlton House Tce
Carlton Gardens
The Mall
15
13
Downing St
Horse Guards Rd
King Charles St
2
Cabinet War Rooms & Churchill Museum
Westminster Pier
Westminster
Great George St
Parliament Sq
Parliament Sq
St Margaret
Big Ben
Houses of Parliament
Westminster Abbey
Old Queen St
Dartmouth St
St James's
St James's Park Lake
St James's Park
4
Jermyn St
St James's Sq
St James's Sq
Ormond Yard
White's
10
White Cube Gallery
Pall Mall
Marlborough Rd
Cleveland Row
8
St James's Palace
Stable Yard Rd (Private)
Queen Victoria Memorial
Birdcage Walk
Spur Rd
Piccadilly
Royal Academy of Arts
9
16
Duke St
20
Bury St
19
St James's St
King St
Park Pl
St James's Pl
Burlington Arc
17
18
Old Bond St
14
Albemarle St
Dover St
Piccadilly
21
Berkeley St
Green Park
Queen's Walk
Green Park
6
Green Park
Constitution Hill
3
Changing of the Guard
Buckingham
A
B
C
D
E
1
2
3
4

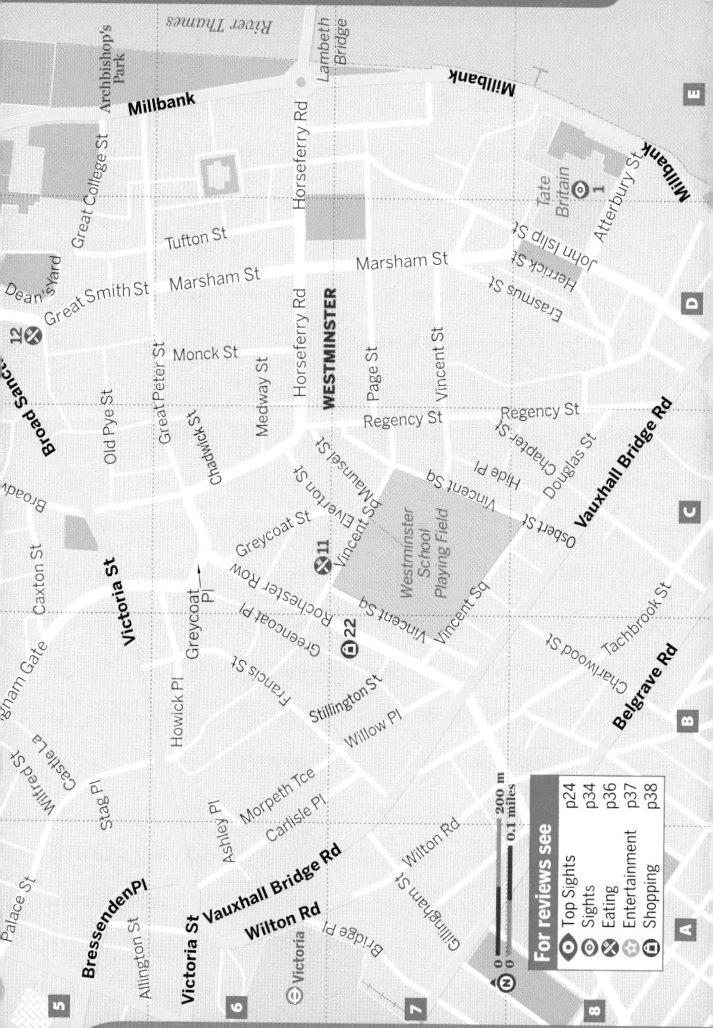
River Thames
Archbishop's Park
Lambeth Bridge
Millbank
Great College St
Horseferry Rd
Tufton St
Marsham St
Dean's Yard
Great Smith St
Tate Britain
1
John Islip St
Herrick St
Atterbury St
Erasmus St
12
Broad Sanctuary
Monck St
WESTMINSTER
Page St
Vincent St
Old Pye St
Great Peter St
Medway St
Chadwick St
Regency St
Chapter St
Hide Pl
Douglas St
Vauxhall Bridge Rd
Broadway
Maunsel St
Elverton St
Vincent Sq
Osbert St
Caxton St
Victoria St
Greycoat St
11
Westminster School Playing Field
Greycoat Pl
Rochester Row
Greencoat Pl
22
Tachbrook St
Charlwood St
Belgrave Rd
Buckingham Gate
Howick Pl
Francis St
Stillington St
Willow Pl
Castle La
Wilfred St
Stag Pl
Ashley Pl
Morpeth Tce
Carlisle Pl
Palace St
Bressenden Pl
Allington St
Wilton Rd
Gillingham St
Bridge Pl
Victoria
200 m
0.1 miles
For reviews see
Top Sights p24
Sights p34
Eating p36
Entertainment p37
Shopping p38
A
B
C
D
E
5
6
7
8

Sights

Tate Britain

GALLERY

1 Map p32, E8

The other, older Tate sibling, this august Portland Stone edifice on the riverside celebrates paintings from the 16th to the 20th century. It embraces works by Gainsborough, Hogarth, Constable, Francis Bacon and most famously, Turner (leaving his name to the controversial annual prize, displayed here). (www.tate.org.uk; Millbank; admission free, prices vary for temporary exhibitions, free tours; 10am-6pm, to 10pm first Friday of month, tours 11am, noon, 2pm, 3pm Mon-Fri, noon & 3pm Sat & Sun; ; Pimlico)

Cabinet War Rooms & Churchill Museum

MUSEUM

2 Map p32, D3

For much of WWII, Britain's steadfast prime minister lived like a rabbit in a warren of tunnels beneath Whitehall, coordinating the Allied resistance on a Bakelite telephone. The austere Cabinet War Rooms remain much as Churchill left them, complete with maps of Allied advances on the walls and a doodle of Adolf on the walls. The attached Churchill Museum features stirring recordings of the great orator's speeches. (cwr.iwm.org.uk; Clive Steps, King Charles St; adult/under 16yr £16/free; 9.30am-6pm, last entry 5pm; Westminster)

Changing of the Guard

CEREMONY

3 Map p32, A4

At 11.30am daily from May to July (on alternate days weather permitting from August to March), the old guard (Foot Guards of the Household Regiment) comes off duty to be replaced by the new guard on the forecourt of Buckingham Palace. Highly popular, the show lasts about half an hour (brace for crowds).

St James's Park

PARK

4 Map p32, C3

Despite its proximity to Buckingham Palace and Downing St, St James's Park remains a place for ordinary folk, feeding the ducks and tame squirrels, gawping at the pelicans and sinking into rentable deck chairs. An unexpected gem is the park's lovely allotment, which you can wander around (May to October). (The Mall; 5am-dusk; St James's Park)

Take a Break In the middle of the park is the excellent Inn the Park café (p37).

Top Tip

Tate to Tate Boat

The ultra-handy and colourful **Tate Boat** (one way adult £5) links the Tate Britain to the Tate Modern (p104) every 40 minutes from 10.17am to 5.04pm.

Horse Guards Parade

Banqueting House HISTORIC BUILDING

5 Map p32, E2

This is the only surviving part of the huge Tudor Whitehall Palace, designed by Inigo Jones as England's first purely Renaissance building, and which burned down in 1698. Charles I was executed on a scaffold built against a 1st-floor window here in 1649. In a vast hall on the 1st floor are nine ceiling panels painted by Rubens in 1635. (Whitehall SW1; adult/child £5/free; 10am-5pm Mon-Sat; Westminster)

Green Park PARK

6 Map p32, A2

Less manicured and crowded than the adjoining St James's, this park has wonderful, huge oaks and hilly meadows. It was once a duelling ground and served as a vegetable garden during WWII. (Piccadilly W1; 5am-dusk; Green Park)

Horse Guards Parade HISTORIC SITE

7 Map p32, D2

In a more accessible version of Buckingham Palace's Changing of the Guard, the mounted troopers of the Household Cavalry change guard here daily, at the official entrance to the royal palaces (opposite Banqueting House). A lite-pomp version takes place at 4pm when the dismounted guards are changed. This will be the pitch for the beach volleyball during the London 2012 Olympics. (Changing of the Guard 11am Mon-Sat, 10am Sun; Westminster)

Understand

No 10 Downing Street

It's charming that the official seat of the British prime minister is a bog-standard Georgian town-house in Whitehall. Unless you have permission to file a petition, however, the closest you'll get to the famous black door is the gate on Whitehall (south of Banqueting House on the other side of the road). (www.number10.gov.uk; 10 Downing St; ⊖Westminster or Charing Cross)

St James's Palace

PALACE

8 Map p32, B2

The striking Tudor gatehouse of St James's Palace is the only surviving part of a building initiated by the palace-mad Henry VIII in 1530. This was the official residence of kings and queens for more than three centuries. Princess Diana hated it, living here until her divorce from Charles in 1996, when she moved to Kensington Palace (p138) (Cleveland Row SW1; closed to the public; ⊖Green Park)

Royal Academy of Arts

CULTURAL BUILDING

9 Map p32, B1

Britain's first art school was founded in 1768. The collection contains works by past and present Academicians, including John Constable, Sir Joshua Reynolds, JMW Turner and Norman Foster. Highlights are displayed in the John Madejski Fine Rooms, accessible by free guided tours. (www.royalacademy.org.uk; Burlington House, Piccadilly W1; 10am-6pm Sat-Thu, to 10pm Fri; ⊖Green Park)

White Cube Gallery

GALLERY

10 Map p32, B1

This white, angular sister to the Hoxton art gallery hosted Tracey Emin's first exhibition in five years, 'Those who suffer Love', in 2009. Together with Damien Hirst's 'For the Love of God' exhibition two years before, it brought back some of the publicity for the (now not-so-young) Young British Artists (YBAs). (www.whitecube.com; 25-26 Mason's Yard SW1; 10am-6pm Tue-Sat; ⊖Green Park or Piccadilly Circus)

Eating

Vincent Rooms

MODERN EUROPEAN £

11 Map p32, C6

Offer yourself up as a guinea pig for the student chefs where celebrity chef Jamie Oliver trained. Service is eager to please, the atmosphere in both the Brasserie and the Escoffier Room is smarter than expected, and the food (including excellent vegie options) ranges from wonderful to exquisite. (7802 8391; www.thevincentrooms.com; Westminster Kingsway College, Vincent Sq SW1; mains £6-10.50; lunch Mon-Fri, dinner selected evenings only; ⊖Victoria)

Cinnamon Club

INDIAN £££

12 Map p32, D5

Domed skylights, high ceilings, parquet flooring and a book-lined mezzanine concoct an atmosphere reminiscent of a colonial club. The food is sumptuous: breakfasts range from European-style eggs to Indian *uttapams* (stuffed crispy rice pancake). If money is no object, embark on a culinary adventure with one of the tasting menus. (☎7222 2555; www.cinnamonclub.com; Old Westminster Library, 30-32 Great Smith St; mains £14-32; closed Sun; St James's Park)

Inn the Park

BRITISH ££

13 Map p32, D2

This stunning wooden cafe and restaurant is run by Irish wonder chef Oliver Peyton and offers cakes and tea as well as excellent British food with a monthly-changing menu. The terrace, overlooking one of the fountains in St James's Park with views of Whitehall's grand buildings, is wonderful on spring and summer days; dinner here is lovely. (☎7451 9999; www.innthepark.com; St James's Park SW1; mains £14-19; 8am-11pm; Westminster)

Top Tip

Westminster Nightlife?

Westminster and Whitehall are totally deserted in the evenings, with little in the way of bars or restaurants. It's pretty much the same story for St James's. If you find yourself in Westminster in the early evening, head north to vibrant Soho for fantastic bars and restaurants, or to the lively streets surrounding Covent Garden.

Wolseley

BRASSERIE ££

14 Map p32, A1

This erstwhile Bentley car showroom has been transformed into an opulent Viennese-style brasserie, with golden chandeliers and stunning black-and-white tiled floors. It's a great place for spotting celebrities. Afternoon tea is a lavish affair, with the Wolseley's very own afternoon blend of English breakfast tea. (www.thewolseley.com; 160 Piccadilly W1; cream/afternoon tea £9/21; daily; Green Park)

Entertainment

Institute of Contemporary Arts

ARTS CENTRE

15 Map p32, D2

Ever since Picasso and Henry Moore had their first UK shows here, the institute has sat on the cutting edge of the British arts world, with an excellent range of shows, exhibitions and films adopting a leftfield lean. There's also the **ICA Bar & Restaurant** and an excellent bookshop. (www.ica.org.uk; The Mall SW1; noon-11pm Wed, to 1am Thu-Sat, to 9pm Sun; wi-fi; Charing Cross or Piccadilly Circus)

Burlington Arcade

Shopping

Fortnum & Mason DEPARTMENT STORE

16 Map p32, B1

This legendary store started business in 1707, recycling half-burned candles from the royal household and selling them on at a profit. Today Fortnum's is London's most elegant department store (staff still dress in old-fashioned tailcoats) – it's worth a trip just to see the window displays. Downstairs is an elegant wine bar designed by the man behind the Wolseley. (www.fortnumandmason.co.uk; 181 Piccadilly; ⊖Piccadilly Circus or Green Park)

Burlington Arcade SHOPPING CENTRE

17 Map p32, A1

On the western side of Burlington House (home of the Royal Academy of Arts) is Burlington Arcade: a long, covered shopping street built in 1819. Today it is a charming shopping precinct for the very wealthy and is most famous for the Burlington Beadles, uniformed guards who make up the 'smallest private police force in existence'. (www.burlington-arcade.co.uk; 51 Piccadilly W1; ⊖Green Park)

Penhaligon's BEAUTY

18 Map p32, A1

In an antidote to soulless duty-free shopping, Penhaligon's attendants will ask you about your favourite aromas, take you on an exploratory tour of their signature range and help you discover new scents. All products are made in Devon, England – from traditional perfumes to home fragrances and bath and body products. (www.penhaligons.com; 16-17 Burlington Arcade W1; ⊖Piccadilly or Green Park)

DR Harris

BEAUTY

19 Map p32, B1

Operating as chemist and perfumer since 1790 (and the Prince of Wales's royal pharmacist), DR Harris is the place to buy your moustache wax and grab a bottle of Crystal Eye Drops to combat red eye after a late night. It also sells a hangover cure: a bitter, herbal concoction called DR Harris Pick-Me-Up. (www.drharris.co.uk; 29 St James's St SW1; closed Sun; ⊖Green Park)

Understand

Smash & Grab

Burlington Arcade was the scene of a dramatic robbery in June 1964 when a Jaguar Mark 10 sped along the narrow arcade before disgorging masked men who made off with £35,000 worth of jewellery from the Goldsmiths and Silversmiths Association shop. The Jaguar – the only car to have ever driven down the arcade – then reversed back up the arcade and sped off.

Taylor of Old Bond Street

BEAUTY

20 Map p32, B1

Plying its trade since 1854, this shop has contributed generously to the expression 'well-groomed gentleman', stocking every conceivable sort of razor, shaving brush and flavour of shaving soap. (www.tayloroldbondst.co.uk; 74 Jermyn St SW1; closed Sun; ⊖Green Park)

Minamoto Kitchoan

FOOD

21 Map p32, A1

Walking into this Japanese sweet shop is a mind-blowing experience. *Wagashi* – Japanese sweets – are made out of all sorts of beans and rice and shaped into glazed red cherries, green-bean bunches or spiky kidney bean rolls. Sit down and enjoy with a complimentary green tea, or buy a box for a sure-hit souvenir. (www.kitchoan.com; 44 Piccadilly W1; closed Sun; ⊖Piccadilly Circus)

Shepherds

GIFTS

22 Map p32, B7

Suckers for fine stationery, leather boxes, elegant albums and exquisite paper will get their fix at this wonderful bookbindery. (www.bookbinding.co.uk; 76 Rochester Row SW1; closed Sun; ⊖Victoria)

Top Sights
Kew Gardens

Getting There

⊖ **Underground** Kew Gardens (District line and Overground).

National Rail Trains from Waterloo stop at Kew Bridge station.

River Boat Thames River Boats (www.wpsa.co.uk).

The 121-hectare gardens at Kew are the finest product of the British botanical imagination and really should not be missed. As well as being a public garden, Kew is a pre-eminent research centre, maintaining its reputation as having the largest collection of plants in the world. No worries if you don't know your golden slipper orchid from your fengoky or your quiver tree from your alang-alang, a visit to Kew is a journey of discovery for everyone.

Palm House, Kew Gardens

Don't Miss

Palm House

The enormous and iconic 700 glass-paned Palm House, a domed hothouse of metal and curved sheets of glass dating from 1848, houses a splendid display of exotic tropical greenery; the aerial walkway offers a parrots'-eye view of the lush vegetation.

Princess of Wales Conservatory

Further north, the stunning Princess of Wales Conservatory houses plants in 10 different climatic zones – everything from a desert to a mangrove swamp.

Temperate House

The beautiful Temperate House (north of the pagoda) is the world's largest surviving Victorian glasshouse, an astonishing feat of architecture housing an equally sublime collection of plants.

Rhizotron & Xstrata Treetop Walkway

In the Arboretum – a short walk from Temperate House – this fascinating and much-enjoyed walkway takes you underground and then 18 metres up in the air into the tree canopy.

Kew Palace

Red-brick **Kew Palace** (adult/child £5.30/free; 10am-5.30pm late Mar-late Oct) in the northwest of the gardens is a former royal residence, built in 1631. Don't miss the restored Georgian rooms and Princess Elizabeth's wonderful doll's house.

Chinese Pagoda

Kew's celebrated 163-ft tall, eight-sided Chinese Pagoda (1762), designed by William Chambers (who designed Somerset House), is one of the garden's architectural icons.

www.kew.org

Kew Rd TW9

adult/child £14/free

gardens 9.30am-6.30pm Mon-Fri, to 7.30pm Sat & Sun Apr-Aug, 9.30am-6pm Sep & Oct, 9.30am-4.15pm Nov-Feb, glasshouses 9.30am-5.30pm Apr-Oct, 9.30am-3.45pm Nov-Feb

/ Kew Gardens

Top Tips

- Jump aboard the Kew Explorer (adult/child £4/1) to hop on and off at stops around the grounds.
- Kids can explore the fun-filled Treehouse Towers (a great outdoor play area) and Climbers and Creepers (an interactive botanical play zone).

Take a Break

In a spiffing grade-1-listed 18th century building near Kew Palace you'll find the **Orangery** (mains £7.50-9.50; 10am-3.15pm, later in spring, summer & autumn;).

Explore

National Gallery & Covent Garden

At the centre of the West End – London's physical, cultural and social heart – the neighbourhood around the National Gallery & Covent Garden is a sightseeing mecca. This is London's busiest area, with a grand convergence of monumental history, stylish restaurants, standout entertainment choices and pubs. And if you're also in town to shop, you'll be in seventh heaven here.

The Sights in a Day

Start with the **National Gallery** (p44), but aim for a selective tour of your favourite artists. **Trafalgar Square** (p50) is perfect for a break and sublime views, but the **National Portrait Gallery** (p50) has some outstanding exhibits. Lunch can be expediently supplied by the splendid **National Dining Rooms** (p45) in the Sainsbury Wing of the National Gallery.

Walk off your meal, heading east along The Strand to browse around **Covent Garden Piazza** (p51), shopping, exploring and watching the street performers. The **London Transport Museum** (p52) is excellent, especially if you've kids. **Somerset House** (p51), a gorgeous neo-classical building containing the impressive **Courtauld Gallery** (p52) entertains with outdoor films in summer and ice-skating in winter.

Have a table booked at **Bocca di Lupo** (p53) for superb Italian dining before catching neon **Piccadilly Circus** (p50) at night. Sink a drink at **Academy** (p55) or **Gordon's Wine Bar** (p56) but ensure you have tickets for a West End musical, theatre or opera to round off the night.

For a local's day in Soho, see p46.

Top Sights

Local Life

Best of London

Getting There

⊖ **Underground** Piccadilly Circus, Leicester Sq and Covent Garden (all Piccadilly Line) or Leicester Sq, Charing Cross and Embankment (all Northern Line).

Top Sights
National Gallery

With more than 2000 Western European paintings on display, this is one of the largest galleries in the world. But it's the quality rather than quantity of the works that impresses most. There are seminal paintings from every important epoch in the history of art, including works by Leonardo da Vinci, Michelangelo, Titian, Velázquez, Turner, Van Gogh and Renoir, just to name a few.

Map p48, E5

www.nationalgallery.org.uk

Trafalgar Sq WC2

admission free

10am-6pm Sat-Thu, to 9pm Fri

Charing Cross or Leicester Sq

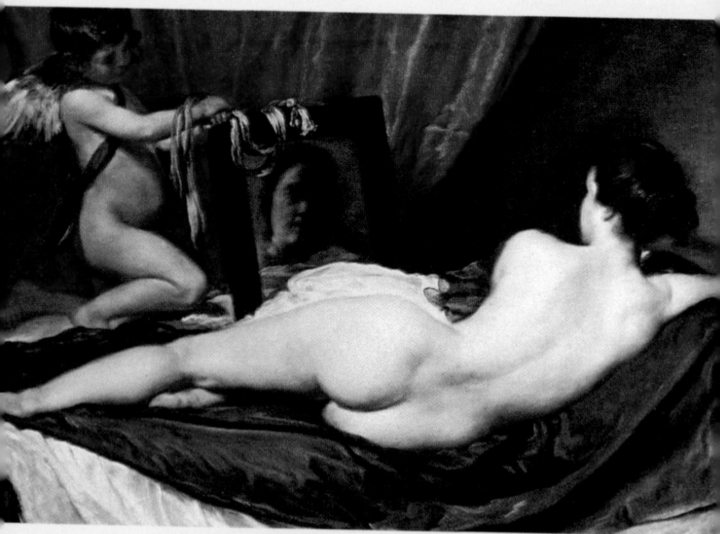

Rokeby Venus by Velázquez, National Gallery

Don't Miss

Sainsbury Wing

The Sainsbury Wing (1260–1510) houses plenty of fine religious paintings commissioned for private devotion as well more unusual masterpieces such as Boticelli's *Venus & Mars*.

West Wing & North Wing

The High Renaissance (1510–1600) is covered in the West Wing with Michelangelo, Correggio, El Greco and Bronzino, while Rubens, Rembrandt and Caravaggio are in the North Wing (1600–1700). There are two self-portraits of Rembrandt and the beautiful *Rokeby Venus* by Velázquez.

East Wing

The East Wing (1700–1900) houses a magnificent collection of 18th-century British landscape artists such as Gainsborough, Constable and Turner, and highbrow impressionist and postimpressionist masterpieces.

Rain, Steam & Speed: The Great Western Railway

ROOM 34

This magnificent oil painting from Turner was created in 1844. Generally considered to depict the Maidenhead Railway Bridge, the painting reveals the forces reshaping the world at the time: railways, speed and a reinterpretation of the use of light, atmosphere and colour in art.

Sunflowers

ROOM 45

One of several Sunflower still lifes painted by the artist in late 1888, this Van Gogh masterpiece displays a variety of then innovative artistic techniques while the saturating vividness of the colour conveys a powerful sense of affirmation.

Top Tips

- Free one-hour introductory guided tours leave from the information desk in the Sainsbury Wing daily at 11.30am and 2.30pm.
- Aim for late night visits on Friday, when the gallery is open till 9pm.
- There are special trails and activity sheets for children.
- Check out the ArtStart computer for a tailor-made itinerary through the gallery.

Take a Break

For sustenance, look no further than the **National Dining Rooms** (www.peytonandbyrne.co.uk; Sainsbury Wing, National Gallery, Trafalgar Sq WC2; mains £15; 10am-5.30pm Sat-Thu, to 8.30pm Fri) in the Sainsbury Wing, run by Irish chef Oliver Peyton and providing high-quality British food and all-day bakery.

Portrait (p55) in the National Portrait Gallery blends fine food with fine views.

Local Life
A Stroll Around Soho

Soho may come into its own in the evenings, but daytime guarantees other surprises and opportunities to be charmed by the area's bohemian and bookish leanings, vitality, diversity, architectural narratives and creative energy. Thread your way from Chinatown through intriguing backstreets, genteel squares and street markets to one of the neighbourhood's signature bars.

1 Explore Chinatown

Just north of Leicester Sq tube station are Lisle and Gerrard Sts, the focal point for London's Chinese community. A tight tangle of supermarkets, roast-duck houses and dim sum canteens, London's Chinatown isn't as big as Chinatowns in many other cities, but it's bubbly and indelibly Cantonese in flavour.

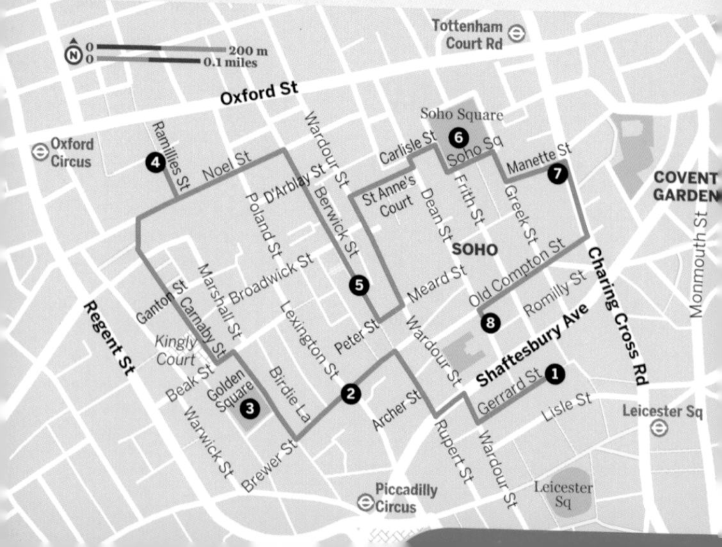

❷ Browse vintage mags

Pop into the **Vintage Magazine Store** (39-43 Brewer St) to look through its riveting range of back issue magazines, old movie posters and retro merchandise. With over a quarter of a million issues in stock, the shop is stuffed with gift ideas and treasures for collectors or just the plain curious.

❸ Relax in Golden Square

North of Brewer St, historic Golden Square – featured in Charles Dickens' *The Life and Adventures of Nicholas Nickleby* – was once part of an area called Windmill Fields, after a famous windmill that stood nearby. This lovely 17th century square was in all probability Christopher Wren's design; the garden in the middle is a relaxing place to find a bench.

❹ Visit the Photographers' Gallery

The fantastic **Photographers' Gallery** (www.photonet.org.uk; 16-18 Ramillies St W1; admission free) was set to re-open in early 2012, with three floors of exhibition space, a new cafe and a shop brimming with prints and photography books. The gallery awards the prestigious annual Deutsche Börse Photography Prize; past winners include Andreas Gursky, Boris Mikhailov and Juergen Teller.

❺ Pick up picnic supplies in Berwick Street Market

Offering a range of fruit and veg, **Berwick Street Market** (Berwick St W1; ⏲9am-5pm Mon-Sat) has managed to hang onto its prime location since the 1840s. It's a great place to put together a picnic or shop for a prepared meal. Berwick St is famously the location of the cover shot of the Oasis album, *(What's the Story) Morning Glory?*

❻ Stopover in Soho Square

Cut through tiny St Anne's Court to Dean St (where Karl Marx and his family lived from 1851 to 1856, at No 28). Leafy **Soho Square** beyond is where people come to laze in the sun on warm days. Laid out in 1681, it was originally named King's Sq, explaining the statue of Charles II standing in its northern half.

❼ Browse Foyles

Even the most obscure titles await discovery at **Foyles** (www.foyles.co.uk; 113-119 Charing Cross Rd WC2), London's legendary bookshop and a vast Charing Cross Rd institution since 1903. The lovely cafe is on the 1st floor, and Ray's Jazz Shop is up on the 5th floor.

❽ Quaff wine in French House

Walk down Old Compton St (the epicentre of the gay village) to Soho's legendary boho boozer, **French House** (www.frenchhousesoho.com; 49 Dean St W1), the meeting place of Free French Forces during WWII; de Gaulle is said to have often drunk here, while Dylan Thomas, Peter O'Toole and Francis Bacon frequently ended up horizontal.

A
B
C
D
1
2
3
4
5
Mortimer St
Riding Wells St
Berners St
Newman St
Gresse St
Rathbone Pl
Little Portland St
Margaret St
Great Titchfield St
Great Portland St
Eastcastle St
Winsley St
Perry's Pl
Hanway St
Great Russell
Tottenham Court Rd
Tottenham Court Rd
Oxford St
Oxford St
25
Sutton Row
Great Chapel St
Wardour St
Berwick St
Poland St
Ramillies St
Oxford Circus
36
33
27
32
Soho Sq
Manette St
34
Noel St
D'Arblay St
43
Great Marlborough St
Frith St
Dean St
Wardour St
Greek St
20
39
10
16
11
Regent St
Kingly St
Poland St
Ingestre Pl
30
Broadwick St
24
Meard St
41
14
Marshall St
Ganton St
Carnaby St
Old Compton St
SOHO
Beak St
Lexington St
Peter St
23
38
Kingly Court
Rupert St
Shaftesbury Ave
19
Wardour St
Birdie La
Brewer St
Great Windmill St
13
Gerrard St
Leicester
Warwick St
Clifford St
17
Heddon St
Sherwood St
Denman St
Leicester Sq
Leicester Sq
Glasshouse St
Piccadilly Circus
Oxendon St
31
0 200 m
0 0.1 miles
Regent St
3
Piccadilly Circus
Panton St
Jermyn St
Haymarket
Whitcomb
Piccadilly
Eagle Pl
Regent St
St Alban's St
Suffolk St
40
9
St James's Piccadilly
Duke of York St
ST JAMES'S
Charles II St
Pall M
For reviews see
Top Sights p44
Sights p50
Eating p53
Drinking p55
Entertainment p57
Shopping p59

E
F
G
H
1
2
3
4
5
High Holborn
Holborn
HOLBORN
New Oxford St
High Holborn
Bloomsbury St
Museum St
Newton St
Whetstone Park
6
Sir John Soane's Museum
Lincoln's Inn Fields
Gate St
Lincoln's Inn Fields
Oxford St
Bucknall St
Grape St
Drury La
Stukely St
Macklin St
Parker St
Great Queen St
Wild Ct
Kingsway
Sardinia St
St Giles High St
Endell St
Shorts Gardens
Betterton St
Shelton St
12
COVENT GARDEN
Wild St
New Compton St
Shaftesbury Ave
Monmouth St
Neal St
44
35
Earlham St
Long Acre
Broad Ct
Drury La
Kemble St
Kean St
Crown Ct
Bow St
Russell St
Drury La
Flower Market
Neal St
Covent Garden
29
Tavistock St
Aldwych
West St
Langley St
Mercer St
James St
Wellington St
Catherine St
Litchfield St
Charing Cross Rd
Long Acre
Floral St
42
Covent Garden
London Transport Museum
37
15
4
7
Bow St
Rose St
21
Covent Garden Piazza
Tavistock St
Strand
Garrick St
King St
Exeter St
Somerset House
Southampton St
Henrietta St
New Row
Savoy St
Lancaster Pl
5
18
Bedfordbury
Maiden La
Bedford St
St Martin's La
Carting La
Chandos Pl
Savoy Pl
National Portrait Gallery
William IV St
Strand
Adam St
John Adam St
Victoria Embankment
2
National Gallery
8
St Martin-in-the-Fields
Villiers St
Victoria Embankment Gardens
River Thames
26
22
Trafalgar Square
1
Craven St
Charing Cross

Sights

Trafalgar Square
SQUARE

1 ◉ Map p48, E5

This grand piazza commemorates the victory of the Royal Navy at the Battle of Trafalgar against the French and Spanish navies in 1805. The 52m-high **Nelson's Column** honours Lord Admiral Horatio Nelson, who led the fleet's victory over Napoleon. The four enormous bronze lion statues were sculpted by Sir Edwin Landseer and cast with seized Spanish and French cannons. (◉Charing Cross or Leicester Sq)

National Portrait Gallery
GALLERY

2 ◉ Map p48, E5

Almost an annexe to the National Gallery, the NPG focuses on putting faces to the famous names in British history, from medieval lords and ladies to modern-day celebs. The gallery hosts brilliant temporary exhibitions and the excellent audioguides (£3) allow you to hear the voices of some of the people portrayed. (www.npg.org.uk; St Martin's Pl WC2; admission free; prices vary for temporary exhibitions; ◷10am-6pm, to 9pm Thu & Fri; ◉Charing Cross or Leicester Sq)

Take a Break Portrait (p55), on the gallery's 3rd floor, offers outstanding food and views.

Piccadilly Circus
LANDMARK

3 ◉ Map p48, C4

Piccadilly Circus is postcard London, buzzing with the liveliness that makes it exciting to be in town. At the centre of the circus is the famous aluminium statue, known as the Angel of Christian Charity, dedicated to the philanthropist and child-labour abolitionist Lord Shaftesbury. The angel

Understand
The Fourth Plinth

Three of the four plinths at Trafalgar Square's corners are occupied by notables but one, originally intended for a statue of William IV, has remained largely vacant for the past 150 years. The Royal Society of Arts conceived the **Fourth Plinth Project** (www.london.gov.uk/fourthplinth) in 1999, for works by contemporary artists. Of three commissioned works, thought-provoking pieces included *Ecce Homo* by Mark Wallinger (1999), a life-size statue of Jesus, tiny in contrast to the enormous plinth and Rachel Whiteread's *Monument* (2001), a resin copy of the plinth, turned upside down.

The Mayor's office has since taken over the Fourth Plinth Project, continuing with the left-field contemporary-art theme. One of the more memorable commissions was Anthony Gormley's *One & Other* (2009), presenting the plinth as a space for individuals to occupy.

MARK DAFFEY/LONELY PLANET IMAGES ©

Somerset House

has been mistaken for Eros, the God of Love, but actually depicts Anteros. (Piccadilly Circus)

Covent Garden Piazza SQUARE

4 Map p48, G3

London's first planned square is now the exclusive reserve of tourists who flock here to shop in the quaint old arcades, and be entertained by buskers and street performers. On its western flank is **St Paul's Church** (www.actorschurch.org; Bedford St WC2; 8.30am-5.30pm Mon-Fri, 9am-1pm Sun). Check out the lovely courtyard at the back of the church, perfect for a picnic. (Covent Garden)

Somerset House HISTORIC BUILDING

5 Map p48, H4

With its 55 dancing fountains, this splendid Palladian masterpiece was designed by William Chambers in 1775 for royal societies and now contains the Courtauld Gallery, a standout gallery connected to the Courtauld Institute of Arts; the Embankment Galleries host regular photographic exhibitions. (www.somerset-house.org.uk; The Strand WC2; admission free to courtyard & terrace; house 10am-6pm, Great Court 7.30am-11pm; Temple or Covent Garden)

Sir John Soane's Museum

MUSEUM

6 Map p48, H1

This is one of the most fascinating sights in London. Sir John Soane was the architectural genius behind the Bank of England, and his former home is now a museum containing all the bits of architectural bric-a-brac that Soane accumulated. The candlelit evenings (first Tuesday of the month) are magical (but queues are long). (www.soane.org; 13 Lincoln's Inn Fields WC2; admission free; 10am-5pm Tue-Sat, 6-9pm 1st Tue of month; Holborn)

Courtauld Gallery

GALLERY

Inside Somerset House (see 5 Map p48, H4), this upscale gallery boasts a collection of impressionist and post-impressionist works, including daubings by Cézanne, Degas, Gauguin, Monet, Matisse, Renoir and Van Gogh. There are free, 15-minute lunchtime talks on specific works/themes at 1.15pm every Monday and Friday. (www.courtauld.ac.uk; The Strand WC2; adult/child £6/free, 10am-2pm Mon free for all; 10am-6pm)

London Transport Museum

MUSEUM

7 Map p48, G3

There's something nostalgic about London's public transport – it must be the old red double-decker buses. Adults will appreciate the history at this revitalised museum, expensively refurbished in 2007; kids will love the old-fashioned vehicles. Browse the museum shop for original souvenirs, including a great selection of posters. (www.ltmuseum.co.uk; Covent Garden Piazza WC2; adult/child £13.50/free; 10am-6pm Sat-Thu, 11am-6pm Fri; Covent Garden)

> Top Tip
>
> **Skate by The Strand**
>
> The courtyard of Somerset House is transformed into a popular ice rink in winter and used for concerts and events in summer; the **Summer Screen** (when the Great Court turns into an outdoor cinema for 10 evenings in early August) is particularly popular – book ahead. Behind the house, there's a sunny terrace and cafe overlooking the embankment.

St Martin-in-the-Fields

CHURCH

8 Map p48, F5

This 'royal parish church', a delightful fusion of classical and baroque styles, was completed by James Gibbs in 1726. Well known for its excellent classical music concerts, many by candlelight, it also has a wonderful cafe in the crypt that hosts jazz evenings once a week. (www.stmartin-in-the-fields.org; Trafalgar Sq WC2; 8am-6.30pm, evening concerts 7.30pm; Charing Cross)

St James's Piccadilly

CHURCH

9 Map p48, B5

This redbrick Christopher Wren church is a gem. It appeals to all comers, housing a counselling service, and staging lunchtime and evening concerts, an antiques market (10am to 5pm Tuesday) and an arts and crafts fair (10am to 6pm Wednesday to Saturday). The current (glass fibre) spire, although designed by Wren, dates from 1968 (the church was badly damaged by the Luftwaffe in 1940). (197 Piccadilly W1; 8am-7pm; Piccadilly Circus)

Take a Break **Caffe Nero** (Map p48, B5; 35 Jermyn St SW1; 7am-7pm Mon-Fri, 8am-7pm Sat, 9am-7pm Sun), right next to St James's, is ideal for coffee, sandwiches and pastries.

Eating

Yauatcha

CHINESE **££**

10 Map p48, C3

This most glamorous of dim sum restaurants, housed in the award-winning Ingeni building, is divided into two parts. The upstairs dining room offers a blue-bathed oasis of calm from the chaos of Berwick Street Market, while downstairs has a smarter, more atmospheric feel with constellations of 'star' lights. Both offer exquisite dim sum as well as a fabulous range of teas. (www.yauatcha.com; 15 Broadwick St W1; dim sum £4-16; lunch & dinner; Oxford Circus)

Mooli's

INDIAN **£**

11 Map p48, D3

Mooli's is a cheerful little eatery serving fresh, homemade rotis (soft bread) with delicious filling (meat as well as paneer and chickpeas). There are also homemade chutneys and mango *lassis* (traditional yoghurt drinks), real lemonade and a nice selection of bottled beers. (www.moolis.com; 50 Frith St W1; roti wrap £5; noon-10pm Mon-Wed, to 11.30pm Thu-Sat; Tottenham Court Rd)

Great Queen Street

BRITISH **££**

12 Map p48, G2

Great Queen Street's menu is seasonal (and changes daily), with an emphasis on quality, hearty dishes and good ingredients – there are always delicious stews, roasts and simple fish dishes. The atmosphere is lively, with a small bar downstairs. The staff are knowledgeable, the wine list is strong and booking is essential. (7242 0622; 32 Great Queen St WC2; mains £9-18; lunch & dinner Mon-Sat, lunch Sun; Covent Garden or Holborn)

Bocca di Lupo

ITALIAN **££**

13 Map p48, C4

Hidden on a dark Soho backstreet, Bocca radiates elegant sophistication. It features dishes from across Italy (the menu tells you which region they're from) and every main can be served as a small or large portion. With an array of Italian wines and fantastic desserts to enjoy, it's often full – book ahead. (7734 2223; www.boccadilupo.com; 12 Archer St W1; mains £8.50-17.50; lunch & dinner Mon-Sat, lunch Sun; Piccadilly Circus)

Diners at Momo

Bar Shu

CHINESE ££

14 Map p48, D3

With dishes redolent of smoked chillies and the all-important peppercorn (*huajiao*), Bar Shu offers authentic Sichuan cuisine. Service can be a little brusque but the food is delicious and the portions huge. (www.bar-shu.co.uk; 28 Frith St W1; mains £8-20; lunch & dinner; Leicester Sq)

Ben's Cookies

BAKERY £

15 Map p48, G3

The cookies at Ben's could be the best in the history of cookie-making. There are 18 varieties, from triple chocolate to peanut butter, oatmeal and raisin to chocolate and orange, all wonderfully gooey and often warm (they're baked fresh on the premises throughout the day). (www.benscookies.com; 13a The Piazza, Covent Garden WC2; cookie £1.50; 10am-8pm Mon-Sat, 11am-7pm Sun; Covent Garden)

Dean Street Townhouse

TEAHOUSE

16 Map p48, C3

Afternoon tea in the parlour of the Dean Street Townhouse hardly gets better; it's old world cosy, with upholstered furniture and a roaring fireplace, and the pastries are divine. In summer, you can enjoy eating at one of the few tables on the street terrace. (www.deanstreettownhouse.com; 69-71 Dean St W1; tea £16; daily; ; Tottenham Court Rd)

Momo

MOROCCAN £££

17 Map p48, A4

This atmospheric Moroccan restaurant is staffed by all-dancing, tambourine-playing waiters. It manages to be all things to all diners, from romantic couples to raucous office-party ravers. Service is very friendly and dishes are as exciting as you dare to be. There's outside seating in the warmer months. (7434 4040; www.momoresto.com; 25 Heddon St W1; mains £18-25, 2-/3-course set lunches £15/19; closed Sun lunch; Piccadilly Circus)

J Sheekey

SEAFOOD £££

18 Map p48, E4

With a pedigree stretching back to 1896, J Sheekey specialises in finely prepared Atlantic salmon, razor shells and other fruits from the seas around Great Britain. The oyster-bar, popular with pre- and post-dinner punters, is another highlight. (7240 2565; www.j-sheekey.co.uk; 28-32 St Martin's Ct; mains £15-42; lunch & dinner; Leicester Sq)

Drinking

Experimental Cocktail Club

COCKTAIL BAR

19 Map p48, D3

The interior of this sensational cocktail bar, with its soft lighting, mirrors, bare brick wall and elegant furnishings matches the sophistication of the cocktails: rare and original spirits (purple shiso-infused Ketel One Vodka), vintage Martinis, Billecart and Krug Champagne and homemade fruit syrups. A £5 cover charge stands after 11pm. (www.experimentalcocktailclublondon.com; 3a Gerrard St W1; 6pm-3am Mon-Sat, 5pm-midnight Sun; Leicester Sq or Piccadilly Circus)

Local Life

Portrait

The **Portrait** (Map p48, E5; 7312 2490; 3rd fl, National Portrait Gallery, St Martin's Pl WC2; mains £14-29; lunch 11.45am-3pm daily, dinner 5.30pm-8.15pm Thu-Sat; Charing Cross) restaurant on the top floor of the National Portrait Gallery has superb views towards Westminster and does wonderful food, including decadent afternoon teas.

Academy

COCKTAIL BAR

20 Map p48, D3

A long-standing Soho favourite, the Academy has some of the best cocktails in town. The menu is the size of a small book but, fear not, just tell the bartender what you feel like and they'll mix you something divine. (www.labbaruk.com; 12 Old Compton St W1; 4pm-midnight Mon-Sat, to 10.30pm Sun; Leicester Sq or Tottenham Court Rd)

Top Tip

West End on the cheap

London, the West End especially, can be an expensive destination but there are plenty of tricks to make your pennies last. Many of the top museums are free so give them priority over the more commercial attractions. The West End is also compact, so walk, take the bus (cheaper than the tube) or hop on a Barclay's bike (p214). Finally, go out early; most bars in the West End offer happy hour until 8pm or 9pm and, when it's over, head to the pub for a good ol' pint instead of a fancy cocktail.

Lamb & Flag

PUB

21 Map p48, F3

Pocket-sized but packed with history and charm, the Lamb & Flag is still going strong after more than 350 years. Rain or shine, you'll have to elbow your way to the bar through the merry crowd quaffing outside. Inside, it's all brass fittings and creaky wooden floors. (33 Rose St WC2; daily; Covent Garden or Leicester Sq)

Gordon's Wine Bar

WINE BAR

22 Map p48, G5

Gordon's is a victim of its own success: relentlessly busy, so unless you get a jump on the office crowd who arrive around 6pm, forget nabbing a table. It's cavernous, dark and atmospheric, the French and New World wines are heady and reasonably priced; bread, cheese and olives are fine accompaniments. (www.gordonswinebar.com; 47 Villiers St WC2; daily; Embankment or Charing Cross)

Madame Jo Jo's

CLUB

23 Map p48, C3

The subterranean crimson cabaret bar comes into its own with Kitsch Cabaret on Saturday and Burlesque Idol on Fridays. Keb Darge's Lost & Found night on Saturday is legendary, attracting a cool crew of breakers and jazz dancers. It's Tranny Shack UK (drag queen night) on Wednesdays. (www.madamejojos.com; 8 Brewer St W1; daily; Leicester Sq or Piccadilly Circus)

Endurance

PUB

24 Map p48, C3

A Soho favourite, the Endurance has a retro jukebox full of indie hits, good wine, draught ales and decent food; Sundays tend to be quiet. The crowd frequently spills outside in the evening, and daytime drinks afford good takes on the Berwick Street Market buzz. (90 Berwick St W1; daily; Oxford Circus or Piccadilly Circus)

Edge

GAY

25 Map p48, C2

Overlooking Soho Square, the Edge, in all its four-storey glory, is London's largest gay bar and heaves every night of the week: there are dancers, waiters in bunny (or other) outfits, good music and a generally superfriendly vibe. There's a heavy straight presence, due to its proximity to Oxford St. (www.edgesoho.co.uk; 11 Soho Sq W1; ⌚to 1am Mon-Sat, to 11.30pm Sun; ⊖Tottenham Court Rd)

Heaven

GAY

26 Map p48, F5

Under the arches beneath Charing Cross station, Heaven has a long-standing reputation for good clubbing. Monday's Popcorn night (mixed dance party, all-welcome door policy) has to be one of the best. The celebrated G-A-Y also takes place here on Thursday (G-A-Y Porn Idol), Friday (G-A-Y Camp Attack) and Saturday (plain ol' G-A-Y). (www.heavennightclub-london.com; Villiers St WC2; ⌚11pm-6am Mon, 11pm-4am Thu & Fri, 10pm-5am Sat; ⊖Embankment or Charing Cross)

Top Tip

An Afternoon at the Opera

Midweek matinees at the Royal Opera House are usually much cheaper than evening performances, with restricted-view seats costing as little as £7. There are same-day tickets (one per customer available to the first 67 people in the queue) from 10am for £8 to £40. Half-price stand-by tickets are only occasionally available. Otherwise, full-price tickets go for anything up to £120.

Candy Bar

LESBIAN

27 Map p48, C2

This brilliant bar has been the centre of London's small but fun lesbian scene for years and is showing no signs of waning. Busy most nights of the week, this is very much a girls' space (one male guest per two women are allowed though). (www.candybarsoho.com; 4 Carlisle St W1; ⌚to midnight Sun-Thu, to 2am Fri & Sat; ⊖Tottenham Court Rd)

Entertainment

12 Bar

LIVE MUSIC

28 Map p48, E2

Small, intimate, with a rough and ready feel, the 12 Bar is one of our favourite live music venues, with solo acts or bands performing every night of the week. The emphasis is on songwriting and the music is very much indie rock, with anything from folk and jazzy influences to punk and metal sounds. (www.12barclub.com; Denmark St WC2; ⌚7pm-3am Mon-Sat, to 12.30am Sun; ⊖Tottenham Court Rd)

Royal Opera House

OPERA

29 Map p48, G3

The £210 million redevelopment for the millennium gave classic opera a fantastic setting, and coming here for a night is a sumptuous prospect. Although the program has been fluffed up by modern influences, the main attractions here are still the classical ballet and opera – all are wonderful productions and feature world-class performers. (www.roh.org.uk; Bow St WC2; daily; Covent Garden)

Ronnie Scott's

JAZZ

30 Map p48, D3

The iconic London nightspot is still pulling in the biggest names in jazz from around the world: Miles Davis, Charlie Parker, Thelonious Monk and Ella Fitzgerald have all played here. Door staff can be terribly rude and the service slow, but that's how it's always been. Gigs are nightly and usually last until 2am. Expect to pay between £18 and £40. (www.ronniescotts.co.uk; 47 Frith St W1; daily; Leicester Sq)

Comedy Store

COMEDY

31 Map p48, D4

One of London's first (and still one of its best) comedy clubs, the Comedy Store attracts some of the biggest names. Wednesday and Sunday night's Comedy Store Players is the most famous improvisation outfit, with the wonderful Josie Lawrence; on Thursdays, Fridays and Saturdays it's Best in Stand Up. Tickets around £20. (www.thecomedystore.co.uk; Haymarket House, 1a Oxendon St SW1; daily; Piccadilly Circus)

Top Tip

West End Budget Flicks

Ticket prices at Leicester Sq cinemas are scandalous, so wait for the first-runs to finish and head to the **Prince Charles** (Map p48, D4; www.princecharlescinema.com; Leicester Pl WC2; Leicester Sq), central London's cheapest cinema, where non-members only have to pay £5.50 to £6.50 (or £8 to £10 for new releases). There are also mini-festivals, Q&As with film directors, old classics and, most famously, sing-along screenings.

Borderline

CONCERT VENUE

32 Map p48, D2

Through the Tex-Mex entrance off Orange Yard and down into the basement you'll find a 275-person capacity venue that really punches above its weight. Crowded House, REM, Blur, Counting Crows, PJ Harvey, Lenny Kravitz, Debbie Harry, and sundry anonymous indie outfits, have all played here. The crowd's full of music journos and talent-spotting record-company A&Rs. (http://venues.meanfiddler.com/borderline/home; Orange Yard W1; most nights, check website; Tottenham Court Rd)

Pizza Express Jazz Club

JAZZ

33 Map p48, C2

It's a bit of a strange arrangement, having a small basement venue beneath the main chain restaurant, but this is one of London's most popular jazz venues. Lots of big names perform here, as well as promising artists – Norah Jones, Jamie Cullum and Amy Winehouse all played here in their early days. Admission is £15 to £20. (www.pizzaexpresslive.com; 10 Dean St W1; daily; Tottenham Court Rd)

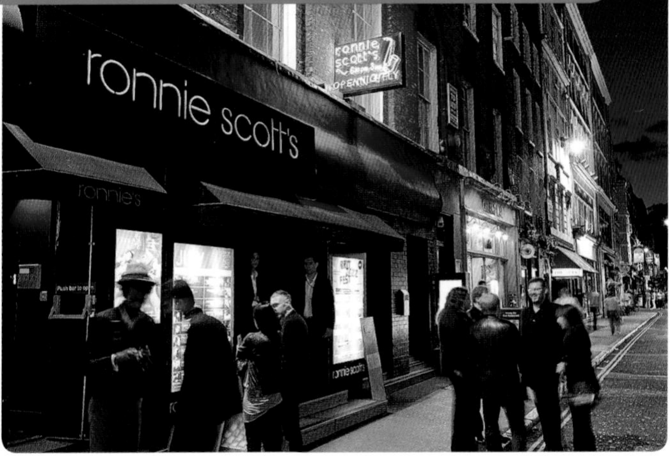

Ronnie Scott's

Soho Theatre
THEATRE

34 Map p48, C2

Soho Theatre has developed a superb reputation for showcasing new writing talent and quality comedy. It's also hosted some top-notch stand up or sketch-based comedians; US acts (such as Louis CK and Kirsten Schaal) frequently come here to perform. Tickets cost £10 to £20. (www.sohotheatre.com; 21 Dean St W1; daily; Tottenham Court Rd)

Donmar Warehouse
THEATRE

35 Map p48, F2

The small Donmar Warehouse is the 'thinking man's theatre' in London. Artistic director Michael Grandage stages interesting and somewhat inventive productions such as Ibsen's *A Doll's House* with Gillian Anderson and *Hamlet* with Jude Law. (www.donmarwarehouse.com; 41 Earlham St WC2; daily; Covent Garden)

Shopping

Joy
FASHION

36 Map p48, C2

Joy is an artistic blend of high street and vintage: there are excellent clothes, from silk dresses for women, fabulous shirts for men and timeless t-shirts for both, as well as such funky gadgets as a floating radio duck and dollar and euro-shaped ice cube trays. Conventional shoppers abstain! (www.joythestore.com; 162-170 Wardour St W1; Oxford Circus or Tottenham Court Rd)

Understand

Regent Street

Regent Street is the curving border dividing Soho's hoi polloi from the high-society residents of Mayfair. Designed by John Nash as a ceremonial route, it was meant to link the Prince Regent's long-demolished city dwelling with the 'wilds' of Regent's Park, and was conceived by the architect as a grand thoroughfare that would be the centrepiece of a new grid for this part of town. Alas, it was never to be – too many toes were being stepped on and Nash had to downscale his plan.

There are some elegant shop fronts that look older than their 1920s origins (when the street was remodelled) but chain stores have almost completely taken over. The street's most famous retail outlet is undoubtedly Hamleys. Regent Street is also famous for its Christmas lights displays, which are turned on in great pomp in late November every year.

Stanfords BOOKS

37 Map p48, F3

Travellers have been coming to Stanfords of Long Acre for well over a century. Inside you'll find London's best selection of guidebooks, travel literature, maps and nifty travel gifts. Ernest Shackleton, David Livingstone, Captain Scott, Amy Johnson and even Brad Pitt have all been customers. (www.stanfords.co.uk; 12-14 Long Acre; ⊖Covent Garden or Leicester Sq)

Hamleys TOYS

38 Map p48, A3

Live demonstrations add an interactive element at London's most famous toy shop. Selling everything from puzzles and pogo-sticks to Lego and Xbox games, the shop gets packed – only the brave or masochistic visit on weekends. (www.hamleys.com; 188-196 Regent St; ⊖Oxford Circus)

Liberty DEPARTMENT STORE

39 Map p48, A3

Step into another era at this old-fashioned, mock-Tudor department store, best known for its printed fabrics, homewares and exotic rugs. 'Liberty prints' still appear regularly on the pages of *Vogue* and *Elle*. (www.liberty.co.uk; Regent St; ⊖Oxford Circus)

Waterstone's BOOKS

40 Map p48, B5

This is the largest bookshop in Europe, with four floors of reading material and a fabulous top-floor bar/restaurant for sweeping views across London's rooftops. The staff are knowledgeable and there are regular author readings and signings. (www.waterstones.com; 203-206 Piccadilly; ⊖Piccadilly Circus)

Vintage House

DRINK

41 Map p48, D3

A whisky connoisseur's paradise, this shop stocks more than 1000 single-malt Scotches, from smooth Macallan to peaty Lagavulin. It also stocks a huge array of spirits and liqueurs that you wouldn't find in your average wine shop. (42 Old Compton St W1; 9am-11pm Mon-Fri, 9.30am-11pm Sat, noon-10pm Sun; Leicester Sq)

Ted Baker

FASHION

42 Map p48, F3

The one-time Glaswegian tailoring shop has grown into a superb clothing brand, offering elegant attire for both sexes. Ted's forte is its formalwear, with beautiful dresses for women (lots of daring prints and exquisite material) and sharp tailoring for men; the casual collections (denim, beachwear etc) are excellent too. (www.tedbaker.com; 9-10 Floral St WC2; Covent Garden)

Sister Ray

MUSIC

43 Map p48, C2

If you were a fan of the late, great John Peel on the BBC/BBC World Service, this specialist in innovative, experimental and indie music (vinyl and CD) is just right for you. (www.sisterray.co.uk; 34-35 Berwick St W1; Oxford Circus or Tottenham Court Rd)

Neal's Yard Dairy

FOOD

44 Map p48, F2

A fabulous, smelly cheese house that would fit in rural England, this place is proof that the British can match the French when it comes to big rolls of ripe cheese. There are more than 70 varieties that you can taste, including independent farmhouse brands. Condiments, pickles, jams and chutneys are also available. (www.nealsyarddairy.co.uk; 17 Shorts Gardens WC2; closed Sun; Covent Garden)

Explore

British Museum & Bloomsbury

Bookish Bloomsbury puts a more leisurely and genteel spin on central London. Home to the British Museum, the British Library, universities, publishing houses, literary pubs and gorgeous Georgian squares, Bloomsbury is deeply, but accessibly, cultured. You could spend all day in the British Museum, but there's a tantalising choice of options outside, with excellent pubs and restaurants nearby.

The Sights in a Day

The **British Museum** (p64) is one of London's top sights, so get here early to do it justice. You will need at least the entire morning here to make any headway, so plan to see the highlights, including the Parthenon Marbles, the Rosetta Stone and the Mummy of Katebet. Pop down to **St George's Bloomsbury** (p74) for a dose of fine ecclesiastical architecture and to **New London Architecture** (p73) for a handle on the city's latest architectural sensations.

Have lunch at **Abeno** (p74) or **Chilli Cool** (p75) before finding out what the wonderfully eclectic **Wellcome Collection** (p72) is all about. Bibliophiles and library lovers will find the **British Library** (p72) a true eye-opener.

Bloomsbury has an alluring selection of international restaurants for dinner, such as **Hakkasan** (p75) or **Diwana Bhel Poori House** (p75). Embark on a local pub crawl via the neighbourhood's historic and literary watering holes (p77) or drop by the **100 Club** (p78) to see what's on the music menu.

For a local's day in Bloomsbury, see p68.

Top Sights

British Museum (p64)

Local Life

A Literary Walk Around Bloomsbury (p68)

Best of London

Museums & Galleries
British Museum (p64)

Historic Pubs
Queen's Larder (p77)

Unusual Sights
Wellcome Collection (p72)

For Kids
British Museum (p64)

Getting There

Underground Take the train to Tottenham Court Rd (Northern Line or Central Line), Goodge St (Northern Line), Russell Sq (Piccadilly Line) or Euston Sq (Circle, Hammersmith & City and Metropolitan lines).

Bus For the British Museum and Russell Sq, take the handy 24-hour bus 7 along Oxford St; bus 91 runs from Whitehall/Trafalgar Square to the British Library.

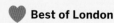

Top Sights
British Museum

The British Museum draws an average of five million visitors each year. It's an exhilarating stampede through world cultures, with galleries devoted to ancient civilisations, from Egypt to Western Asia, the Middle East, the Romans and Greece, India, Africa, prehistoric and Roman Britain and medieval antiquities. Founded in 1753 following the bequest of royal physician Hans Sloane's 'cabinet of curiosities', the museum expanded its collection through judicious acquisitions and the controversial plundering of empire.

Map p70, D6

www.britishmuseum.org

Great Russell St WC1

admission free, £3 donation suggested

10am-5.30pm Sat-Thu, to 8.30pm Fri

Tottenham Court Rd or Russell Sq

Ancient Egypt collection, British Museum

Don't Miss

Great Court

Covered with a spectacular glass-and-steel roof designed by Norman Foster in 2000, the Great Court is the largest covered public square in Europe. In its centre is the world-famous Reading Room, formerly the British Library, which has been frequented by all the big brains of history, from Mahatma Gandhi to Karl Marx.

Ancient Egypt

The star of the show at the British Museum is the Ancient Egypt collection. It comprises sculptures, fine jewellery, papyrus texts, coffins and mummies, including the beautiful and intriguing Mummy of Katebet (room 63). Perhaps the most prized item in the collection is the Rosetta Stone (room 4), the key to deciphering Egyptian hieroglyphics.

Parthenon Sculptures

ROOM 18

Another highlight of the museum is the **Parthenon Sculptures** (aka Parthenon Marbles). The marble works are thought to show the great procession to the temple that took place during the Panathenaic Festival, on the birthday of Athena, one of the grandest events in the Greek world.

Mosaic Mask of Tezcatlipoca

ROOM 27

Kids will love the Mexican gallery, with the 15th-century Aztec Mosaic Mask of Tezcatlipoca (or Skull of the Smoking Mirror), a human skull decorated with turquoise mosaic. Believed to represent Tezcatlipoca, a creator deity, the skull actually employs a real human skull as a base for its construction, emblazoned with turquoise, lignite, pyrite and shell.

Top Tips

- There are 15 free 30- to 40-minute eyeOpener tours of individual galleries throughout the day.
- The museum has also developed excellent audioguides (adult/child £5/3.50).
- Download one- or three-hour itineraries from the museum's website that take in various highlights.
- A major new extension called the World Conservation and Exhibitions Centre is being built in the museum's northwestern corner. Due for completion in late 2013, it will host a special exhibition space and state-of-the-art facilities for the preservation and research of the museum's collections.

Take a Break

The British Museum is vast so you'll need to recharge. Abeno (p74) is nearby for scrumptious savoury pancakes and other dishes from Japan.

China, South Asia & Southeast Asia

ROOM 33

Visit this magnificent gallery, where the impact of Buddhism and other religious beliefs is explored through a stunning collection of objects from China, Tibet, Thailand, Cambodia and other Eastern nations and civilisations. The Qing dynasty gilt bronze mandala is a gorgeous Chinese specimen with pronounced Tibetan Lamaist motifs.

Roman and Medieval Britain

ROOMS 40 TO 51

Amid all the highlights from ancient Egypt, Greece and Rome, it almost comes as a surprise to see treasures from Britain and nearby Europe (rooms 40 to 51). Many of course, go back to Roman times, when the empire spread across much of the continent, but not all.

Sutton Hoo Ship-Burial

ROOM 41

This elaborate Anglo-Saxon burial site from Suffolk (Eastern England) dates back to the 7th century; items include coins and a stunning helmet complete with face mask.

Lindow Man

ROOM 50

The Lindow Man is the remains of a 1st-century man discovered in a bog near Manchester in northern England in 1984. Thanks to the conditions in the bog, many of the internal organs, skin and hair were preserved and scientists were able to determine the nature of Lindow Man's death: an axe stroke to the head and garrotted.

Oxus Treasure

ROOM 52

Dating largely from the 5th to 4th centuries BC, this dazzling collection of around 170 pieces of Achaemenid Persian metalwork was found by the River Oxus, possibly once displayed in a temple. The collection features a host of objects, including model chariots, bracelets, statuettes, vessels and other skilfully fashioned gold and silver pieces.

King's Library

To square the circle, check out the King's Library. Not only is it a stunning neoclassical space, it also goes back to how we got interested in the history of civilisations, and how disciplines such as biology, archaeology, linguistics and geography all emerged during the 18th century ('the Enlightenment') in a quest for knowledge.

British Museum Floorplan

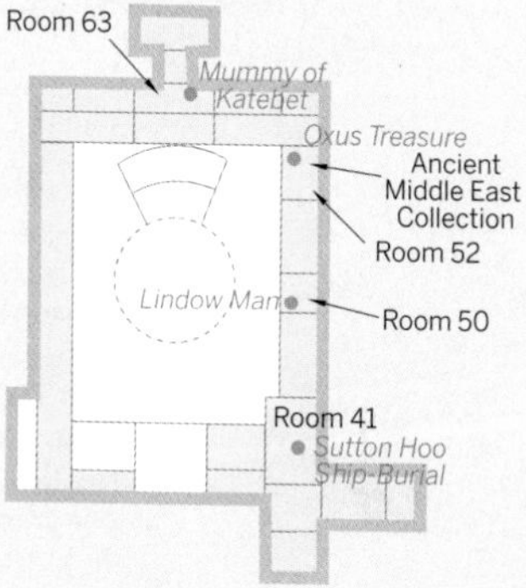

Upper Floor

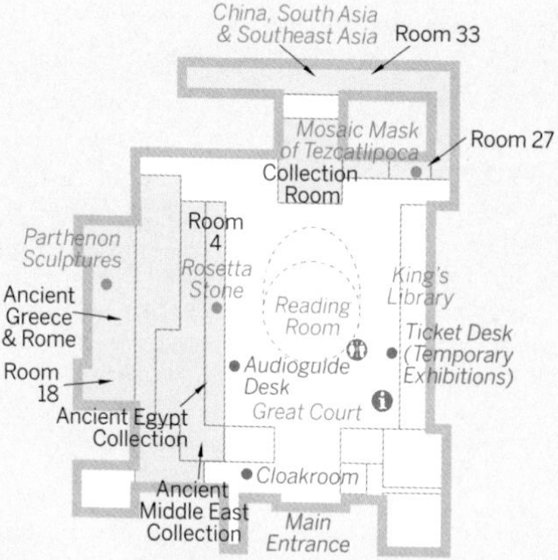

Ground Floor

Local Life
A Literary Walk Around Bloomsbury

Bloomsbury is indelibly associated with the literary circles that made this part of London their home. Virginia Woolf, WB Yeats, Sylvia Plath, TS Eliot, Charles Dickens and other titans of English literature have all left their names associated with properties delightfully dotted around Bloomsbury and its attractive squares.

1 Bedford Square
An eye-catching symbiosis of Bloomsbury's creative heritage and architectural charms, Bedford Square is London's best preserved Georgian square. The main offices of publishing house Bloomsbury Publishing is at No 50. Sir Anthony Hope Hawkins, author of *The Prisoner of Zenda*, lived at No 41 while the Pre-Raphaelite Brotherhood was founded in 1848 round the corner at 7 Gower St.

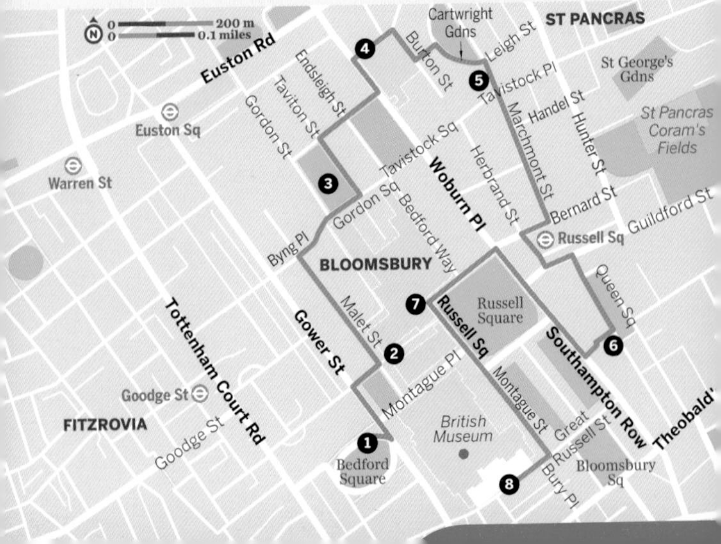

❷ Stroll past Senate House

Along student-thronged Malet St, the splendid but intimidating art deco Senate House served as the Ministry of Information in WWII, providing the inspiration for George Orwell's Ministry of Truth in his dystopian 1948 novel, *Nineteen Eighty-Four*. George Orwell's wife, Eileen worked in the censorship department between 1939 and 1942.

❸ Stop off in Gordon Square

Once a private square, Gordon Square is open to the public and it's a lovely place for a rest. Locals sit out on benches reading, chatting and eating sandwiches when the sun shines over Bloomsbury.

❹ WB Yeats & Woburn Walk

Irish poet and playwright WB Yeats lived at No 5 Woburn Walk, a genteel lane just south of the church of St Pancras. A leading figure of the Celtic Revival that promoted the native heritage of Ireland and author of *The Tower*, WB Yeats was born in Dublin, but spent many years in London.

❺ Rest your legs in the Lord John Russell

Locals drink and dine at this great **pub** (91-93 Marchmont St WC1) with a fantastic range of beers and a decent lunch menu, including tasty fish and chips. It's a traditional one-room London bar with a cosy atmosphere where chatting is the norm.

❻ Pop into St George the Martyr

The 18th century church of **St George the Martyr** (44 Queen Sq) across from the historic Queen's Larder pub (p77) at the south end of Queen Sq was the site of the marriage of Ted Hughes and Sylvia Plath on 16 June 1956. The couple chose this date (commemorating Bloomsday) to tie the knot, in honour of James Joyce.

❼ Faber & Faber

The former offices of Faber & Faber are at the northwest corner of Russell Square, by the main buildings of the School of Oriental and African Studies, marked with a plaque to TS Eliot, the American poet and playwright and first editor at Faber. The gardens at the centre of Russell Square are excellent for recuperation on a park bench under the trees.

❽ Drinks at the Museum Tavern

Karl Marx used to down a well-earned pint at the **Museum Tavern** (49 Great Russell St WC1; ⊖Tottenham Court Rd or Holborn) after a hard day inventing communism in the British Museum Reading Room. This is also where George Orwell boozed after his literary musings. It's a lovely traditional pub set around a long bar and is popular with academics, students, loyal regulars and tourists alike.

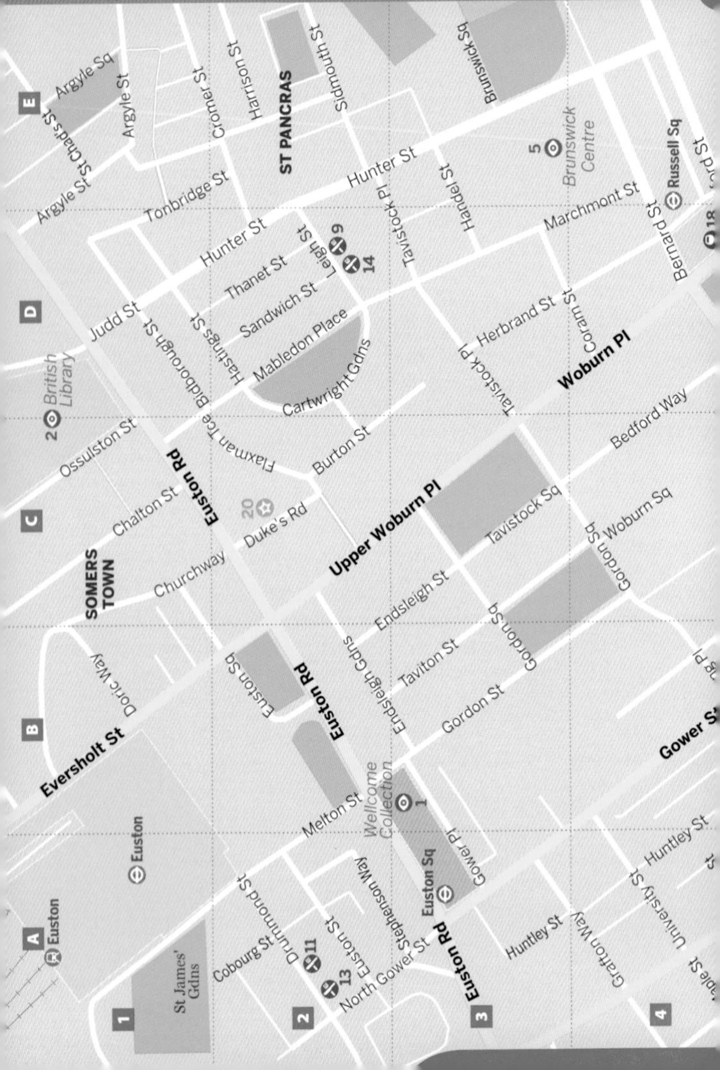

A
B
C
D
E
1
2
3
4
Argyle Sq
Argyle St
St Chad's St
Cromer St
Harrison St
ST PANCRAS
Sidmouth St
Brunswick Sq
Brunswick Centre
5
Hunter St
Tonbridge St
Judd St
Thanet St
Sandwich St
Leigh St
9
14
Tavistock Pl
Handel St
Marchmont St
Bernard St
Russell Sq
British Library
2
Bidborough St
Hastings St
Mabledon Place
Cartwright Gdns
Herbrand St
Coram St
Woburn Pl
Ossulston St
Euston Rd
Flaxman Tce
Burton St
Bedford Way
Chalton St
20
Duke's Rd
Upper Woburn Pl
Tavistock Sq
Woburn Sq
Gordon Sq
SOMERS TOWN
Churchway
Endsleigh St
Endsleigh Gdns
Euston Sq
Taviton St
Gordon St
Doric Way
Eversholt St
Gower St
Wellcome Collection
1
Melton St
Euston
Gower Pl
Huntley St
University St
Stephenson Way
Drummond St
Cobourg St
Euston St
North Gower St
11
13
St James' Gdns
Grafton Way

Russell Sq
Southampton Row
Queen Sq
Bedford Pl
Bloomsbury Sq
Bloomsbury Way
Barter St
Bury Pl
Montague St
British Museum
Great Russell St
Little Russell St
Museum St
St George's Bloomsbury
Bloomsbury St
Montague Pl
Bedford Square
Streatham St
New Oxford St
Bucknall St
Shaftesbury Ave
Neal St
St Giles High St
Tottenham Court Rd
Centre Point
Charing Cross Rd
SOHO
Sutton Row
Soho Sq
Soho St
Oxford St
Hanway St
Hanway Pl
Gresse St
Rathbone Pl
Perry's Pl
Great Chapel St
Noel St
Newman St
Wardour St
Berwick St
Poland St
Bedford Ave
Morwell St
New London Architecture
Store St
Alfred Pl
Chenies St
Percy St
Windmill St
Charlotte St
Rathbone St
Goodge St
Pollock's Toy Museum
Tottenham Court Rd
FITZROVIA
Whitfield St
Charlotte St
Tottenham St
Newman St
Berners Mews
Berners St
Torrington
200 m
0.1 miles
For reviews see
Top Sights p64
Sights p72
Eating p74
Drinking p77
Entertainment p78
Shopping p78
A
B
C
D
E
5
6
7
8
N
1
2
3
4
6
7
8
10
12
15
16
17
19
21
22
23
24

Sights

Wellcome Collection

1 Map p70, B3

The Wellcome Collection styles itself as a 'destination for the incurably curious', exploring the links between medicine, science, life and art. The heart of the permanent collection is pharmacist, entrepreneur and collector, Sir Henry Wellcome's (1853–1936) collection of objects from around the world. The museum also runs outstanding temporary exhibitions on topics roaming the frontiers of modern medicine. (www.wellcomecollection.org; 183 Euston Rd NW1; admission free; 10am-6pm Tue-Sat, to 10pm Thu, 11am-6pm Sun; Euston Sq or Euston)

British Library

2 Map p70, C1

The nation's principal copyright library, the British Library stocks one copy of every British and Irish publication as well as historic manuscripts, books and maps from the British Museum. Don't miss the Sir John Ritblat Gallery, where the library keeps its most precious documents, including a Gutenberg Bible (1455). Other highlights include the King's Library and the Philatelic Exhibition. (www.bl.uk; 96 Euston Rd NW1; admission free; 9.30am-6pm Mon & Wed-Fri, to 8pm Tue, to 5pm Sat, 11am-5pm Sun; King's Cross St Pancras)

Take a Break Feast on great Sichuan dishes at Chilli Cool (p75)

Understand

British Library

In 1998 the British Library moved to its new premises between King's Cross and Euston stations. At a cost of £500 million, it was Britain's most expensive building, and not one that is universally loved. Colin St John Wilson's exterior of straight lines of red brick, which Prince Charles reckoned was akin to a 'secret-police building', may not be to all tastes. But even those who don't like the building from the outside will be won over by the spectacularly cool and spacious interior.

What you can see of the British Library is basically the tip of the iceberg. Under your feet, on four basement levels run some 186 miles of shelving where the library keeps its records and treasures. The library currently contains 14 million books, 920,000 journal and newspaper titles, 58 million patents, and some 3 million sound recordings.

An exhibition at the Wellcome Collection

New London Architecture

ARCHITECTURE

3 Map p70, B6

For updates on the latest architectural designs in London, check out what's on view at New London Architecture. A large model of the capital also shows the extent of the 2012 Olympics plans and various neighbourhood regeneration programs. Photographs and details of individual buildings help you locate each new structure, so that you can go and see it in real life. (www.newlondonarchitecture.org; Bldg Centre, 26 Store St WC1; 9.30am-6pm Mon-Fri, 10am-5pm Sat; Goodge St)

Pollock's Toy Museum

MUSEUM

4 Map p70, A6

Aimed at both kids and adults, this museum is simultaneously creepy and mesmerising. Walk in via its shop and climb up a rickety narrow staircase, where displays begin with framed dolls from Latin America, Africa, India and Europe. Upstairs is the museum's collection of toy theatres, many made by Benjamin Pollock himself, the leading Victorian manufacturer of the popular sets. (www.pollockstoymuseum.com; 1 Scala St W1; adult/child £5/3; 10am-5pm Mon-Sat; Goodge St)

Understand

A History of the World in 100 Objects

In 2010, the British Museum launched an outstanding radio series on BBC Radio 4 called *A History of the World in 100 Objects*. The series, presented by British Museum director Neil MacGregor, retraces two million years of history through 100 objects from the museum's collections. Each object is described in a 15-minute program, its relevance and significance analysed. The series is hugely informative and anyone with access to an MP3 player would be encouraged to download the podcasts, available from www.bbc.co.uk/ahistoryoftheworld/programme. That way, you could even listen to the program while looking at the artefact in the museum. Neil MacGregor has also written a book on the topic, *A History of the World in 100 Objects*, published by Allen Lane (2010).

Brunswick Centre MALL

5 Map p70, E3

This now-wonderful 1960s complex consists of apartments, restaurants, shops and a cinema. A £24 million project transformed it from a dreary, stern space to a lovely, cream-coloured airy square in 2006, and the centre is now packed with people seven days a week. For more information and a complete listing of shops and restaurants, check the website. (www.brunswick.co.uk; The Brunswick WC1; Russell Sq)

St George's Bloomsbury CHURCH

6 Map p70, E7

Superbly restored in 2005, this Nicholas Hawksmoor church (1731) is distinguished by its classical portico of Corinthian capitals and a steeple that was inspired by the Mausoleum of Halicarnassus. It is topped with a statue of George I in Roman dress. Check the website for details on concert performances. (www.stgeorgesbloomsbury.org.uk; Bloomsbury Way WC1; 9.30am-5.30pm Mon-Fri, 10.30am-12.30pm Sun; Holborn or Tottenham Court Rd)

Eating

Abeno JAPANESE ££

7 Map p70, D7

This understated Japanese restaurant specialises in *okonomiyaki*, a savoury pancake from Osaka. The pancakes consist of cabbage, egg and flour combined with the ingredients of your choice (over two dozen varieties, from sliced meats and vegetables to egg, noodles and cheese), cooked on the hotplate at your table. The more traditional teppan-yaki and *yakisoba* dishes are also beautifully presented. (www.abeno.co.uk; 47 Museum St WC1; mains £7.50-18; lunch & dinner; Tottenham Court Rd)

Hummus Bros

MIDDLE EASTERN £

8 Map p70, E6

The deal at this very popular outlet is a bowl of filling hummus with your choice of topping (such as beef, chicken or tabouli) eaten with warm pita bread. It's very filling and you can eat in or take away. (www.hbros.co.uk; Victoria House, 37-63 Southampton Row WC1; mains £2.50-6; 11am-9pm Mon-Fri; ; ; Holborn)

Chilli Cool

CHINESE ££

9 Map p70, D2

For genuine Sichuan cuisine, look no further than Chilli Cool. The restaurant itself is nothing to write home about but it's the food people come for: hot pots, dan dan noodles, Gong Bao chicken and all the Sichuan favourites, which the clientele (almost exclusively Chinese) merrily tucks into. (www.chillicool.com; 15 Leigh St WC1; mains £7-19; lunch & dinner; Russell Sq)

Hakkasan

CHINESE £££

10 Map p70, B7

This basement restaurant successfully combines celebrity status, stunning design, persuasive cocktails and sophisticated Chinese food. The low, nightclub-style lighting (lots of red) makes it a good spot for dating or a night out with friends. For dinner in the main dining room, book far in advance. Do what savvy Londoners do and have lunch in the more informal Ling Ling lounge. (7927 7000; www.hakkasan.com; 8 Hanway Pl W1; mains £9.50-42; Tottenham Court Rd)

Diwana Bhel Poori House

INDIAN £

11 Map p70, A2

Arguably one London's best Indian vegetarian restaurants, Diwana specialises in Bombay-style *bhel poori* (a sweet-and-sour, soft and crunchy 'party mix' snack) and dosas (filled pancakes made from rice flour). You can try *thalis*, which offer a selection of tasty treats and the all-you-can-eat lunchtime buffet is legendary. (7387 5556; 121-123 Drummond St; mains £7-9; noon-midnight; Euston or Euston Sq)

Local Life

Afternoon Tea in Bloomsbury

Bea's of Bloomsbury (Map p70; www.beasofbloomsbury.com; 44 Theobalds Rd WC1; tea £15; daily; Holborn or Chancery Lane) made its name with signature cupcakes, so it was only natural for them to offer a full afternoon tea too. The cafe is tiny but original, with its mix of open kitchen and boutique decor. It's located a 10 minute walk east of the British Museum.

Fino

SPANISH ££

12 Map p70, A6

Set in a glamorous basement, critically-acclaimed Fino is a tapas restaurant with a difference. Try the Jerusalem artichoke cooked with mint, the prawn tortilla with wild garlic or the foie gras with chilli jam for a feast of innovative and delightful Spanish cooking. Enter from Rathbone St. (www.finorestaurant.com; 33 Charlotte St W1; tapas £4-17; lunch Mon-Fri, dinner Mon-Sat; Goodge St)

Ravi Shankar

INDIAN £

13 Map p70, A2

Another reliable *bhel poori* (a vegetarian restaurant named after the dish of the same name containing puffed rice and a mix of vegetables) house on Drummond St, this place with the memorable name is a good second choice if you can't get a table at Diwana. (133-135 Drummond St NW1; mains £6-10; lunch & dinner; Euston or Euston Sq)

North Sea Fish Restaurant

FISH & CHIPS ££

14 Map p70, D2

The North Sea sets out to cook fresh fish and potatoes – a simple ambition in which it succeeds admirably. Look forward to jumbo-sized plaice or halibut steaks, deep-fried or grilled, and a huge serving of chips. There's takeaway next door if you can't face

Staff prepare for lunch at Hakkasan (p75)

the soulless dining room. (www.northseafishrestaurant.co.uk; 7-8 Leigh St WC1; mains £9-20; closed Sun; Russell Sq)

Drinking

Newman Arms

PUB

15 Map p70, A7

A lovely local and also one of the few family-run pubs in central London, Newman Arms is a one-tiny-room affair with a 150-year history. George Orwell and Dylan Thomas were regulars in their day, and a scene from Michael Powell's *Peeping Tom* was filmed in the passageway alongside the pub in 1960. An excellent pie room is upstairs. (www.newmanarms.co.uk; 23 Rathbone St W1; daily; Goodge St or Tottenham Court Rd)

Queen's Larder

PUB

16 Map p70, E5

In a lovely square southeast of Russell Square, this pub is so called because Queen Charlotte, wife of 'Mad' King George III, rented part of the pub's cellar to store special foods for him while he was being treated nearby. It's a tiny but wonderfully cosy pub; there are benches outside for fair-weather fans and a good dining room upstairs. (www.queenslarder.co.uk; 1 Queen Sq WC1; daily; Russell Sq)

Bradley's Spanish Bar

BAR

17 Map p70, B8

Only vaguely Spanish in decor, but Bradley's wins amigos for its choice of booze: San Miguel, Cruzcampo, Tinto de Verano (red wine with rum and lemonade) and – teenager favourite – Sangria. Punters are squeezed under low ceilings in the nooks of the basement, while a vintage vinyl jukebox plays rock tunes of your choice. (42-44 Hanway St W1; daily; Tottenham Court Rd)

Tempus Bar

BAR

18 Map p70, D4

Nestled behind the awesome Victorian Gothic facade of the Hotel Russell, Tempus is a nice change from traditional pubs. With grand Edwardian decor, huge leather armchairs and table service, prices are a little inflated but there is a good selection of cocktails and wines, and you're generally guaranteed a seat. (Hotel Russell, Russell Sq WC1; daily; Russell Sq)

Fitzroy Tavern

PUB

19 Map p70, B6

In the years before and after WWII, the Fitzroy was the hangout of such literary colossi as George Orwell and Dylan Thomas. Today it's a typical downtown boozer, and part of the popular Sam Smith's chain, which means plenty of ales and specialist beers at bargain prices. (16 Charlotte St; closed Sun; Goodge St)

Entertainment

Place

DANCE

20 Map p70, C2

An exciting modern dance venue, the Place was the birthplace of modern British dance. It concentrates on challenging, contemporary and experimental choreography. Behind the late-Victorian facade you'll find a 300-seat theatre, an arty, creative cafe atmosphere and six training studios. The Place sponsors an annual award, 'Place Prize', which seeks out new and outstanding dance talent. Tickets cost £5 to £15. (www.theplace.org.uk; 17 Duke's Rd WC1; daily; Euston Square)

100 Club

LIVE MUSIC

21 Map p70, A8

This legendary London venue has always concentrated on jazz, but it's also spreading its wings to swing and rock. It once showcased Chris Barber, BB King and the Stones, and was at the centre of the punk revolution as well as the '90s indie scene. It hosts dancing swing gigs and local jazz musicians, as well as the occasional big name. (www.the100club.co.uk; 100 Oxford St W1; daily; Tottenham Court Rd)

Shopping

Bang Bang Exchange

VINTAGE

22 Map p70, A6

Got some designer pieces you're tired of? Bang Bang exchanges, buys and sells vintage pieces, proving the saying 'One girl's faded Prada dress is another girl's top new wardrobe piece'. (www.myspace.com/bangbangexchange; 21 Goodge St W1; Goodge St)

Understand

Squares of Bloomsbury

At the very heart of Bloomsbury is **Russell Square**. Originally laid out in 1800 by Humphrey Repton, it was dark and bushy until the striking facelift that pruned the trees, tidied up the plants and gave it a 10m-high fountain.

The centre of literary Bloomsbury was **Gordon Square** (p68) where, at various times, Bertrand Russell lived at No 57, Lytton Strachey at No 51 and Vanessa and Clive Bell, John Maynard Keynes and the Woolf family at No 46. Strachey, Dora Carrington and Lydia Lopokova (the future wife of Maynard Keynes) all took turns living at No 41. Not all the buildings, many of which now belong to the university, are marked with blue plaques.

Lovely **Bedford Square** is the only completely Georgian square still surviving in Bloomsbury.

Queen's Larder (p77)

London Review Bookshop BOOKS

23 Map p70, E6

The bookshop of *London Review of Books* literary magazine doesn't believe in piles of books, stocking a cautious but helpfully wide-range of titles in one or two copies only. It often hosts high-profile author talks; there is also a charming cafe where you can peruse your new purchases. (www.lrb.co.uk; 14 Bury Pl WC1; ⊖Russell Sq or Holborn)

On the Beat MUSIC

24 Map p70, B7

Mostly '60s and '70s retro – along with helpful staff – in a tiny room plastered with posters. (22 Hanway St W1; ⊖Tottenham Court Rd)

Explore

St Paul's & the City

For its size, the City punches well above its weight for attractions, with an embarrassment of sightseeing riches. The heavyweights – the Tower of London and St Paul's – are a must, but combine the other top sights with explorations of the City's lesser-known delights and quieter corners; the scores of churches make peaceful stops along the way.

The Sights in a Day

Make it an early start to get a jump on the crowds beginning to besiege the **Tower of London** (p86). Explore **Tower Bridge** (p92; check the website the day before to see if the bridge is due to be raised) and have a table booked for lunch at **Wine Library** (p97).

Pay a visit to **All Hallows-by-the-Tower** (p93) and consider climbing **Monument** (p93) or marvelling at the glittering technical sophistication of the **Lloyd's of London** building (p94). Rest your legs and quaff afternoon tea in the **Restaurant at St Paul's** (p95), or in the crypt of St-Mary-le-Bow at the **Cafe Below** (p95). Devote the rest of the afternoon to **St Paul's Cathedral** (p82), including climbing the cathedral's staggering dome for choice views. If you've any time spare, peruse the **Museum of London** (p92).

Catch an evening musical performance at the **Barbican** (p99) or embark on a tour of local historic pubs, including **Ye Olde Watling** (p98), **Ye Olde Cheshire Cheese** (p99) and the **Black Friar** (p98), but note some City pubs are shut at weekends. Shoreditch (p100) also makes a fine alternative for an entertaining and memorable evening out in London.

Top Sights

St Paul's Cathedral (p82)

Tower of London (p86)

Best of London

Modern Architecture

30 St Mary Axe (p95)

Lloyd's of London (p94)

Early Architecture

Tower of London (p89)

All Hallows-by-the-Tower (p93)

Churches

St Paul's Cathedral (p82)

All Hallows-by-the-Tower (p93)

St Bartholomew-the-Great (p93)

St Stephen Walbrook (p93)

St Mary Woolnoth (p93)

St Mary-le-Bow (p93)

Getting There

Underground. Handiest stations are St Paul's (Central Line) and Bank (Central, Northern, DLR and Waterloo & City lines), but Blackfriars (Circle and District lines), Barbican (Circle, Metropolitan and Hammersmith & City lines) and Tower Hill (Circle & District lines) are also useful.

Bus Useful routes include bus 8, 15, 11 and 26.

Top Sights
St Paul's Cathedral

Towering over Ludgate Hill, in a superb position that has been a place of worship for over 1400 years, St Paul's Cathedral is one of London's most majestic structures. For Londoners, the vast dome, which still manages to dominate the skyline despite the far higher skyscrapers of the Square Mile, is a symbol of resilience and pride, standing tall for over 300 years. Viewing Sir Christopher Wren's masterwork from the inside, and climbing to its height for sweeping views, is exhilarating.

Map p90, C3

www.stpauls.co.uk

St Paul's Churchyard EC4

adult/child £14.50/5.50

8.30am-4.30pm Mon-Sat, last admission 4pm

St Paul's

Dome and Whispering Gallery, St Paul's Cathedral

Don't Miss

Dome

London's largest church dome – the structure actually consists of three domes, one inside the other – made the cathedral Wren's tour de force. Exactly 528 stairs take you to the top, but it's a three-stage journey. Through a door on the western side of the southern transept and some 30m and precisely 257 steps above, you reach the interior walkway around the dome's base.

Whispering Gallery & Stone Gallery

The Whispering Gallery is the first level of your ascent towards the dome. It is so called because if you talk close to the wall it carries your words around to the opposite side, 32m away. Climbing even more steps (another 119) brings you to the Stone Gallery, an exterior viewing platform rather obscured by pillars and other safety prevention measures.

Golden Gallery

The remaining 152 iron steps to the **Golden Gallery** are steeper and narrower than the steps below but climbing them is really worth the effort. From here, 85m above London, you can enjoy superb 360-degree views of the city.

Epitaph & Duke of Wellington Memorial

Just beneath the dome is a compass and epitaph written for Wren by his son: *Lector, si monumentum requiris, circumspice* (Reader, if you seek his monument, look around you). In the northern aisle you'll find the grandiose Duke of Wellington Memorial (1875).

☑ Top Tips

- Join one of the free 90-minute tours.
- To go at your own pace, pick up one of the free 45-minute iPod tours (in multiple languages) at the entrance.
- Anyone can use the facilities in the cathedral crypt (for free), entering via the side door under the north transept; you can enter the cafe, restaurant and shop, use the toilet, shelter from bad weather, or even just enjoy a packed lunch here.
- Enquire at the desk just past the entrance about short introductory talks.
- If you're a group of five, consider the one-hour Triforium tour.

Take a Break

The Restaurant at St Paul's (p95) in the crypt offers good-value lunches.

The **Crypt Café** (dishes £5.65-7.40; 🕘9am-5pm Mon-Sat, noon-4pm Sun) is handy for light meals.

The Light of the World

In the north transept chapel is Pre-Raphaelite artist Holman Hunt's iconic painting, *The Light of the World,* which depicts Christ knocking at an overgrown door that, symbolically, can only be opened from the inside.

Quire

Progressing east into the cathedral's heart is the spectacular quire (or chancel) – its ceilings and arches dazzling with green, blue, red and gold mosaics – and the high altar. The ornately carved choir stalls by Grinling Gibbons on either side of the quire are exquisite, as are the ornamental wrought-iron gates, separating the aisles from the altar, by Jean Tijou.

American Memorial Chapel

Walk around the altar, with its massive gilded oak canopy, to the American Memorial Chapel, a memorial to the 28,000 Americans based in Britain who lost their lives during WWII.

Crypt

On the eastern side of the north and south transepts, stairs lead down to the crypt and OBE Chapel where services are held for members of the Order of the British Empire. There are memorials to Florence Nightingale, Lord Kitchener and others; the Duke of Wellington, Christopher Wren and Admiral Nelson are buried here, the latter in a black sarcophagus.

St Paul's Cathedral Floorplan

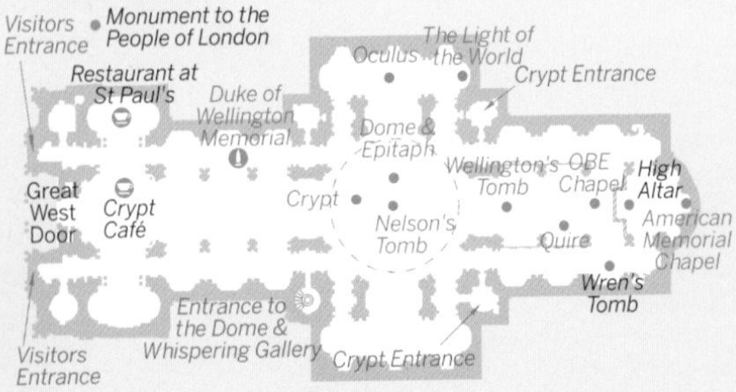

Ground Floor & Crypt

Oculus

The Oculus, opened in 2010 in the former treasury, projects four short films onto its walls. (You'll need to have picked up the iPod audiotour to hear the sound.) If you're not keen on scaling the dome, you can experience it here, audiovisually, from the ground.

Monument to the People of London

Just outside the north transept, there's a simple monument to the people of London, honouring the 32,000 civilians killed (and another 50,000 seriously injured) in the city during WWII.

Temple Bar

To the left as you face the entrance stairway is Temple Bar, one of the original gateways to the City of London. This medieval stone archway once straddled Fleet St at a site marked by a griffin but was removed to Middlesex in 1878. Temple Bar was restored and made a triumphal return to London alongside the redevelopment of Paternoster Sq in 2003.

St Paul's Cathedral

Tours

Joining a tour is one of the best ways to explore the cathedral and allows access to the Geometric Staircase and Chapel of St Michael and St George. Tours are usually held four times a day; book at the desk just past the entrance. The Triforium tour (minimum five people) also takes in the library and Wren's Great Model.

Top Sights
Tower of London

The absolute kernel of London, with a history as bleak and bloody as it is fascinating, the Tower of London is one of London's superlative sights. Begun during the reign of William the Conqueror (1066–87), the Tower is actually a castle, and has served through history as a palace, observatory, storehouse and mint. But it is, of course, most famous for its grizzly past as a prison and site of execution. Despite ever-inflating ticket prices and crowds, it remains a must-see.

Map p90, H5

www.hrp.org.uk

Tower Hill EC3

adult/child £20/11

9am-5.30pm Tue-Sat, 10am-5.30pm Sun & Mon, closes 4.30pm daily Nov-Feb

Tower Hill

Tower of London

Don't Miss

Crown Jewels

Waterloo Barracks is home to the magnificent Crown Jewels. A travelator conveys you past the dozen or so crowns that are the centrepiece, including the £27.5-million Imperial State Crown, set with diamonds (precisely 2868 of them), sapphires, emeralds, rubies and pearls, and the platinum crown of the late Queen Mother, Elizabeth, famously set with the 105-carat Koh-i-Noor (Mountain of Light) diamond.

White Tower

Begun in 1078, this was the original 'Tower' of London, built as a palace and fortress. By modern standards it's not tall, but in the Middle Ages it would have dwarfed the surrounding huts of the peasantry. Inside, along with St John's Chapel, the tower has retained a couple of remnants of Norman architecture, including a fireplace and *garderobe* (lavatory).

Royal Armouries

Housed within the White Tower, this fabulous collection of cannons, guns and suits of armour for men and horses includes Henry VIII's suit of armour, made for the monarch in his forties, the 2m suit of armour made for John of Gaunt and, alongside it, a tiny child's suit of armour designed for James I's young son, Henry.

Chapel Royal of St Peter ad Vincula

At the culmination of your tour, the Chapel Royal of St Peter ad Vincula (St Peter in Chains) is a rare example of ecclesiastical Tudor architecture and the burial place of those beheaded on the scaffold outside, most notably Anne Boleyn, Catherine Howard and Lady Jane Grey. Inside (accessible

Top Tips

- Tag along with one of the Yeoman Warder's tours.
- Avoid immense queues and arrive as early as you can to see the Crown Jewels.
- Book online for cheaper tickets; tickets bought in advance are valid for seven days from the selected date.
- If you've a question, put it to one of the Yeoman Warders who are happy to help.

Take a Break

The red-brick **New Armouries Cafe** (9.30am-4pm Tue-Sat, 10.30am-4pm Sun & Mon), in the southeastern corner of the inner courtyard offers hot meals and sandwiches.

Fortify yourself with wine and eats at nearby Wine Library (p97), but book ahead if lunching.

only via tour) are monuments to luminaries from the Tower's history.

Tower Green Scaffold Site

Anne Boleyn, Catherine Howard, Margaret Pole (countess of Salisbury) and 16-year-old Lady Jane Grey were among privileged individuals executed here. The site is commemorated by a sculpture from artist Brian Catling, and a remembrance poem. To the left of the scaffold site is the Beauchamp Tower, where high-ranking prisoners have left behind melancholic inscriptions.

Bloody Tower

The Bloody Tower takes its nickname from the 'princes in the tower', Edward V and his younger brother, held here and later murdered. Their uncle Richard III usually takes the blame, but an exhibition allows you to vote for your prime suspect. There are also exhibits on Elizabethan adventurer Sir Walter Raleigh, imprisoned here three times by Elizabeth I.

Medieval Palace

Inside St Thomas' Tower, discover what the hall and bedchamber of Edward I might once have looked like. Opposite St Thomas' Tower is Wakefield Tower, built by Henry III between 1220 and 1240 and enticingly furnished with a replica throne and candelabra to give an impression of how it might have looked in Edward I's day.

Bowyer Tower

Behind the Waterloo Barracks is the Bowyer Tower, where George, Duke of Clarence, brother and rival of Edward IV, was imprisoned and, according to a long-standing legend that has never been proved, was drowned in a barrel of malmsey (sweet Madeira wine).

East Wall Walk

The huge inner wall of the Tower was added to the fortress in 1220 by Henry III. This walk begins in the 13th-century Salt Tower, takes in Broad Arrow and Constable Towers and ends with Martin Tower, housing an exhibition of original coronation regalia. Colonel Thomas Blood, disguised as a clergyman, attempted to steal the Crown Jewels from Martin Tower in 1671.

Bell Tower

Housing the curfew bells, the Bell Tower was a one-time lock-up to Thomas More. The politician and author of *Utopia* was imprisoned here in 1534 before his execution for refusing to recognise King Henry VIII as head of the Church of England in place of the Pope.

Tours

While Yeoman Warders officially guard the tower and Crown Jewels at night, their main role is as tour guides (and to pose for photographs with curious foreigners). These tours, which are often extremely amusing and always informative, leave from the Middle Tower every 30 minutes from 10am to 3.30pm (2.30pm in winter).

Understand

Tower of London

Yeoman Warders

Yeoman Warders have been guarding the tower since 1485. There are 35 of them and, to qualify for the job, a minimum of 22 years in the British Armed Forces is mandatory. They all live within the tower walls and are known affectionately as 'beefeaters'. The origin of this name is unknown, although it possibly refers to the large rations of beef given to them in past times.

The Ravens

Legend has it that Charles II requested that ravens always be kept at the Tower as the kingdom would fall apart if they left. Other camps, however, maintain this may well be a Victorian fairy story. There are usually eight ravens permanently at the Tower and their wings are clipped to placate the superstitious.

Ceremonies at the Tower

This elaborate locking of the main gates has been performed daily without fail for more than 700 years. The ceremony begins at 9.53pm precisely, and it's all over by 10pm. Even when a bomb hit the Tower of London during the Blitz, the ceremony was only delayed by 30 minutes. Entry to the ceremony begins at 9.30pm and is free but, in a suitably antiquated style, you have to apply for tickets by post, as demand is so high. See the Tower website for details.

More accessible is the official unlocking of the Tower, which takes place every day at 9am. The keys are escorted by a military guard and the doors are unlocked by a Yeoman Warder. With fewer visitors around, this is a great time to arrive, although you'll have to wait until 10am on a Sunday or Monday to begin your visit.

Koh-i-Noor Diamond

Surrounded by myth and legend, the 14th-century Koh-i-Noor diamond has been claimed by both India and Afghanistan. It reputedly confers enormous power on its owner, but male owners are destined for a tormented death. The Crown Jewels display was due to be redesigned for the Queen's Diamond Jubilee in June 2012.

A
B
C
D
1
2
3
4
5
Farringdon
Cowcross St
St John St
Barbican
Beech St
Silk St
22
Kirby St
Greville St
Long La
Smithfield Market
Charterhouse St
23
West Smithfield
Little Britain
Fore St
Museum of London
1
HOLBORN
Farringdon St
Snow Hill
Hosier La
Cock La
Giltspur St
London Wall
Basinghall St
Noble St
Wood St
St Andrew St
Shoe La
Holborn Viaduct
Angel St
Gresham St
Newgate St
Stonecutter St
Limeburner La
Central Criminal Court
Foster La
Bride St
15
13
King St
St Paul's
Wood St
21
Cheapside
St Paul's Churchyard
Poultry
Fleet St
Ludgate Hill
St Paul's Cathedral
12
City Thameslink
Bouverie St
Whitefriars St
Salisbury Ct
New Bridge St
St Paul's Churchyard
Watling St
Bow La
Carter La
20
Cannon St
11
Tudor St
Temple Ave
18
Puddle Dock
Queen Victoria St
Mansion House
Queen St
Cloak
Blackfriars
Castle Baynard St
White Lion Hill
Upper Thames St
Victoria Embankment
Blackfriars Bridge
Millennium Bridge
0
400 m
0
0.2 miles
Southwark Bridge
Bankside
Park St
Clin
For reviews see
Top Sights p82
Sights p92
Eating p95
Drinking p98
Entertainment p99
Shopping p99

E
F
G
H
1
2
3
4
5
Exchange Square
Lamb St
Spitalfields Market
Wilkes St
Fournier St
Brushfield St
Sun St
Wilson St
Moorgate
South Pl
Eldon St
Liverpool St
Finsbury Circus
Moorgate
London Wall
Blomfield St
Liverpool St
Bishopsgate
New St
Artillery La
White's Row
Commercial St
Fashion St
Brune St
Middlesex St
Wentworth St
Wormwood St
Houndsditch
Camomile St
Petticoat Lane Market
Goulston St
Old Castle St
17
Bishopsgate
St Mary Axe
Bevis Marks
Bury St
Duke's Pl
Aldgate
Aldgate High St
Lothbury
Bank of England Museum
9
Threadneedle St
Princes St
14
Mansion House
Cornhill
Birchin La
19
Bank
8
Leadenhall St
Lloyd's of London
Creechurch La
Mitre St
Jewry St
Billiter St
Fenchurch St
Minories
Mansell St
King William St
Lombard St
Gracechurch St
Lime St
Stephen Walbrook
Fenchurch St
Vine St
America Sq
Crutched Friars
Cannon St
Cannon St
Philpot La
Rood La
Mincing La
Mark La
5
St Olave
Roman Wall
Pepys St
Tower Gateway DLR
16
Trinity Square Gardens
7
Roman Wall
Shorter St
Tower Hill
L Pountney La
Arthur St
Monument
Monument St
Great Tower St
4
Monument
Angel Pass
Lower Thames St
Byward St
3
All Hallows-by-the-Tower
Tower of London
Old Billingsgate Market
Lower Thames St
Tower Bridge Approach
River Thames
London Bridge
Tower of London
The Queen's Walk
Tooley St
2
Tower Bridge

Sights

Museum of London

MUSEUM

1 Map p90, C2

One of the capital's best museums, this presents a fascinating and highly informative journey from Anglo-Saxon village to 21st-century metropolis. Exhibits run from ancient settlements through the Roman era to Saxon, medieval, Tudor and Stuart London and on to the excellent modern galleries, opened in 2010. There's also a great shop and two cafes. (www.museumoflondon.org.uk; London Wall EC2; admission free; 10am-6pm; Barbican or St Paul's)

Tower Bridge

BRIDGE

2 Map p90, H5

According to legend, the German Luftwaffe left this famous bridge intact to act as a navigation aid for bombings raids on London in WWII. True or not, the upper gallery offers a bombardier's view over the river, and there's an exhibition on the steam-powered swing bridge, which still lifts around 1000 times a year for vessels (check web for times). (www.towerbridge.org.uk; adult/child £8/3.40; 10am-6.30pm Apr-Oct, 9.30am-6pm Nov-Mar, last admission 1hr before closing; Tower Hill)

Tower Bridge

All Hallows-by-the-Tower

CHURCH

3 Map p90, G4

All Hallows has stood here since AD 675, and the highlight is undoubtedly its atmospheric Saxon undercroft (crypt), where you'll find a pavement of reused Roman tiles and walls of the 7th-century Saxon church. Above ground it's a pleasant enough church, rebuilt after WWII. From April to September, there are free 20-minute tours at 2pm each day. (www.ahbtt.org.uk; Byward St EC3; admission free; 8am-6pm Mon-Fri, 10am-5pm Sat & Sun; Tower Hill)

Monument

MONUMENT

4 Map p90, E4

Christopher Wren and Dr Robert Hooke's memorial to the Great Fire of London stands 202ft tall – the exact distance to the bakery where the Great Fire started in 1666. The Monument would have towered over London, when first built. Climbing up the column's 311 steps rewards you with some of the best 360-degree views over town. (www.themonument.info; Monument St EC3; adult/child £3/1.50; 9.30am-5.30pm, last admission 5pm; Monument)

St Olave

CHURCH

5 Map p90, G4

St Olave's was built in the mid-15th century, and restored in the 1950s. Most famous of those who worshipped at the church is Samuel Pepys, who is buried here with his

Understand

Churches of the City

As befits the oldest part of London, the City has plenty of historic churches where you can explore some of the oldest architecture in town. Houses of worship include:

- **All Hallows-by-the-Tower**
- **St Olave**
- **St Stephen Walbrook** (p94)
- **St Mary Woolnoth** (9.30am-4.30pm Mon-Fri; Bank)
- **St Mary-le-Bow** (www.stmarylebow.co.uk; Cheapside EC2; 7.30am-6pm Mon-Wed, to 6.30pm Thu, to 4pm Fri; Bank or St Paul's)
- **St Lawrence Jewry** (www.stlawrencejewry.org.uk; Gresham St EC2; 8am-4pm; Bank)
- **St Bartholomew-the-Great** (www.greatstbarts.com; West Smithfield EC1; adult/concession £4/3.50; 8.30am-5pm Mon-Fri, 10.30am-4pm Sat, 8.30am-8pm Sun; Farringdon or Barbican)
- **St Bride's, Fleet Street** (www.stbrides.com; St Bride's Lane EC4; 8am-6pm Mon-Fri, hours vary Sat, 10am-6.30pm Sun; St Paul's or Blackfriars)
- **Temple Church** (p186)

wife, Elizabeth. Dickens called the place 'St Ghastly Grim' because of the skulls above its entrance, but today it's a lovely little spot. (www.sanctuaryinthecity.net; 8 Hart St EC3; admission free; 9am-5pm Mon-Fri, closed Aug; Tower Hill)

St Stephen Walbrook CHURCH

6 Map p90, E3

Widely considered to be the finest of Wren's City churches and a forerunner to St Paul's Cathedral, this 17th century building is indisputably impressive. Some 16 pillars with Corinthian capitals rise up to support its dome and ceiling, while a large, cream-coloured boulder lies at the heart of its roomy central space. The modern altar is by sculptor Henry Moore. (www.ststephenwalbrook.net; 39 Walbrook EC4; admission free; 10am-4pm Mon-Fri; Bank)

Local Life

Tale of Two Cities

While about 300,000 people work in the City of London, only 8000 actually live here. To really appreciate its frantic industry and hum, you're best to come during the week, which is when you'll find everything open. It empties quickly in the evening, though, as its workers retreat to the suburbs. Weekends have a very different appeal, giving you a lot more space for quiet contemplation, although you'll find most places shut tight until Monday. All of the big-hitting sights, however, open on at least one weekend day.

Trinity Square Gardens GARDENS

7 Map p90, G4

Trinity Square Gardens was once the site of the Tower Hill scaffold where many met their fate, the last in 1747. On a grassy area next to Tower Hill tube station's main exit there's a stretch of the medieval wall built on Roman foundations; there's more of the Roman wall around the corner from the station, in the forecourt of the Grange Hotel. (8-14 Cooper's Row; Tower Hill)

Lloyd's of London BUILDING

8 Map p90, F3

People still stop to gawp at the stainless-steel external ducting and staircases of the Lloyd's of London building. A creation of Richard Rogers, its brave-new-world postmodernism concocts a dramatic contrast with the olde-worlde Leadenhall Market next door. While you can watch people whizzing up and down the building's external all-glass lifts, sadly you can't experience it yourself. (www.lloyds.com; 1 Lime St EC3; Aldgate or Bank)

Bank of England Museum MUSEUM

9 Map p90, E3

The centrepiece of this museum – which explores the evolution of money and the history of this venerable institution – is a reconstruction of Soane's original stock office, complete with mahogany counters. Adjacent rooms are packed with exhibits, ranging from silverware and coins to a gold bar you can lift up, as well as the muskets once used to defend the bank. (www.bankofengland.co.uk; Bartholomew Lane EC2; admission free; 10am-5pm Mon-Fri; Bank)

Mansion House
HISTORIC BUILDING

10 Map p90, E3

The imposing Mansion House is the official residence of the Lord Mayor of London and features magnificent interiors, an impressive art collection and a stunning banqueting hall. It's not open to the public except on the weekly tour, which leaves from the porch entrance on Walbrook. The tour is limited to 40 people; tickets are sold on a first-come-first-served basis. (www.cityoflondon.gov.uk; The City of London, EC4; guided tour adult/concession £6/4; tour 2pm Tue; Bank)

Eating

Sweeting's
SEAFOOD ££

11 Map p90, D3

A City institution, Sweeting's has been serving customers since 1889. It hasn't changed much, with its small sit-down dining area, mosaic floor and narrow counters, behind which stand waiters in white aprons. Dishes include sustainably sourced fish of all kinds (grilled, fried or poached), potted shrimps, eels and Sweeting's celebrated fish pie. (www.sweetingsrestaurant.com; 39 Queen Victoria St EC4; mains £13.50-32; lunch Mon-Fri; Mansion House)

Understand

The Gherkin

Built in 2002–03 and known to one and all as 'the Gherkin', **30 St Mary Axe** (www.30stmaryaxe.co.uk; 30 St Mary Axe EC3; Aldgate or Bank) remains London's most distinctive skyscraper, dominating the city despite actually being slightly smaller than the neighbouring NatWest Tower. Sir Norman Foster's phallic sci-fi exterior has become an emblem of modern London as recognisable as Big Ben or the London Eye.

Café Below
CAFE £

12 Map p90, D3

This atmospheric cafe and restaurant in the crypt of St Mary-le-Bow church has good value menus, offering such tasty dishes as fish cakes/steak sandwiches at lunch and fillet of sea bream/courgette filo pie in the evening. There's also a better-than-average choice for vegetarians. In summer there are tables outside on the tree-lined courtyard next to the church. (www.cafebelow.co.uk; St Mary-le-Bow church, Cheapside EC2; mains £8-12; 7.30am-9pm Mon-Fri; ; Mansion House)

Restaurant at St Paul's
MODERN BRITISH ££

Set in the crypt of St Paul's Cathedral (see Map p90, C3), this restaurant has a short and simple menu offering two- or three-course lunches; options range

Understand
The Great Fire of London

As nearly all its buildings were constructed from wood, London had for centuries been prone to conflagration, but the mother of all blazes broke out on 2 September 1666 in a bakery in Pudding Lane in the City.

It didn't seem like much to begin with – the mayor himself dismissed it as being easily extinguished before going back to bed – but the unusual September heat combined with rising winds to spark a tinderbox effect. The fire raged out of control for days, reducing some 80% of London to carbon. Only eight people died (officially at least), but most of London's medieval, Tudor and Jacobean architecture was destroyed. The fire was finally stopped (at Fetter Lane, on the very edge of London) by blowing up all the buildings in the inferno's path. It is hard to overstate the scale of the destruction – 89 churches and more than 13,000 houses were razed, leaving tens of thousands of people homeless. Many Londoners left for the countryside, or sought their fortunes in the New World.

from potted lemon-and-thyme chicken to pork loin chop with a rarebit glaze. It also does a good-value daily express lunch (£15, including a glass of wine) and afternoon tea (served until 4.30pm Monday to Saturday). (www.restaurantatstpauls.co.uk; St Paul's Cathedral, St Paul's Churchyard EC4; 2/3 courses £22/26; noon-3pm; ; St Paul's)

City Càphê
VIETNAMESE £

13 Map p90, D3

Down a quiet little lane off Cheapside, this small cafe attracts queues of City workers for its excellent and good-value Vietnamese street food to eat in or takeaway. Choose from *pho* (noodle soup), salads or summer rolls, or go for the classic (and very reasonable) *banh mi* (baguettes), which are simply delicious. (www.citycaphe.com; 17 Ironmonger Lane EC2; dishes £4-7; 11.30am-3pm Mon-Fri; Bank)

Sauterelle
MODERN FRENCH £££

Up on the mezzanine level of the ornate Royal Exchange (see 14 Map p90, E3), Sauterelle ('grasshopper' in French) offers distinct yet subtly flavoured fine dining, where beautifully cooked and presented dishes are accompanied by a comprehensive and well-chosen wine list. The setting is particularly romantic, with views to the covered courtyard below. Set menus (two/three courses £20/23.50) are good value. (7618 2483; www.sauterelle-restaurant.co.uk; Royal Exchange EC3; mains £18-31; Mon-Fri; Bank)

Royal Exchange Grand Café & Bar
MODERN EUROPEAN ££

14 Map p90, E3

This cafe sits in the middle of the covered courtyard of the beautiful Royal Exchange building. The food runs the gamut from breakfast, salads and sandwiches to oysters and duck confit. (www.danddlondon.com; Royal Exchange EC3; mains £12-16.50; ⊘8am-11pm Mon-Fri; ⊖Bank)

Bar Battu
FRENCH ££

15 Map p90, D3

This intimate place has a fantastic range of 'natural' wines and an enticing selection of dishes to accompany your tipple. From a sumptuous *boudin noir* (blood sausage) to grilled lemon sole, the food is well-executed, and smaller plates and charcuterie are also available. (☑7036 6100; www.barbattu.com; 48 Gresham St EC2; mains £11.50-24.50; ⊘11.30am-11pm Mon-Fri; ⊛; ⊖Bank)

Wine Library
MODERN EUROPEAN ££

16 Map p90, H4

A great place for a light but boozy lunch in the City; buy a bottle of wine at retail price (no mark-up, £7.25 corkage fee) from the large selection on offer at the vaulted-cellar restaurant and then snack on a set plate of delicious pâtés, cheeses and salads. Reservations

Royal Exchange Grand Café & Bar

recommended for lunch. (☎7481 0415; www.winelibrary.co.uk; 43 Trinity Sq EC3; set meals £17.25; ⏲11.30am-3pm Mon, 11.30am-8pm Tue-Fri; ⊖Tower Hill)

Drinking

Vertigo 42

BAR

17 Map p90, F2

On the 42nd floor of a 183m-high tower, this circular bar has expansive views over the city that range for miles on a clear day, becoming stunning at sunset. The classic drinks list is pricier than average – wine by the glass starts from £9.20 and champagne and cocktails from £14, with a limited food menu. Reservations are essential. (☎7877 7842; www.vertigo42.co.uk; Tower 42, 25 Old Broad St EC2; ⏲noon-4.30pm & 5-11pm Mon-Fri, from 5pm Sat; ⊖Liverpool St or Bank)

Local Life

Free View

Designed by Jean Nouvel, **One New Change** (Map p90, C3; www.onenewchange.com; Cheapside EC2; ⊖St Paul's), a recently opened shopping centre, houses mainly run-of-the-mill, high-street brands, but take the lift to its 6th floor and a great open viewing platform will reward you with up-close views of the dome of St Paul's Cathedral and out over London.

Black Friar

PUB

18 Map p90, B4

The interior of the Black Friar is an Arts and Crafts makeover dating back to 1905 and the pub name on the exterior is fashioned from a marvellous mosaic. Built on the site of a Dominican monastery, the theme is appealingly celebrated throughout the pub. Unusually for this part of town, it opens at the weekend. (174 Queen Victoria St EC4; ⊖Blackfriars)

Counting House

PUB

19 Map p90, F3

It's claimed that old banks – with their counters and basement vaults – make perfect homes for pubs, and this award winner certainly looks and feels comfortable in the former headquarters of NatWest with its domed skylight and beautifully appointed main bar. It's a favourite of City boys – who come for the good range of real ales and speciality pies (£9.75). (50 Cornhill EC3; ⏲Mon-Fri; 📶; ⊖Bank or Monument)

Ye Olde Watling

PUB

20 Map p90, D3

This small strip behind St Paul's has an almost village-like feel to it, and the centre of the village is definitely Ye Olde Watling, an old timer with a gorgeous wooden bar that is always busy from 5pm. Food is served and there's a taste-before-you-buy policy for the great selection of real ales. (29 Watling St EC4; ⏲Mon-Fri; ⊖Mansion House)

Barbican

Ye Olde Cheshire Cheese

PUB

21 Map p90, A3

The entrance to this historic pub is via a narrow alley off Fleet St. Past customers have included Dr Johnson, Thackeray and Dickens. Despite (or possibly because of) this the Cheshire feels like a bit of a museum piece, and a fairly shabby one at that. Nevertheless it's one of London's most famous pubs and well worth popping in for a pint. (Wine Office Ct, 145 Fleet St EC4; Mon-Sat; Blackfriars)

Entertainment

Barbican

ARTS CENTRE

22 Map p90, D1

Home to the wonderful London Symphony Orchestra, the Barbican also has an associate orchestra, the lesser-known BBC Symphony Orchestra, which plays regularly, as do scores of leading international musicians across the genres of jazz, folk, world and soul. The centre is also acclaimed for its dance performances and film-goers will love the brilliant sloping seating that guarantees a full-screen view to all. (7638 8891; www.barbican.org.uk; Silk St EC2; Moorgate or Barbican)

Shopping

Smithfield Market

MARKET

23 Map p90, B1

Central London's last surviving meat market, Smithfield Market was built on the site of the notorious St Bartholomew's fair, where witches were traditionally burned at the stake. Today it's a very smart annexe of Clerkenwell and full of bars and restaurants, while the market itself is a wonderful building. Visit before 7am to see it in full swing. (www.smithfieldmarket.com; West Smithfield EC1; 3am-noon Mon-Fri; Farringdon)

Local Life
A Night out in Shoreditch

Getting There

Overground Shoreditch High St and Hoxton are handy stops on the overground.

Underground Old St is a useful station, on the Northern Line (and National Rail).

After a day's sightseeing, night owls can wing over to Shoreditch for a taste of its slick bars, cutting-edge clubs, funky restaurants and spot-on pubs catering to a local creative/media diaspora fleeing high rents elsewhere. Once working class but now gentrified, the neighbourhood spills over into hip Hoxton where the night's partying continues.

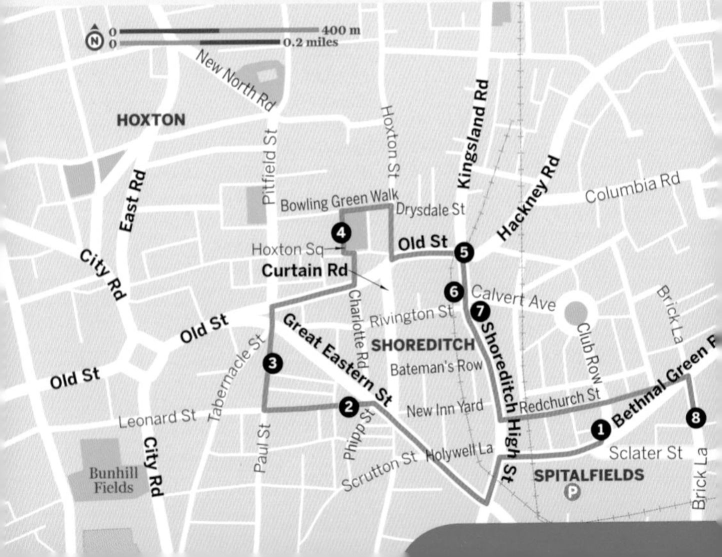

1 Dine at Les Trois Garçons

The name prepares you for the truly excellent French menu at this Victorian pub and restaurant, but perhaps not for its camp decor. Stuffed or bronze animals fill every surface at **Les Trois Garçons** (7613 1924; www.lestroisgarcons.com; 1 Club Row E1; 2/3 courses £39.50/45.50; closed dinner Sun), while chandeliers dangle between suspended handbags.

2 Drink at Book Club

A spacious former Victorian warehouse, the **Book Club** (www.wearetbc.com; 100 Leonard St EC2; 8am-midnight Sun-Wed, to 2am Thu-Sat;) has offbeat events (spoken word, dance lessons, life drawing), as well as DJ nights (punk, ska and '60s pop to electro, house and disco). Food is available day and night.

3 Mingle with the Suits

This handsome and buzzing pub, the **Princess of Shoreditch** (7729 9270; www.theprincessofshoreditch.com; 76 Paul St EC2; mains £10-13;) is frequented by City suits and media types. Food is very well done, with daily specials and polite service backed up by a comprehensive wine list and a good ale selection. Head up the spiral staircase to the more refined (and slightly pricier) 1st-floor dining space (reservations advised).

4 Mix up a Cocktail

The menu at **Happiness Forgets** (www.happinessforgets.com; 8-9 Hoxton Sq N1; 5-11pm Mon-Sat;) promises you mixed drinks and mischief at this low-lit, basement bar with good-value cocktails in a relaxed and intimate setting.

5 Hit the Dance Floor

It doesn't look like much, but **Catch** (www.thecatchbar.com; 22 Kingsland Rd E2; 6pm-midnight Mon-Wed, to 2am Thu-Sat, 7pm-1am Sun) is one of the best nights out in Shoreditch. Upstairs: '90s to funk and hip hop, new and established bands. Downstairs: a big house-party vibe with DJs (free).

6 Club it at Cargo

One of London's most eclectic clubs, **Cargo** (www.cargo-london.com; 83 Rivington St EC2; noon-1am Mon-Thu, noon-3am Fri, 6pm-3am Sat, noon-midnight Sun) boasts a dance-floor room, bar and outside terrace. The music policy is innovative and varied, with plenty of up-and-coming bands also on the menu (food available throughout the day).

7 Get a Pick-Me-Up at Bridge

Late night caffeine? **Bridge** (15 Kingsland Rd E2; noon-1am Sun-Thu, to 2am Fri & Sat;) sells coffee and snacks, but check out the Rococo salon-cum-boudoir upstairs that resembles something decorated by the bastard love child of Louis XIV and your eccentric auntie with all the cats. The downstairs bar retains a distinctive Italian theme with a fantastic old-fashioned till.

8 Grab a Late Night Snack

Round off a full night with a late night bagel on Brick Lane. You won't find fresher (or cheaper) bagels anywhere in London than at **Brick Lane Beigel Bake** (159 Brick Lane E2; filled bagels £1.50-3.50; 24hr) and delicatessen; just ask any taxi driver.

Explore

Tate Modern & South Bank

The South Bank today has transformed into one of London's must-see neighbourhoods. A roll call of riverside sights lines the Thames, commencing with the London Eye, running past the cultural enclave of the Southbank Centre and on to the outstanding Tate Modern, the Millennium Bridge, Shakespeare's Globe, waterside pubs, a cathedral and one of London's most-visited food markets.

The Sights in a Day

Pre-booked ticket for the **London Eye** (p110) in hand, enjoy a leisurely revolution in the city skies for astronomical views (if the weather's clear). If you've children in tow, the nearby **Sea Life London Aquarium** (p112) is a hit with kids. For culture, explore the creative horizons of the **Southbank Centre** (p118) before restoring calories at **Canteen** (p115) or feast on the views at **Skylon** (p113).

Sashay along the South Bank to descend the ramp into the industrial bowels of the **Tate Modern** (p104). If you've a taste for modern and contemporary art, the whole afternoon may vanish. Try to grab a photograph of St Paul's Cathedral on the far side of the elegant **Millennium Bridge** (p111) and consider a tour of the iconic **Shakespeare's Globe** (p117). Further east, follow your nostrils to aromatic **Borough Market** (p118) for gastronomic exploration.

Dine at **Roast** (p115) above Borough Market or at **Magdalen** (p114) along Tooley St, before sinking a drink in the historic **George Inn** (p116) on Borough High St. Theatre lovers will have tickets booked for the **National Theatre** (p117) or the **Old Vic** (p118).

Top Sights

Tate Modern (p104)

Best of London

Eating

Laughing Gravy (p113)

Skylon (p113)

Magdalen (p114)

Oxo Tower Restaurant & Brasserie (p114)

Entertainment

National Theatre (p117)

Shakespeare's Globe (p117)

Royal Festival Hall (p118)

Drinking

George Inn (p116)

Markets

Borough Market (p118)

Getting There

Underground Waterloo, Southwark, London Bridge and Bermondsey stations are all on the Jubilee Line.

Underground The Northern Line runs through London Bridge and Waterloo (the Bakerloo and Waterloo & City lines serve the latter).

Top Sights
Tate Modern

The public's love affair with this phenomenally successful modern art gallery shows no sign of cooling a decade after it opened. In fact, so enraptured are art goers with the Tate Modern that over 50 million visitors flocked to the former power station in its first 10 years. The world's most popular art gallery is naturally one of the most-visited sights in London and is set to expand even further in 2012 by converting two of the power station's huge subterranean oil tanks into display space.

Map p108, D2

www.tate.org.uk/modern

Bankside SE1

admission free/suggested donation £3

10am-6pm Sun-Thu, to 10pm Fri & Sat

Southwark or London Bridge

Tate Modern

Don't Miss

Turbine Hall

First to greet you as you pour down the ramp off Holland St (the main entrance), the cavernous 3300-sq-metre Turbine Hall originally housed the power station's humungous turbines. Today the Turbine Hall has been transformed into a commanding space for large-scale, temporary exhibitions.

Unilever Series

Some art critics swipe at the populism of this annual commission, designed for display in Turbine Hall, but others insist this makes art and sculpture more accessible. Past works have included Carsten Höller's funfair-like slides *Test Site;* Doris Salcedo's enormous fissure in the floor *Shibboleth* and Chinese artist Ai Weiwei's thoughtful and compelling *Sunflower Seeds* – a huge carpet of hand-painted ceramic seeds.

Permanent Collection

LEVELS 3 & 5

Tate Modern's permanent collection is now arranged by both theme and chronology. More than 60,000 works are on constant rotation, and the curators have at their disposal paintings by Georges Braque, Henri Matisse, Piet Mondrian, Andy Warhol, Mark Rothko and Jackson Pollock, as well as pieces by Joseph Beuys, Damien Hirst, Rebecca Horn, Claes Oldenburg, Auguste Rodin and others.

Surrealism

LEVEL 3

Poetry and Dream submerges the viewer in the fantastic mindscapes of Yves Tanguy, Max Ernst, Paul Delvaux and other artists either directly connected with surrealism or influenced by the

Top Tips

- Free guided tours depart at 11am, noon, 2pm and 3pm daily.
- The Tate Modern is open late night Friday and Saturday till 10pm.
- To reach the Tate Britain (p34), hop on the Tate Boat (p34).
- Don't miss the wonderful views of the Thames and St Paul's, particularly from the restaurant-bar on the 7th level and the espresso bar on the 4th.
- The Interactive Zone on the Level 5 concourse has free-to-use interactive resources on the collection.

Take a Break

The **Tate Modern Restaurant** (lunch Sun-Thu, lunch & dinner Fri & Sat) on level 7 is an excellent choice for a main meal, morning coffee or afternoon tea, with panoramic vistas.

Head west to the Oxo Tower Restaurant & Brasserie (p114) for fantastic food and glorious views.

Understand

Tate of the Art

Swiss architects Herzog & de Meuron scooped the prestigious Pritzker Prize in 2001 for their transformation of empty Bankside Power Station, built between 1947 and 1963 and shut by high oil prices in 1981. The conversion of power station into a now-iconic art gallery displayed an inspired and visionary use of space and architecture. Meanwhile, the transformation continues with the 2012 conversion of two underground oil tanks into further gallery space. Visitors will have to wait until 2016 for the opening of the Tate Modern's funky 11-storey geometric extension, also designed by Herzog & de Meuron. The extension will similarly be constructed of brick, but artistically devised as a lattice through which interior lights will be visible at eventide.

movement. Works by Joan Miró, Paul Klee and Alberto Giacometti display the dreamlike form and content of the school, while other canvases reveal the convergence of abstract principles with surreal techniques and themes.

Special Exhibitions

LEVEL 4

Special exhibitions (which carry an admission charge) constantly feed fresh ideas into the Tate Modern. Past exhibitions have included retrospectives on Edward Hopper, Frida Kahlo, August Strindberg, Nazism and 'Degenerate' Art, local 'bad boys' Gilbert & George, Joan Miró, Gauguin, Arshile Gorky, Futurism, Kandinsky and Rothko. Some exhibitions are also held on level 2.

Dynamic Contrasts

LEVEL 5

Focussing on early-20th-century avant-garde movements, including cubism, futurism and vorticism, States of Flux opens with a dramatic pairing of Umberto Boccioni's *Unique Forms of Continuity in Space* and Roy Lichtenstein's pop icon *'Whaam!'*, pieces separated by half a century. Ground-breaking works from Georges Braque, Picasso and other cubists lie beyond.

Pop

LEVEL 5

American Pop Art is also explored in States of Flux, with vibrant and colourful works from Roy Lichtenstein, Andy Warhol and other pop artists commenting on the culture of post-war consumerism. Other pop works, including works by such artists as Robert Rauschenberg, veer in more abstract directions.

Energy & Process

LEVEL 5

The main focus of this gallery is Arte Povera, a radical art movement closely associated with Italian artists in the

Tate Modern, designed by Herzog & de Meuron

late 1960s. A hallmark of the style was the employment of a diverse range of materials in the creation of sculpture, attempting to involve the intrinsic energy of those materials in the art work, while moving away from more traditional substances.

Architecture

The 200m-long Tate Modern is an imposing sight. The conversion of the empty Bankside Power Station – all 4.2 million bricks of it – to art gallery in 2000 was a design triumph. Leaving the building's single central 99m-high chimney, adding a two-storey glass box onto the roof and employing the cavernous Turbine Hall as a dramatic entrance space were three strokes of genius.

A
B
C
D
1
2
3
4
5
Strand
Aldwych
Strand
Temple
Victoria Embankment
Blackfriars
Puddle Dock
Blackfriars Bridge
Waterloo Bridge
River Thames
14
Barge House St
30
26
23
Waterloo Rd
Upper Ground
Stamford St
Hatfields St
Southwark St
Tate Modern
Holland St
Hungerford Bridge
24
Coin St
SOUTHWARK
Meymott St
Great Suffolk St
Belvedere Rd
22
Waterloo East
Joan St
London Eye Millennium Pier
1
Jubilee Gdns
York Rd
SOUTH BANK
Exton St
Alaska St
Wootton St
Southwark
15
20
Union
London Eye
Waterloo
Waterloo
Waterloo Rd
Cons St
The Cut
25
Mitre Rd
Ufford St
Blackfriars Rd
Surrey Row
Sea Life London Aquarium
7
Westminster Bridge
Lower Marsh
Baylis Rd
12
BOROUGH
Webber St
Lancaster St
17
Waterloo Rd
Westminster Bridge Rd
Carlisle La
Lambeth North
Pearman St
Borough Rd
0 400 m
0 0.2 miles
Kennington Rd
St George's Rd
For reviews see
Top Sights p104
Sights p110
Eating p113
Drinking p116
Entertainment p117
Shopping p118
LAMBETH
Lambeth Rd
Imperial War Museum
3
West Square Gdns
Garden Row
London Rd
Elephant & Castle

E
F
G
H
1
2
3
4
5
Queen Victoria St
Mansion House
Cannon St
Cannon St
Gracechurch St
Fenchurch St
Queen St
Upper Thames St
King William St
Monument
Byward St
Lower Thames St
Millennium Bridge
Southwark Bridge
Old Billingsgate Market
London Bridge
Tower of London
Shakespeare's Globe
2
Bankside
River Thames
21
London Bridge Experience & London Tombs
HMS Belfast
6
Park St
Southwark Bridge Rd
Clink St
Southwark Cathedral
Montague Cl
Winchester Walk
4
9
Sumner St
19
London Bridge
8
10
London Dungeon
Battle Br La
The Queen's Walk
Stoney St
28
27
London Bridge
City Hall
11
William Curtis Park
Great Guildford St
16
Borough Market
Old Operating Theatre Museum & Herb Garret
18
London Br St
Tooley St
St Thomas St
13
Shand St
Copperfield St
Redcross Way
Borough High St
Newcomen St
Weston St
Snowsfields
Crucifix La
Druid St
Kipling St
Lant St
Borough
Long La
Leathermarket St
Bermondsey St
Tower Bridge Rd
Southwark Bridge Rd
Borough
BERMONDSEY
Trinity St
Long La
Newington Causeway
Harper Rd
29
Abbey St
Decima St
Bermondsey Market
Rothsay St
Great Dover St
Grange Rd
Falmouth Rd
Pages Wk
New Kent Rd
Elephant & Castle
New Kent Rd

Sights

London Eye
FERRIS WHEEL

1 Map p108, A3

The landmark 135m-tall London Eye fundamentally altered the South Bank skyline. A ride – or 'flight', as it is called here – in one of the wheel's 32 glass-enclosed eye pods, holding up to 28 people, takes a gracefully slow 30 minutes. Weather permitting, you can see 25 miles in every direction from the top of the western hemisphere's tallest Ferris wheel. (0870 500 0600; www.londoneye.com; Jubilee Gardens SE1; adult/child £18.50/9.50; 10am-8.30pm Oct-Mar, to 9pm Apr-Jun, to 9.30pm Jul & Aug, 10am-8.30pm Sep-Mar; ; Waterloo)

Shakespeare's Globe
THEATRE

2 Map p108, E2

Shakespeare's Globe consists of the authentically reconstructed Globe Theatre (p116) and, beneath it, an exhibition hall, entry to which includes a tour (departing every 15 to 30 minutes) of the theatre. When matinees are being staged, the tour shifts to the nearby historic Rose Theatre. (information 7902 1400, bookings 7401 9919; www.shakespeares-globe.org; 21 New Globe Walk SE1; exhibition incl guided tour adult/child £11.50/7; 9am-12.30 & 1-5pm Mon-Sat, 9am-11.30am & noon-5pm Sun late Apr–mid-Oct, 9am-5pm mid-Oct–late Apr; Mansion House or London Bridge)

> Top Tip
>
> **London Eye Tickets**
>
> The London Eye draws 3.5 million visitors annually and at peak times (July, August and school holidays) it can seem like they are all there in the queue with you; save money and shorten queues by buying tickets online, or cough up an extra £10 to showcase your fast-track swagger. Alternatively, visit before 11am or after 3pm to avoid peak density.

Imperial War Museum
MUSEUM

3 Map p108, C5

Fronted by a pair of intimidating 15in naval guns that could lob a 1938lb shell over 16 miles, this riveting museum is housed in what was once Bethlehem Royal Hospwital, commonly known as Bedlam. Although the museum's focus is officially on military action involving British or Commonwealth troops during the 20th century, it rolls out the carpet to war in the wider sense. (www.iwm.org.uk; Lambeth Rd SE1; admission free; 10am-6pm; Lambeth North)

Take a Break Masters Super Fish (p115) serves up a fine lunch.

Southwark Cathedral
CHURCH

4 Map p108, F2

The earliest surviving parts of this fascinating, but small, cathedral are the retrochoir at the eastern end, which was part of the 13th-century Priory of St Mary Overie (from 'St Mary over the Water'), some ancient arcading by

Millennium Bridge to Tate Modern (p104)

the southwest door, 12th-century wall cores in the north transept and an arch that dates to the original Norman church. Most of the cathedral, however, is Victorian. (www.southwark.anglican.org /cathedral; Montague Close SE1; admission free, requested donation £4; ◷8am-6pm Mon-Fri, from 9am Sat & Sun; ⊖London Bridge)

Millennium Bridge
BRIDGE

5 ◉ Map p108, E1

The elegant Millennium Bridge staples the south bank of the Thames in front of Tate Modern with the north bank at the steps of Peter's Hill below St Paul's Cathedral. The low-slung frame designed by Sir Norman Foster and Antony Caro looks spectacular, particularly lit up at night with fibre optics, and

the view of St Paul's from the South Bank is one of London's iconic images. (⊖Mansion House, Blackfriars or Southwark; ⊠London Bridge or Blackfriars)

HMS Belfast
SHIP

6 ◉ Map p108, H2

White Ensign flapping on the Thames breeze, HMS *Belfast* is a magnet for naval-gazing kids. This large, light cruiser served in WWII, helping to sink the German battleship *Scharnhorst* and shelling the Normandy coast on D-Day. Visit the admiral's cabin or peer through the sights of the 4in HA/ LA guns on the open deck. (www.iwm. org.uk; Morgan's Lane, Tooley St SE1; adult/ child £13.50/free; ◷10am-6pm Mar-Oct, to 5pm Nov-Feb; ⊖London Bridge)

Top Tip

Walking the South Bank

The drawcard sights stretch west-east in a manageable riverside melange, so doing it on foot is the best way. To collect the main sights along the South Bank, trace the Silver Jubilee Walk and the South Bank section of the Thames Path along the southern riverbank, with occasional inroads south for shopping, dining and drinking recommendations.

Sea Life London Aquarium

AQUARIUM

7 Map p108, A3

Completed in 1922, grand County Hall contains this excellent aquarium, one of the largest in Europe. Fish and other creatures from the briny deep are grouped in 15 zones according to their geographic origin. There are over 40 sharks, a newly arrived colony of gentoo penguins, ever-popular clownfish and a rewarding rainforests section. (www.sealife.co.uk; Riverside Bldg, County Hall, Westminster Bridge Rd SE1; adult/child £17/12.50; 10am-6pm Mon-Thu, to 7pm Fri-Sun; ; Westminster or Waterloo)

Old Operating Theatre Museum & Herb Garret

MUSEUM

8 Map p108, G2

The highlight of this unique museum, 32-steps up the spiral stairway in the tower of St Thomas Church (1703) focuses on the nastiness of 19th-century hospital treatment. A fiendish array of amputation knives presages the 19th-century operating theatre where doctors operated in rough-and-ready (pre-ether, pre-chloroform, pre-antiseptic) conditions. Contact the museum for details of their spooky Surgery by Gaslight evenings. (7188 2679; www.thegarret.org.uk; 9a St Thomas St SE1; adult/child £6/4; 10.30am-4.45pm; London Bridge)

London Bridge Experience & London Tombs

MUSEUM

9 Map p108, G2

Stuffed away in the vaults beneath so-called New London Bridge (dating back to 1831), this is London's most famous spot. It's essentially for kids, so the roll call includes 'the Keeper of the Heads', who preserved the severed heads of the executed for display on the bridge, plus tombs and plague pits with rodents (animatronics) and zombies-from-nowhere. Save up to 50% by buying online. (0800 043 4666; www.londonbridgeexperience.com; 2-4 Tooley St SE1; adult/child £23/17; 10am-5pm Mon-Fri, 10am-6pm Sat & Sun; London Bridge)

London Dungeon

MUSEUM

10 Map p108, G2

Under the arches of the Tooley St railway bridge, the London Dungeon has been milking its reputation since 1974. Stagger through the Labyrinth of Lost Souls, followed by a peep at the Great Plague and a close shave with Sweeney Todd. The best bits are the fairground-ride boat to Traitor's Gate, the Extremis Drop Ride to Doom and

Vengeance – a spookily entertaining '5D laser ride'. (www.thedungeons.com; 28-34 Tooley St SE1; adult/child £23/17; usually 10am-5pm; London Bridge)

City Hall

BUILDING

11 Map p108, H2

Home to the Mayor of London, bulbous City Hall was designed by Foster and Partners. The 45m, glass-clad building has been compared to Darth Vader's helmet, a woodlouse and a 'glass gonad'. The scoop amphitheatre outside the building is the venue for a variety of free entertainment, from music to theatre in warmer weather. (7983 4100; www.london.gov.uk; The Queen's Walk SE1; admission free; 8.30am-6pm Mon-Thu, to 5.30pm Fri; ; Tower Hill or London Bridge)

Eating

Laughing Gravy

BRITISH **££**

12 Map p108, D4

It's hard not to warm to this cosy and very relaxed restaurant and bar in a former foundry building. Recently steered in a lucratively fresh direction by new owners, this is a true gem, with a sure-fire menu that combines locally sourced food and the culinary talent of chef Michael Facey, with splendid roasts on Sunday. (7998 1707; www.thelaughinggravy.co.uk; 154 Blackfriars Rd SE1; mains £8.50-17.50; 11am-late Mon-Fri, 5.30pm-late Sat, noon-6pm Sun; Southwark)

Skylon

INTERNATIONAL **££**

This excellent restaurant on the top of the refurbished Royal Festival Hall (see 24 Map p108, A2) is divided into grillroom and fine-dining sections by a large bar (open 11am to 1am). The decor is cutting-edge 1950s: muted colours and period chairs (trendy then, trendier now) while floor-to-ceiling windows bathe you in magnificent views of the Thames and the City. Dress smart casual. (7654 7800; www.skylonrestaurant.co.uk; 3rd fl, Royal Festival Hall, South Bank Centre, Belvedere Rd SE1; grillroom mains £12.50-19.50, restaurant 2-/3-course meal £40/45; grillroom noon-11pm, restaurant lunch daily, dinner to 10.30pm Mon-Sat; Waterloo)

Local Life

Pie & Mash

Those curious to find out how Londoners once ate before everything went chic and ethnic should visit a traditional pie 'n' mash shop. **M Manze** (Map p108, H5; 87 Tower Bridge Rd SE1; 11am-2pm Mon, 10.30am-2pm Tue-Thu, 10am-2.15pm Fri, 10am-2.45pm Sat; London Bridge) dates to 1902 and is a classic operation, from the lovely tile work to the traditional working-man's menu: pie and mash (£3.20), pie and liquor (£2.25) and you can take your eels jellied or stewed (£3.20).

VIEW PICTURES LTD / ALAMY ©

Roast restaurant

Magdalen

MODERN BRITISH **££**

13 ✗ Map p108, H3

You can't go wrong with this stylish dining room (with a couple of tables optimistically positioned on the pavement outside). The Modern British fare adds its own appetising spin to familiar dishes (grilled calves' kidneys, creamed onion and sage, smoked haddock *choucroute*). The welcome is warm and the service excellent; a true diamond in the rough. (www.magdalenrestaurant.co.uk; 152 Tooley St SE1; mains £13.50-21, 2-/3-course set lunch £15.50/18.50; ⊘closed lunch Sat & all day Sun; ⊖London Bridge)

Oxo Tower Restaurant & Brasserie

INTERNATIONAL **£££**

14 ✗ Map p108, C2

The Oxo Tower's conversion with this 8th floor restaurant helped spur much of the local dining renaissance. In the stunning glassed-in terrace you get a front-row seat for London's best view: pay for this handsomely in the brasserie and stratospherically in the restaurant. Fish dishes usually comprise half the fusion menu, but vegetarians and vegans will feel at home. (www.harveynichols.com/restaurants/oxo-tower-london; 8th fl, Barge House St SE1; mains £19.50-32.50, 3-course set lunch £35, brasserie 2-/3-course set lunch £22.50/26.50; ⊘lunch & dinner ⊖Waterloo)

Anchor & Hope

GASTROPUB ££

15 Map p108, C3

The hope is that you'll get a table without waiting hours because you can't book at this quintessential gastropub, except for Sunday lunch at 2pm. The anchor is gutsy, British food. Critics love this place to pieces and despite the menu's heavy hitters (pork shoulder or salt marsh lamb shoulder cooked for seven hours), vegetarians aren't totally stranded. (7928 9898; 36 The Cut SE1; mains £11.50-22; closed lunch Mon & dinner Sun; Southwark or Waterloo)

Roast

BRITISH ££

Accessed via an elevator in the middle of Borough Market (see 27 Map p108, F2), this busy modern British eatery sources the meat for its popular roasts from the artisan producers downstairs. Roast also cooks up great breakfasts; if you're on the move, grab snacks from the handy takeout (open till 3pm, except Sunday) outside the main entrance at ground level. (www.roast-restaurant.com; Floral Hall, Borough Market, Borough High St; closed dinner Sun; London Bridge)

Applebee's Fish Café

SEAFOOD ££

16 Map p108, F2

All manner of fresher-than-fresh fish and shellfish dishes are on the ever-changing chalkboard at this excellent fishmonger with a cafe-restaurant attached, but the fish soup as a main is a meal in itself. (www.applebeesfish.com; 5 Stoney St SE1; mains £13.50-39.50, 2-course seasonal set lunch £18.50; lunch and dinner Tue-Sat, closed Sun & Mon; London Bridge)

Canteen

BRITISH ££

Part of the design ethos, the institutional canteen-style furniture – plain wood tables, simple chairs – won't be a hit with everyone, but the outside seating in the shade of big umbrellas behind the Royal Festival Hall (see 24 Map p108, A2) is immensely inviting on sunny days. The British food is homely and no-nonsense: all day breakfasts, shepherd's pie, steak and chips and daily roast. (www.canteen.co.uk; Royal Festival Hall, Belvedere Rd, London SE1; mains £8.50-18.50; 8am-11pm Mon-Fri, 9am-11pm Sat, 9am-10pm Sun; Waterloo)

Masters Super Fish

FISH & CHIPS £

17 Map p108, C4

This popular place serves excellent fish (brought in fresh daily from Billingsgate Market and grilled rather than fried if desired); low on charm but full marks for flavour. (191 Waterloo Rd SE1; mains £8-16; closed Sun; Waterloo)

Top Tip

Beg, Steal or Borough

Freeloaders, gastronomic bargain-hunters and the irrepressibly peckish need to make a pilgrimage to Borough Market (p118) when the munchies strike: loads of freebie samples can be had from the stalls – from tasty titbits to exotic fare!

Understand
A Bard's Eye View of Shakespearian Theatre

The original Globe – known as the 'Wooden O' after its circular shape and roofless centre – was erected in 1599. Rival to the Rose Theatre, all was well but did not end well when the Globe burned to the ground within two hours during a performance of a play about Henry VIII in 1613 (a stage cannon ignited the thatched roof). A tiled replacement was speedily rebuilt only to be closed in 1642 by Puritans, who saw the theatre as the devil's workshop, and it was dismantled two years later.

The new Globe was designed to resemble the original as closely as possible, painstakingly constructed with 600 oak pegs (nary a nail or a screw in the house), specially-fired Tudor bricks and thatching reeds from Norfolk; even the plaster contains goat hair, lime and sand as it did in Shakespeare's time. It even means leaving the arena open to the fickle London skies and roar of passing aircraft, leaving the 700 'groundlings' to stand even in London's notorious downpours.

Drinking

George Inn PUB

18 🍺 Map p108, F3

Owned by the National Trust, London's last surviving galleried coaching inn swims with history. The building is delightfully wonky, but ye gods it gets busy, particularly in summer, when the courtyard is often full to bursting point. (Talbot Yard, 77 Borough High St; ⊘daily; ⊖London Bridge)

Rake PUB

19 🍺 Map p108, F2

The place of superlatives – the only pub actually in Borough Market and the smallest boozer in London – the Rake tucks a strong line up of bitters and real ales (with ⅓ pint measures) into its pea-sized premises. Claustrophobics can find valuable elbow space on the bamboo-decorated decking outside. (14 Winchester Walk SE1; ⊘noon-11pm Mon-Fri, from 10am Sat; ⊖London Bridge)

Baltic BAR

20 🍺 Map p108, D3

This stylish bar at the front of an Eastern European restaurant specialises – not surprisingly – in vodkas; some 50-plus, including bar-infused concoctions, along with cocktails. (www.balticrestaurant.co.uk; 74 Blackfriars Rd SE1; ⊘noon to midnight Mon-Sat, to 10.30pm Sun; ⊖Southwark)

Swan at the Globe BAR–BRASSERIE

At Shakespeare's Globe (see 2 ◉) Map p108, E2), this fine pub-bar (with brasserie) at the piazza level is open for lunch and dinner (lunch only on

Sunday) and has simply glorious views of the Thames and St Paul's on the 1st floor. (www.swanattheglobe.co.uk; 21 New Globe Walk SE1; daily; London Bridge)

Anchor Bankside

PUB

21 Map p108, F2

This riverside boozer dates to the early 17th century (subsequently rebuilt after the Great Fire and again in the 19th century). Trips to the terrace are rewarded with superb views across the Thames but brace for a constant deluge of drinkers. Dictionary writer Samuel Johnson, whose brewer friend owned the joint, drank here as did diarist Samuel Pepys. (34 Park St SE1; daily; London Bridge)

PICTURESOFLONDON/ALAMY ©

Shakespeare's Globe

King's Arms

PUB

22 Map p108, C3

Relaxed and charming when not crowded, this award-winning neighbourhood boozer at the corner of a terraced Waterloo backstreet was a funeral parlour in a previous life, so show some respect. The large traditional bar area, serving up a good selection of ales and bitters, gives way to a fantastically odd conservatory bedecked with junk-store eclectica of local interest, which has decent Thai food. (25 Roupell St SE1; daily; Waterloo or Southwark)

Entertainment

National Theatre

THEATRE

23 Map p108, B2

Another massive concrete block on the South Bank, the National Theatre is going from strength to strength under the directorship of Nicholas Hytner. The three theatre spaces – the Olivier, Lyttleton and Cottesloe – stage different works, so there's always a selection of performances to choose from. (7452 3000; www.nationaltheatre.org.uk; South Bank; Waterloo)

Shakespeare's Globe

THEATRE

The original theatre (see 2 Map p108, E2) where Shakespeare staged his famous plays burned down in 1613, but American director Sam Wanamaker decided to build a perfect replica (p110). Shows here conjure up a powerful sense of the way Shakespeare's work was originally

Top Tip

Shakespeare's Birthday

On the Sunday closest to 23 April (the Bard's birthday), the Globe (p117) hosts an array of fun, free celebratory events in honour of the playwright; contact the theatre for details.

meant to be performed. (information 7902 1400, bookings 7401 9919; www.shakespeares-globe.org; 21 New Globe Walk SE1; daily; St Paul's or London Bridge)

Southbank Centre
CULTURAL CENTRE

24 Map p108, A2

The overhauled **Royal Festival Hall** (located within the Southbank Centre) is London's premier concert venue and seats 3000 in a now acoustic amphitheatre. Catch music and dance performances here and more eclectic gigs at the smaller Queen Elizabeth Hall and Purcell Room. (0844 847 9910; www.southbankcentre.co.uk; Belvedere Rd SE1; daily; Waterloo)

Old Vic
THEATRE

25 Map p108, C3

Never has there been a London theatre with a more famous artistic director. Many were hoping for more from Kevin Spacey's tenure but recent performances seem to have restored the theatre's good reputation. Spacey appears in a couple of shows every year, and Sir Ian McKellen frequently crops up in the Christmas pantomime. (0844 871 7628; www.oldvictheatre.com; The Cut; daily; Waterloo)

BFI Southbank
CINEMA

26 Map p108, B2

The British Film Institute (BFI) maintains the national archives of films and moving images, many of which can be viewed for free in the 'Mediatheque' library. As well as red-carpet events for new releases, there's a regular programme of golden oldies and giant screenings at the Imax (in the middle of the Waterloo Rd roundabout). If you can, visit during the London Film Festival in October. (information 7928 3535, bookings 7928 3232; www.bfi.org.uk; South Bank; 11am-11pm, Mediatheque noon-8pm Tue-Sun; Waterloo)

Shopping

Borough Market
MARKET

27 Map p108, F2

'London's Larder' has enjoyed an astonishing renaissance in the past decade, overflowing with gastronomes and visitors. Along with a section devoted to quality fresh fruit, exotic vegetables and organic meat, there's a fine-foods retail market, with loads of free samples. Takeaway stalls supply gourmet sausages, chorizo sandwiches or quality burgers. The market heaves on Saturdays (get here early). (www.boroughmarket.org.uk; cnr Southwark & Stoney Sts SE1; 11am-5pm Thu, noon-6pm Fri, 8am-5pm Sat; London Bridge)

Royal Festival Hall, Southbank Centre

Konditor & Cook

FOOD

28 Map p108, F2

This elegant cake shop and bakery produces wonderful cakes – lavender and orange, lemon and almond – massive raspberry meringues, cookies (including gingerbread men!) and loaves of warm bread with olives, nuts and spices. There are five other K&C shops on either side of the river. (www.konditorandcook.com; 10 Stoney St SE1; 7.30am-6pm Mon-Fri, 8.30am-5pm Sat; London Bridge)

Bermondsey Market

MARKET

29 Map p108, H4

It was once legal to sell stolen goods here before dawn and although this market is more upright and sedate these days, get here early for the best pickings from cutlery and other old-fashioned silverware, antique porcelain and glassware, paintings and costume jewellery. (www.bermondseysquare.co.uk; Bermondsey Sq; 5am-1pm Fri; Borough or Bermondsey)

South Bank Book Market

BOOKS

30 Map p108, B2

The South Bank Book Market is great for secondhand books long out of print, and is held in all weather in front of the BFI Southbank, under the arches of Waterloo Bridge. (11am-7pm; Riverside Walk SE1; Waterloo)

Top Sights
Hampton Court Palace

Getting There

Train Trains run regularly from Waterloo to Hampton Court, via Wimbledon station.

Boat Westminster Passenger Services Association (7930 2062; www.wpsa.co.uk) run boats from Westminster Pier.

London's most spectacular Tudor palace, 16th-century Hampton Court Palace is steeped in history, from the grand living quarters of Henry VIII to the spectacular gardens, complete with a 300-year-old maze. One of the best days out London has to offer, the palace is mandatory for anyone with an interest in British history, Tudor architecture or gorgeous landscaped gardens. Set aside plenty of time to do it justice (if you arrive by boat from central London, half the day will have vanished already).

Hampton Court Palace

Don't Miss

Clock Court

Passing through the magnificent main gate (Trophy Gate) you arrive first in the Base Court and then the Clock Court, named after the 16th-century astronomical clock that still shows the sun revolving round the earth. The second court is your starting point; from here you can follow any or all of the six sets of rooms in the complex.

Henry VIII's State Apartments

The stairs inside Anne Boleyn's Gateway lead up to Henry VIII's State Apartments, including the Great Hall, the largest single room in the palace, decorated with tapestries and what is considered the country's finest hammer-beam roof. The Horn Room, hung with impressive antlers, leads to the Great Watching Chamber where guards controlled access to the king.

Chapel Royal

Further along the corridor is the beautiful Chapel Royal, built in just nine months and still a place of worship after 450 years. The blue-and-gold vaulted ceiling was originally intended for Christ Church, Oxford, but was installed here instead; the 18th-century reredos was carved by Grinling Gibbons.

Tudor Kitchens

The delightful Tudor kitchens, again accessible from Anne Boleyn's Gateway, once rustled up meals for a royal household of some 1200 people. The kitchens have been fitted out as they might have appeared in Tudor days and palace 'servants' turn the spits, stuff the peacocks and frost the marzipan with real gold leaf. Don't miss the Great Wine Cellar.

0844 482 7777

www.hrp.org.uk/HamptonCourtPalace

Hampton Court Rd, East Molesy KT8

all-inclusive ticket adult/child £16/8

10am-6pm late Mar-Oct, to 4.30pm Nov-late Mar

Hampton Court

Top Tips

- Glide (or slide) on the glittering ice rink at the palace from late November to mid-January.
- Tag along with a costumed guide on fun and informative tours.

Take a Break

Hampton Court Palace is an excellent place for picnicking in the gorgeous gardens.

The **Tiltyard Café** (10am-4.30pm Nov-late Mar 10am-6pm late Mar-Oct) at the palace has a decent menu and lovely views over the garden.

King's Apartments
West of the colonnade in the Clock Court is the entrance to the Wolsey Rooms and the Young Henry VIII Exhibition. East of the colonnade in the Clock Court are stairs to the King's Apartments, a tour of which takes you up the grand King's Staircase, painted by Antonio Verrio. Highlights are the King's Great Bedchamber and the King's Closet (where His Majesty's toilet has a velvet seat).

Queen's Apartments
William's wife, Mary II, had her own Queen's Apartments, accessible up the Queen's Staircase, decorated by William Kent. When Mary died in 1694, work on these was incomplete; they were finished during the reign of George II. Compared with the King's Apartments, those for the queen seem austere, although the Queen's Audience Chamber has an imposing throne.

Georgian Rooms
Also worth seeing are the Georgian Rooms used by George II and Queen Caroline on the last royal visit to the palace in 1737. The first rooms were designed to accommodate George's second son, the Duke of Cumberland, whose bed is woefully tiny for its grand surroundings.

Cartoon Gallery
This is where the real Raphael Cartoons (now in the Victoria & Albert Museum, see p128) used to hang; the ones you see here in the Cartoon Gallery are late-17th-century copies.

Queen's Private Apartments
Beyond the Cartoon Gallery are the Queen's Private Apartments: her drawing room and bedchamber, where she and the king would sleep if they wanted to be alone. Particularly interesting are the Queen's Bathroom, with its tub set on a floor cloth to soak up any spillage, and the Oratory, an attractive room with its exquisite 16th-century Persian carpet.

Garden & Maze
Beyond the palace are the stunning gardens. Look out for the Real Tennis Court, dating from the 1620s. No-one should leave Hampton Court without losing themselves in the famous 800m-long maze, made of hornbeam and yew and planted in 1690. The maze is included in entry, although those not visiting the palace can enter for £3.85 (£2.75/11 for children/families).

Beer & Jazz Festival
Real ale joins jazz at this entertaining jazz festival (www.hamptoncourtbeerandjazz.com), held at the palace in late August. The outdoor festival ranges through the octaves over roughly four days, taking whatever the London weather throws at it (so dress accordingly).

Understand

History of Hampton Court

Like so many royal residences, Hampton Court Palace was not built for the monarchy at all. In 1515 Cardinal Thomas Wolsey, Lord Chancellor of England, built himself a palace in keeping with his sense of self-importance. Unfortunately, even Wolsey couldn't persuade the pope to grant Henry VIII a divorce from Catherine of Aragon and relations between king and chancellor soured. With that in mind, you only need to glance at the palace to see why Wolsey felt obliged to present it to Henry, a monarch not too fond of anyone trying to outdo him. The hapless Wolsey was charged with high treason but died in 1530, before he could come to trial.

As soon as he had his royal hands upon the palace, Henry set to work expanding it, adding the Great Hall, the exquisite Chapel Royal and the sprawling kitchens. By 1540 it had become one of the grandest and most sophisticated palaces in Europe, but Henry only spent an average three weeks a year here. James I kept things ticking over at Hampton Court while Charles I put in a new tennis court and did some serious art-collecting, before finding himself a prisoner in the palace during the Civil War. After the war, puritanical Oliver Cromwell warmed to his own regal proclivities, spending weekends in the comfort of the former Queen's bedroom at the palace and flogging Charles I's art collection. In the late 17th century, William and Mary employed Sir Christopher Wren for extensions: the result is a beautiful blend of Tudor and 'restrained baroque' architecture.

Haunted Hampton Court

With a history as old and as eventful as Hampton Court Palace, a paranormal dimension is surely par for the course. Arrested for adultery and detained in the palace in 1542, Henry's fifth wife, Catherine Howard, was dragged screaming down a gallery at the palace by her guards after an escape bid. Her ghost is said to do a repeat performance to this day in the Haunted Gallery (she must be a tireless ghost as she also haunts the Tower of London). Not to be outshone, the ghostly Grey Lady (supposedly former Tudor servant Dame Sybil Penn) has scared the bejesus out of mere mortals in the Clock Court and the State Apartments.

Explore

Kensington Museums

With its triumvirate of top museums, Kensington is compulsory sightseeing land. Shoppers will adore the King's Rd, mixing with the well-heeled up to Knightsbridge and Harrods via Sloane St, but earmark a sight-packed day for a visit to Hyde Park and conjoined Kensington Gardens. Dining is an experience in itself, with an astonishing choice, whether you're grazing, snacking or simply feasting.

The Sights in a Day

Make a start with the bountiful **Victoria & Albert Museum** (p126), bearing in mind you could easily spend the entire day in this one museum alone. If you've children, start instead with the **Natural History Museum** (p130) or the **Science Museum** (p138), both enthralling for young ones. For lunch, dine at **Refreshment Rooms** (p127) at the V&A.

Clamber up monumental **Wellington Arch** (p139) for the views before exploring stately **Apsley House** (p139) opposite. Set aside the rest of the afternoon exploring **Hyde Park** (p138) and **Kensington Gardens** (p138), including **Kensington Palace** (p138) and the **Albert Memorial** (p139), or if your instinct is shopping, head to **Harvey Nichols** (p145) or **Lulu Guinness** (p145).

Dinner at **Launceston Place** (p140) or **Zuma** (p141) is highly recommended, but aim for sunset with a cocktail at **Galvin at Windows** (p142) or rub shoulders with local drinkers at the **Drayton Arms** (p143). Tickets for a performance at the **Albert Hall** (p144) or the **Royal Court Theatre** (p144) will conclude a sightseeing-packed day with a much needed seat and great entertainment.

For a local's shopping day around Kensington, see p134.

Top Sights

Victoria & Albert Museum (p126)
Natural History Museum (p130)

Local Life

Shopping around Chelsea & Knightsbridge (p134)

Best of London

Museums & Galleries
Victoria & Albert Museum (p126)
Natural History Museum (p130)

Parks & Gardens
Hyde Park (p138)
Kensington Gardens (p138)
Wildlife Garden (p133)

Entertainment
Royal Albert Hall (p144)
Royal Court Theatre (p144)

Museums for Kids
Science Museum (p138)
Natural History Museum (p130)

Getting There

Underground South Kensington, Sloane Sq, Victoria, Knightsbridge, Hyde Park Corner, High St Kensington stations.

Bus Handy routes include 74, 52 and 360.

Top Sights
Victoria & Albert Museum

The Museum of Manufactures, as the V&A was known when it opened in 1852, specialises in decorative art and design with some 4.5 million objects reaching back as far as 3000 years, from Britain and around the globe. The museum boasts an unparalleled collection in a setting as inspiring as the sheer diversity and (often exquisite) rarity of its exhibits. Its original aims – which still hold today – were the 'improvement of public taste in design' and 'applications of fine art to objects of utility'.

Map p136, D4

www.vam.ac.uk

Cromwell Rd SW7

admission free

10am-5.45pm, to 10pm Fri

South Kensington

Sculptures in the British Galleries, Victoria & Albert Museum

Don't Miss

Islamic Middle East Gallery
ROOM 42, LEVEL 1

This gallery holds more than 400 objects from the Islamic Middle East, including ceramics, textiles, carpets, glass and woodwork from the 8th-century caliphate up to the years before WWI.

Ardabil Carpet
ROOM 42, LEVEL 1

The highlight of the Islamic Middle East Gallery is the gorgeous Ardabil Carpet, the world's oldest (and one of the largest) dated carpet. It was completed in 1540, one of a pair commissioned by Shah Tahmasp, then ruler of Iran. The carpet is most astonishing for the artistry of the detailing and the breathtaking subtlety of its design.

China Collection & the Japan Gallery
ROOMS 44, 45 & 47E, LEVEL 1

The TT Tsui China collection (rooms 44 and 47e) displays lovely pieces, including an art deco–style woman's jacket (1925–35) and exquisite Tang dynasty Sancai porcelain. Within the subdued lighting of the Japan Gallery (room 45) stands a fearsome suit of armour in the Domaru style.

Tipu's Tiger
ROOM 41, LEVEL 1

This disquieting 18th-century wood-and-metal mechanical automaton portrays a European being savaged by a tiger. When a handle is turned, an organ hidden within the feline mimics the cries of the dying man, whose arm also rises.

Cast Courts
ROOM 46A, LEVEL 1

One of the museum's highlights is the Cast Courts, containing staggering plaster casts collected in the

Top Tips

- For fewer crowds and more space, visit late on Friday evenings.
- Consider one of the free introductory guided tours, which leave the main reception area every hour from 10.30am to 3.30pm.
- The V&A's temporary exhibitions are compelling and fun (note that admission fees apply).
- The V&A also has an excellent program of talks, workshops and events, plus one of the best museum shops around.
- For fresh air, the landscaped John Madejski Garden is a lovely shaded inner courtyard.

Take a Break

Make for the V&A Café in the magnificent **Refreshment Rooms** (Morris, Gamble and Poynter Rooms), dating from the 1860s.

In the summer, the **Garden Café** (10am-5.15pm) in the John Madejski Garden is open for drinks and snacks.

Victorian era, such as Michelangelo's *David*, acquired in 1858.

Photography Collection
ROOM 38A, LEVEL 1

The photography collection is one of the nation's best, with over 500,000 images collected since 1852.

Raphael Cartoons
48A, LEVEL 1

The highly celebrated Raphael cartoons, which were moved here from Hampton Court Palace in 1865, are designs for tapestries created for the Sistine Chapel.

Fashion Room
ROOM 40, LEVEL 1

Due to reopen in 2012, the Fashion Room is among the most popular, with displays ranging from Elizabethan costumes to Vivienne Westwood gowns, dated 1980s Armani outfits and designs from contemporary catwalks.

Henry VIII's Writing Box
ROOM 58E, LEVEL 2

The British Galleries, featuring every aspect of British design from 1500 to 1900, are divided between levels 2 (1500–1760) and 4 (1760–1900). One highlight is a relic from Henry VIII's reign – an exquisitely ornate walnut and oak 16th-century writing box. The original decorative motifs are superb, including Henry's coat of arms, flanked by Venus (holding Cupid) and Mars.

Great Bed of Ware
ROOM 57, LEVEL 2

There's also the so-called Great Bed of Ware from the late 16th century, big enough to sleep five! With an astounding width of 326cm, the bed even finds mention in William Shakespeare's *Twelfth Night*.

Hereford Screen
LEVEL 3

Designed by Sir George Gilbert Scott, this mighty choir screen is a labour of love, originally fashioned for Hereford Cathedral. An almighty conception of wood, iron, copper, brass and hardstone, there were few parts of the museum that could support its terrific mass.

Jewellery Gallery
ROOMS 91-93, LEVEL 3

The Jewellery Gallery in Materials and Techniques is outstanding, including pieces of exquisite intricacy, from early Egyptian, Greek and Roman jewellery to dazzling tiaras and contemporary designs. The upper level – accessed via the glass and perspex spiral staircase – glitters with jewel-encrusted swords, watches and gold boxes.

20th Century Gallery
ROOMS 74-76, LEVEL 3

The 20th Century Gallery embraces design classics from a Le Corbusier chaise longue to a Sony Walkman, Katherine Hamnett T-shirts and a Nike 'Air Max' shoe from 1992.

Victoria & Albert Floorplan

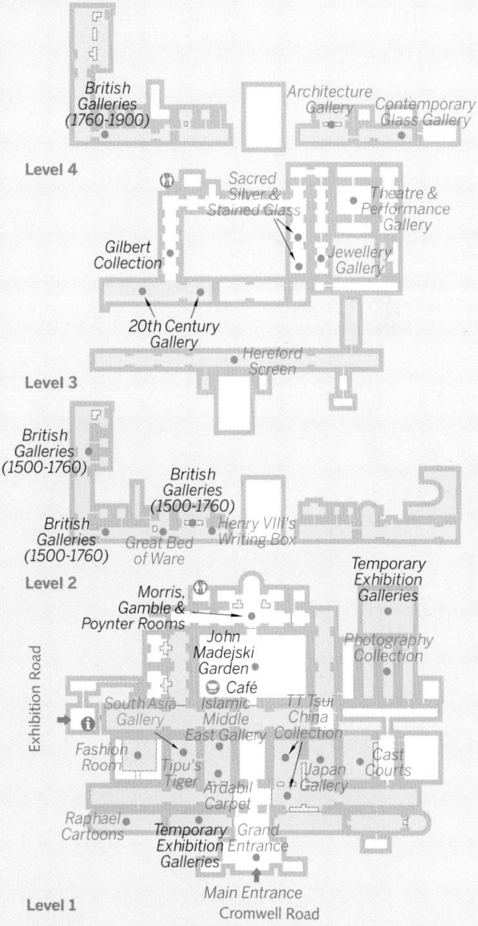
British
Galleries
(1760-1900)
Architecture
Gallery
Contemporary
Glass Gallery
Level 4
Sacred
Silver &
Stained Glass
Theatre &
Performance
Gallery
Gilbert
Collection
Jewellery
Gallery
20th Century
Gallery
Hereford
Screen
Level 3
British
Galleries
(1500-1760)
British
Galleries
(1500-1760)
British
Galleries
(1500-1760)
Great Bed
of Ware
Henry VIII's
Writing Box
Level 2
Temporary
Exhibition
Galleries
Morris,
Gamble &
Poynter Rooms
John
Madejski
Garden
Photography
Collection
Café
Exhibition Road
South Asia
Gallery
Islamic
Middle
East Gallery
TT Tsui
China
Collection
Fashion
Room
Tipu's
Tiger
Ardabil
Carpet
Japan
Gallery
Cast
Courts
Raphael
Cartoons
Temporary
Exhibition
Galleries
Grand
Entrance
Main Entrance
Cromwell Road
Level 1

Top Sights
Natural History Museum

One of London's best-loved museums, this colossal landmark building is infused with the irrepressible Victorian spirit of collecting, cataloguing and interpreting the natural world. A symphony in stone, the main museum building, designed by Alfred Waterhouse with its blue and sand-coloured brick and terracotta, is as much a reason to visit as the world-famous collection within. Kids are the No 1 fans, but adults remain as enamoured of the exhibits as their inquisitive offspring.

Map p136, C4

7942 5000

www.nhm.ac.uk

Cromwell Rd SW7

admission free

10am-5.50pm, to 10pm last Friday of month

South Kensington

Interior of the Natural History Museum

Don't Miss

Architecture

When visiting, admire the astonishing architecture designed by Alfred Waterhouse: with carved pillars, animal bas-reliefs, sculptures of plants and beasts, leaded windows and sublime arches, the museum is a work of art and a labour of love. Beyond the gorgeous arched entrance, examine the lovingly painted ceiling of the Central Hall, with panels depicting plants from across the globe.

Diplodocus Skeleton

CENTRAL HALL

It's hard to match any of the exhibits with the initial sight of the overarching Diplodocus skeleton rising up when you enter the Central Hall just ahead of the main entrance. A herbivorous quadruped, Diplodocus (double beamed lizard) was one of the longest dinosaurs to have lived and weighed in at around twelve to sixteen tons.

Dinosaur Gallery

BLUE ZONE

Children immediately yank their parents to the fantastic dinosaur gallery (Blue Zone). With an impressive overhead walkway past twitchy-looking Velociraptors, it culminates in the museum's star attraction down the ramp: the awesome roaring and tail-flicking animatronics *T. rex*. Make your way back via hands-on exhibits on dinosaurs, including a skeleton of a triceratops (a vegetarian, despite his fearsome appearance).

Green Zone

The galleries here are stuffed with fossils and glass cases of taxidermic birds. Ponder the enormity of the extinct giant ground sloth and visit the excellent Creepy Crawlies room. The thoughtful Ecology section is also here, explaining the

☑ Top Tips

- Try to schedule a visit on the last Friday of the month, when the museum is open till 10pm (except December).
- The monthly Dino Snores sleepover (£46 per child; ⏲7pm-9.50am) is great fun for kids, but book well ahead; if they feel left out, adults can embark on a Night Safari (£28).
- Step-free access for disabled visitors is on Exhibition Rd.

Take a Break

The museum is huge and will drain even the most seasoned museum-goer. Handily located behind the main staircase in the Central Hall, the **Central Hall Café** (⏲10am-5.30pm) serves hot and cold drinks and snacks.

The **Restaurant** (⏲11am-5pm) in the Green Zone serves pizzas, burgers, salads and has a kids menu.

delicate relationship between humans and the world they inhabit.

Blue Whale

BLUE ZONE

Hanging from the ceiling, this life-size mock up of a blue whale is one of the museum's star attractions. Even bigger than the dinosaurs, the Blue Whale (*Balaenoptera musculus*) is the largest creature to have existed, weighing two tons at birth, while adult Blue Whales consume over four tons of krill daily!

Earth Galleries

RED ZONE

The Earth galleries are easily accessed from the Exhibition Rd entrance. Swapping Victorian fustiness for sleek, modern design, the black walls of the Earth Hall are lined with crystals, gems and precious rocks. By the Rio Tinto Atrium escalator, discover how the skull of a mastodon spawned the myth of the Cyclops with the hole in its skull (where the trunk attached).

Earth's Treasury

RED ZONE

Part of the Earth Galleries, Earth's Treasury includes a magnificent collection of colourful minerals, gemstones and rocks ranging across the spectrum from opals to kryptonite-green dioptase and milky-white albite cat's eyes.

The Power Within

RED ZONE

Ride out a tremor in The Power Within (Red Zone), where the mock-up of the Kobe earthquake, a facsimile of a small Japanese grocery shop, shudders in replication of the 1995 earthquake where more than 6000 people perished. Explanations reveal that the Japanese once blamed earthquakes on Namazu, a vast and restless catfish trapped by a rock.

Pele's Hair

RED ZONE

In the Volcanoes section on the upper floors discover how the glistening fibres of 'Pele's Hair' (thin strands of glistening volcanic glass) are a miraculous by-product of volcanic explosions. The 'hair' can result when molten volcanic material is ejected into the air and spun out into fine strands by the wind. (Pele is the goddess of volcanoes in Hawaiian mythology.)

Darwin Centre

ORANGE ZONE

This vast centre focuses on taxonomy (the study of the natural world), with some 450,000 jars of pickled specimens, including an 8.6m-long giant squid called Archie, shown off during free guided tours every half-hour (book in advance). The centre's new feature showcases some 28 million insects and six million plants in 'a giant cocoon'.

Sensational Butterflies

Inside the Sensational Butterflies tunnel tent on the East Lawn, there are swarms of what must originally have been called 'flutter-bys'. It's open

Dinosaur Gallery, Natural History Museum

from 10am to 6pm, mid-April to mid-September (£3.50 for adult/child and £12 for a family).

Wildlife Garden
Home to thousands of British and animal species, the beautiful Wildlife Garden is open from April to October. It displays a range of British lowland habitats, even including a meadow with farm gates and a bee tree with a colony of honey bees. Late summer sees the arrival of Greyface Dartmoor sheep; ornithologists can look out for moorhens, wrens and finches.

Skating at the Museum
In winter months (November to January), a section by the East Lawn of the Natural History Museum is transformed into a glittering and highly popular ice rink. Our advice: book your slot well ahead (www.ticketmaster.co.uk), browse the museum and skate later.

Natural History Museum Shop
Not far from the Cromwell Rd entrance to the museum, the well-stocked shop has bundles of imaginative and educational toys, games, collectibles, stationery and books for young natural historians. It's open from 10am to 5.50pm.

Local Life
Shopping around Chelsea & Knightsbridge

From ever-fashionable Chelsea hub Sloane Sq to the well-groomed swirl of shoppers in Knightsbridge, you'll be rewarded with all-embracing shopping opportunities, from charming bookshops through an inspiring design emporium, rare art nouveau architecture to exclusive handmade shoes. Pick up some souvenirs in London's signature department store and celebrate your smart buys with drinks in a classic British pub.

❶ Peruse art at the Saatchi Gallery

A short walk up the King's Rd from Sloane Sq, the invigorating **Saatchi Gallery** (☎7823 2363; www.saatchi-gallery.co.uk; Duke of York's HQ, King's Rd SW3 4SQ; admission free; ⊙10am-6pm; ⊖Sloane Sq) is a must for art lovers, with this excellent gallery space embracing 6500 sq metres for temporary exhibitions of contemporary international art and sculpture.

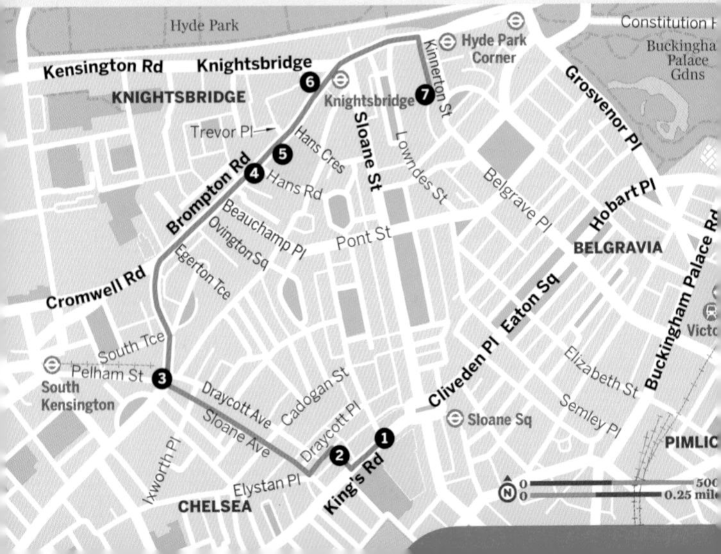

❷ Browse at John Sandoe Books

The perfect antidote to impersonal book superstores, this atmospheric and individual **bookshop** (www.johnsandoe.com; 10 Blacklands Tce SW3; ⏲9.30am-5.30pm Mon-Sat, to 7.30pm Wed, noon-6pm Sun; ⊖Sloane Sq) is a treasure trove of literary gems and hidden surprises. In business for decades, loyal customers swear by it and the knowledgeable booksellers spill forth with well-read pointers.

❸ Check out the Conran Shop

Located within iconic art nouveau Michelin House (p140), this splendid **design shop** (www.conranshop.co.uk; Michelin House, 81 Fulham Rd SW3; ⏲10am-6pm Mon, Tue & Fri, to 7pm Wed & Thu, to 6.30pm Sat, noon-6pm Sun; ⊖South Kensington) constantly rewards visits with ideas, from chic canvases of literary first editions, quirky gifts for the kids, lovely deco-style furniture, trendy minimalist wristwatches and much more.

❹ Size up a pair of Church's shoes

It can take up to eight weeks to make a pair of shoes from **Church's** (www.church-footwear.com; 143 Brompton Rd SW3; ⏲10.30am-6.30pm Mon-Sat, noon-6pm Sun; ⊖Knightsbridge), so they will cost an arm and, more appropriately, a leg, but they have been lovingly produced in Northampton since 1873 with such exquisite care and precision they can last decades.

❺ Explore Harrods

Simultaneously garish and stylish, **Harrods** (☎7730 1234; www.harrods.com; 87-135 Brompton Rd SW1; ⏲10am-8pm Mon-Sat, 11.30am-6pm Sun; ⊖Knightsbridge) is an obligatory stop for everyone from the cash strapped to big, big spenders. Piped opera will be thrown at you as you recoil from the price tags but the stock is astonishing and you'll swoon over the spectacular food hall.

❻ Cutler & Gross

This flagship boutique of **Cutler & Gross** (16 Knightsbridge Green; ⏲9.30am-7pm Mon-Sat, noon-5pm Sun; ⊖Knightsbridge) sells a stunning range of glam, handmade glasses frames and sunglasses to those who want to make a real splash. Colourful frames are hip and distinctive with classic undertones; collections capturing a different stylistic zeitgeist appear regularly. A branch for vintage frames is nearby at 7 Knightsbridge Green.

❼ A beer in the Nag's Head

A gorgeously genteel early-19th-century drinking den located in a serene mews not far from bustling Knightsbridge, the **Nag's Head** (53 Kinnerton St SW1; ⊖Hyde Park Corner) has eccentric decor (think 19th-century cricket prints), traditional wood-panelled charm, a sunken bar and a no-mobile-phones rule. Quiet and relaxed, it's a great place to conclude a day's shopping.

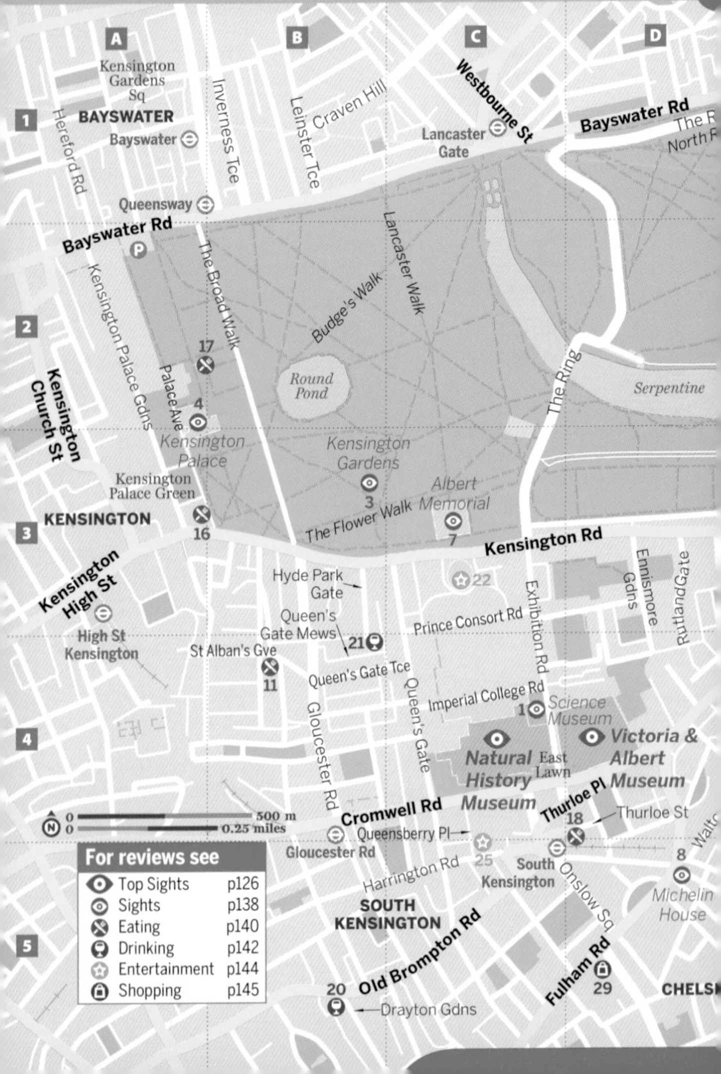
A
B
C
D
1
2
3
4
5
Kensington Gardens Sq
BAYSWATER
Bayswater
Hereford Rd
Inverness Tce
Leinster Tce
Craven Hill
Westbourne St
Lancaster Gate
Bayswater Rd
The Ring
North R
Queensway
Bayswater Rd
The Broad Walk
Lancaster Walk
Budge's Walk
Kensington Palace Gdns
Kensington Church St
Palace Ave
17
4
Round Pond
The Ring
Serpentine
Kensington Palace
Kensington Gardens
Kensington Palace Green
3
Albert Memorial
KENSINGTON
16
The Flower Walk
7
Kensington Rd
Kensington High St
High St Kensington
Hyde Park Gate
22
Ennismore Gdns
Rutland Gate
Queen's Gate Mews
Prince Consort Rd
Exhibition Rd
21
St Alban's Gve
11
Queen's Gate Tce
Imperial College Rd
1
Science Museum
Gloucester Rd
Queen's Gate
Natural History Museum
East Lawn
Victoria & Albert Museum
Thurloe Pl
Thurloe St
0 500 m
0 0.25 miles
Cromwell Rd
18
Queensberry Pl
Gloucester Rd
25
South Kensington
Onslow Sq
8
Harrington Rd
Michelin House
SOUTH KENSINGTON
Old Brompton Rd
Fulham Rd
29
20
Drayton Gdns
CHELS
For reviews see
Top Sights p126
Sights p138
Eating p140
Drinking p142
Entertainment p144
Shopping p145

E
F
G
H
1
2
3
4
5
Marble Arch
10 Marble Arch
Speaker's Corner
North Audley St
Duke St
Brook St
Grosvenor St
Conduit St
Regent St
New Bond St
South Audley St
Park La
Berkeley St
Piccadilly
ST JAMES'S
Charles St
Curzon St
2 Hyde Park
Green Park
19
Hertford St
Piccadilly
Green Park
Queen's Walk
Serpentine Rd
The Mall
Apsley House 5
Rotten Row
NIGHTSBRIDGE
South Carriage Dr
Knightsbridge
6 Wellington Arch
Constitution Hill
Hyde Park Corner
13
Knightsbridge
26
Buckingham Palace Gnds
Lowndes St
Grosvenor Pl
12
Brompton Rd
Birdcage Walk
Buckingham Gate
Belgrave Sq
Belgrave Sq
Palace St
Eaton Pl
Grosvenor Gardens
Hobart Pl
Victoria St
auchamp Pl
Pont St
Sloane St
Buckingham Palace Rd
Westminster Cathedral 9
Eaton Sq
Eaton Sq
Chester Sq
Victoria
Vauxhall Bridge Rd
Cadogan Pl
28
Wilton Rd
24
Belgrave Rd
Sloane Tce
Victoria Coach Station (Arrivals)
14
27
30
23
Draycott Pl
raycott Ave
ane Ave
Lower Sloane St
Sloane Sq
Victoria Coach Station
Warwick Way
PIMLICO
15
King's Rd
stan Pl
Pimlico Rd

Sights

Science Museum

MUSEUM

1 Map p136, C4

With seven floors of interactive and educational exhibits, this scientifically spellbinding museum will mesmerise even the most precocious of young know-it-alls. Some children head for the ground-floor shop's voice warpers, lava lamps, boomerangs, bouncy globes and alien babies, and stay put. Highlights include the Energy Hall on the ground floor and the riveting Flight Gallery on the third floor. (www.sciencemuseum.org.uk; Exhibition Rd SW7; admission free; 10am-6pm; ; South Kensington)

Take a Break Relax at an illuminated table top in the **Deep Blue Cafe** (ground floor level, Wellcome Wing, Science Museum).

Hyde Park

PARK

2 Map p136, F2

London's largest royal park spreads itself over 142 hectares of neatly manicured gardens, wild expanses of overgrown grass and magnificent trees, from misshapen beeches to evergreen monkey puzzles. Hyde Park is separated from Kensington Gardens by the L-shaped **Serpentine**, a small lake that will host the Olympic triathlon and marathon swimming events in 2012. (5.30am-midnight; Hyde Park Corner, Marble Arch, Knightsbridge or Lancaster Gate)

Top Tip

Science Museum for Tots

If you've kids under the age of five, pop down to the basement of the Science Museum to find **The Garden**, where there's a fun-filled play zone, including a water-play area, besieged by tots in red waterproof smocks.

Kensington Gardens

PARK

3 Map p136, B3

Immediately west of Hyde Park and across the Serpentine lake, these gardens are technically part of Kensington Palace. Highlights include the **Serpentine Gallery** (www.serpentinegallery.org; Kensington Gardens W2; 10am-6pm;), one of London's most important contemporary art galleries, the thoughtfully conceived **Princess Diana Memorial Fountain** and George Frampton's celebrated **Peter Pan statue**, close to the lake. (7298 2000; www.royalparks.org.uk; 6am-dusk; Queensway, High St Kensington or Lancaster Gate)

Kensington Palace

HISTORIC BUILDING

4 Map p136, A2

Built in 1605 and most recently restored in 2011, the palace became the favourite royal residence under William and Mary of Orange in 1689, and remained so until George III became king and relocated to Buckingham Palace. In the 17th and 18th centuries, Kensington Palace was variously renovated by Sir Christopher Wren and William Kent. Highlights include the Royal Ceremonial Dress Collection and the Cupola Room. (☎0844 482 7777; www.hrp.org.uk; Kensington Gardens W8; adult/child £12.50/6.25, park & gardens free; ⊙10am-6pm Mar-Sep, to 5pm Oct-Feb; ⊖Queensway or High St Kensington)

Apsley House

HISTORIC BUILDING

5 ◎ Map p136, F3

This stunning house was designed by Robert Adam for Baron Apsley in the late 18th century, but was later sold to the first Duke of Wellington, who lived here until his death in 1852. Wellington memorabilia fills the basement gallery, while the stairwell is dominated by Antonio Canova's staggering 3.4m-high statue of a fig-leafed Napoleon. Don't miss the elaborate Portuguese silver service. (149 Piccadilly W1; adult/child £7/4, with Wellington Arch £8/5; ⊙11am-5pm Wed-Sun Apr-Oct, to 4pm Nov-Mar; ⊖Hyde Park Corner)

Wellington Arch

MONUMENT

6 ◎ Map p136, F3

This magnificent neoclassical 1826 arch, facing Apsley House in the green space strangled by the Hyde Park Corner roundabout is topped by Europe's largest bronze sculpture: *Peace Descending on the Quadriga of War* (1912). Until the 1960s part of the monument served as a tiny police station, but it was opened up to the public as a three-floor exhibition space with unforgettable views. (Hyde Park Corner W1; adult/child £4/3, with Apsley

House £8/5; ⊙10am-5pm Wed-Sun Apr-Oct, to 4pm Nov-Mar; 🛜; ⊖Hyde Park Corner)

Albert Memorial

MONUMENT

7 ◎ Map p136, C3

Designed by George Gilbert Scott, this splendid Victorian confection on the southern edge of Kensington Gardens is a 53m-high, gaudy Gothic memorial from 1872. It's an eye-opening blend of mosaic, gold leaf, marble and Victorian bombast. For a close-up of the memorial's Frieze of Parnassus, join one of the 45-minute tours. (☎7495 0916; tours adult/child £6/5; ⊙tours 2pm & 3pm 1st Sun of the month Mar-Dec; ⊖Knightsbridge or Gloucester Rd)

CHRISTER FREDRIKSSON/LONELY PLANET IMAGES ©

Serpentine Gallery summer cafe, Hyde Park

Michelin House
HISTORIC BUILDING

8 Map p136, D5

Built for Michelin between 1905 and 1911 by François Espinasse, and completely restored in 1985, this magnificent building blurs the line between art nouveau and art deco. The iconic roly-poly Michelin Man (Bibendum) appears in the exquisite modern stained glass (the originals were removed at the outbreak of WWII and subsequently vanished), while the mesmerising lobby is decorated with tiles depicting early-20th-century cars. (81 Fulham Rd SW3; admission free; South Kensington)

Westminster Cathedral
CHURCH

9 Map p136, H4

John Francis Bentley's 19th-century cathedral, the mother church of Roman Catholicism in England and Wales, is a splendid example of neo-Byzantine architecture. Although construction started here in 1896, the gaunt interior remains largely unfinished. The stone bas-reliefs of the Stations of the Cross (1918) by Eric Gill and the views from the 83m-tall bell tower – thankfully, accessible by lift – are impressive. (www.westminstercathedral.org.uk; Victoria St SW1; admission free, exhibition adult/child £5/2.50, joint ticket with tower £8/4, tower £5/2.50; cathedral 7am-7pm, tower 9.30am-12.30pm & 1-5pm daily Apr-Nov, Thu-Sun Dec-Mar, exhibition 9.30am-5pm Mon-Fri, to 6pm Sat & Sun; ; Victoria)

Local Life

Speakers' Corner

The northeastern corner of Hyde Park is traditionally the spot for soapbox ranting. It's the only place in Britain where demonstrators can assemble without police permission. Speakers' Corner was frequented by Karl Marx, Vladimir Lenin, George Orwell and William Morris. If you've got something to get off your chest, do so on Sunday, although you'll mainly have fringe dwellers, religious fanatics and hecklers for company.

Marble Arch
MONUMENT

10 Map p136, E1

Lending its name to the surrounding area, this huge white arch was designed by John Nash in 1827. Facing Speakers' Corner, it was moved here from its original spot in front of Buckingham Palace in 1851; if you're feeling anarchic, walk through the central portal, a privilege reserved by (unenforced) law for the Royal Family and the ceremonial King's Troop Royal Horse Artillery. (Marble Arch)

Eating

Launceston Place
MODERN EUROPEAN ££

11 Map p136, B4

This exceptionally handsome restaurant on a picture-postcard Kensington street of Edwardian houses is super-chic. The food, prepared by chef Tristan Welch, a protégé of Marcus Wareing, tastes as divine as it looks. The adventurous (and flush) will go for the tasting menu (£52). (7937 6912; www.launcestonplace-restaurant.co.uk; 1a Launceston Pl W8; 3-course lunch/Sun lunch/dinner £18/24/42; closed lunch Mon; Gloucester Rd or High St Kensington)

Zuma

JAPANESE £££

12 Map p136, E3

A modern-day take on the traditional Japanese *izakaya* ('a place to stay and drink sake'), where drinking and eating go together in relaxed unison, Zuma oozes style and sophistication. Traditional Japanese materials – wood and stone – combine with modern pronunciation for a highly contemporary feel. Ultimately it's the sushi, sashimi and robata dishes, all excellent and outstandingly presented, that steal the show. (7584 1010; www.zumarestaurant.com; 5 Raphael St SW7; mains £15-75; Knighstbridge)

Dinner by Heston Blumenthal

MODERN BRITISH £££

13 Map p136, E3

The most eagerly awaited restaurant opening of recent years, sumptuously presented Dinner, on the ground floor of the Mandarin Oriental, is a gastronomic tour de force, taking diners on a journey through British culinary history (with inventive modern inflections). The restaurant interior is a design triumph, from the glass-walled kitchen and its overhead clock mechanism to the large windows onto the park. (7201 3833; www.dinnerbyheston.com; Mandarin Oriental Hyde Park, 66 Knightsbridge SW1; set lunch £28, mains £32-72; lunch & dinner; Knightsbridge)

Kazan

TURKISH ££

14 Map p136, H5

Excellent and enjoyable, Kazan gets repeated thumbs up for its set meze platters, shish kebabs and *karniyarik* (lamb-stuffed aubergines). Flavours are rich and full, service attentive and the refreshingly unaffected setting allows you to focus on dining, with one eye on the evening belly dancers that occasionally swivel into view. Seafood and vegetarian options available. (www.kazan-restaurant.com; 93-94 Wilton Rd SW1; mains £12-16, set meals £26-40; Victoria)

Rasoi Vineet Bhatia

INDIAN £££

15 Map p136, E5

When you eventually locate this gorgeous restaurant off the King's Rd

Top Tip

Queen's Life Guard

Catch the Queen's Life Guard (Household Cavalry) departing for Horse Guards Parade at 10.32am (9.32am on Sunday) from Hyde Park Barracks for the daily Changing of the Guard, performing a ritual that dates to 1660. They troop via Hyde Park Corner, Constitution Hill and the Mall.

Understand

Upmarket Eats

Quality gravitates to where the money is, and you'll find some of London's finest establishments in the exclusive hotels and ritzy mews of Chelsea, Belgravia and Knightsbridge. Chic and cosmopolitan South Kensington has always been reliable for pan-European options.

and ring the doorbell, it's like being invited round for dinner at someone's Chelsea residence with a handful of other guests. High on hospitality, seductively decorated and home to stunningly presented Indian cuisine (including a seven-course vegetarian gourmand menu for £79), this is truly what a fine dining experience should be. (☎7225 1881; www.rasoi-uk.com; 10 Lincoln St SW3; 2-/3-/4-course lunch £21/27/32; ⏲lunch Sun-Fri, dinner daily; ⊖Sloane Sq)

Min Jiang

CHINESE £££

16 Map p136, A3

Min Jiang serves up excellent Peking duck (half/whole £27.50/53.50) – cooked in a wood-burning stove – seafood and sumptuously regal views over Kensington Palace and Gardens. The menu is diverse, with a sporadic accent on spice (the Min Jiang is a river in Sichuan), but vaults alarmingly across China from dim sum to stir-fried Mongolian-style ostrich. (www.minjiang.co.uk; 10th fl, Royal Garden Hotel, 2-24 Kensington High St W8; mains £10.50-48; ⊖High St Kensington)

Orangery

TEAHOUSE ££

17 Map p136, A2

The Orangery, housed in an 18th-century conservatory on the grounds of Kensington Palace, is lovely for lunch, especially if the sun is beaming. The standout experience is tea, ranging in price from the Signature Orange Tea (£14.85 per person) to the indulgent heights of the Tregothnan English Tea (£33.75), a champagne-laced feast. (Kensington Palace, Kensington Gardens W8; mains £9.50-14; ⏲10am-6pm Mar-Sep, to 5pm Oct-Feb; ⊖Queensway or High St Kensington)

Gessler at Daquise

POLISH £

18 Map p136, D4

This popular Polish cafe-cum-diner tempts with a good range of vodkas and reasonably priced dishes, including the oft-seen *bigos*, a 'hunter's stew' of cabbage and pork, and ravioli-like *pierogi*. (www.gessleratdaquise.co.uk; 20 Thurloe St SW7; mains £6.50-13.50, set lunch £9.50; ⊖South Kensington)

Drinking

Galvin at Windows

COCKTAIL BAR

19 Map p136, G2

This swish bar on the edge of Hyde Park opens onto stunning views, especially at dusk. Cocktail prices reach similar heights (£13.50 to £15.25) but the leather seats are comfortable and the marble bar is gorgeous.

(www.galvinatwindows.com; London Hilton on Park Lane, 28th fl, 22 Park Lane W1; 10am-1am Mon-Wed, to 3am Thu-Sat, to 11pm Sun; Hyde Park Corner)

Drayton Arms PUB

20 Map p136, B5

This vast Victorian corner boozer is delightful inside and out, with some bijou art nouveau features (sinuous tendrils and curlicues above the windows and the doors), contemporary art on the walls and a fabulous coffered ceiling. The crowd is both hip and down-to-earth; great beer and wine selection. (www.thedraytonarmssw5.co.uk; 153 Old Brompton Rd SW5; noon-midnight Mon-Fri, 10am-midnight Sat & Sun; West Brompton or South Kensington, 430)

Queen's Arms PUB

21 Map p136, B4

Tucked down a quiet mews off Queen's Gate, this place wins bouquets from the many students living in the area as well as from concertgoers heading for the Royal Albert Hall (p144), around the corner. Add to that four beer hand pumps and a decent (mostly gastropub) menu. (www.thequeensarmskensington.co.uk; 30 Queen's Gate Mews SW7; daily; Gloucester Rd)

Orangery, Kensington Palace

Entertainment

Royal Albert Hall

CONCERT VENUE

22 Map p136, C3

This splendid Victorian concert hall hosts classical music, rock and other performances, but is most famously the venue for the BBC-sponsored Proms. Booking is possible, but from mid-July to mid-September Proms punters also queue for £5 standing (or 'promenading') tickets, on sale one hour before curtain-up. Otherwise the box office and prepaid ticket collection counter are both through door 12. (information 7589 3203, bookings 7589 8212; www.royalalberthall.com; Kensington Gore SW7; daily; South Kensington)

Royal Court Theatre

THEATRE

23 Map p136, F5

Equally renowned for staging innovative new plays and old classics, the Royal Court on Sloane Sq is among London's most progressive theatres and has continued to discover major writing talent across the UK under its inspirational artistic director, Dominic Cooke. (7565 5000; www.royalcourttheatre.com; Sloane Sq SW1; daily; Sloane Sq)

Top Tip

Albert Hall Tours

You can take a one-hour front-of-house **guided tour** (7959 0558; adult/concession £8.50/7.50; tours hourly 10.30am-4.30pm most days) of the Albert Hall from the box office at door 12. Ninety-minute **backstage tours** (0845 401 5045; adult £12) are also available, but are far less frequent (roughly one day a month; check website).

Local Life

High Street Kensington

High Street Kensington is a less crowded, more salubrious alternative to Oxford St, with all the high-street chains, plus trendy stores and shops, such as Miss Sixty, Urban Outfitters and Waterstone's booksellers. Snap up antiques along the many shops up Kensington Church St towards Notting Hill.

Cadogan Hall

CONCERT VENUE

24 Map p136, F5

Home of the Royal Philharmonic Orchestra, Cadogan Hall is a major venue for classical music, opera and choral music, with occasional dance, rock and jazz. (7730 4500; www.cadoganhall.com; 5 Sloane Tce SW1; daily; Sloane Sq)

Ciné Lumière

CINEMA

25 Map p136, C5

Ciné Lumière is attached to South Kensington's French Institute, and its large art deco 300-seat *salle* (cinema) screens great international seasons (including the London Spanish Film Festival) and French and other foreign films subtitled in English. (7073 1350; www.institut-francais.org.uk; 17 Queensberry Pl SW7; daily; South Kensington)

Shopping

Harvey Nichols

DEPARTMENT STORE

26 Map p136, E3

At London's temple of high fashion, you'll find Chloé and Balenciaga bags, the city's best denim range, a massive make-up hall with exclusive lines, great jewellery and the fantastic restaurant, Fifth Floor. (www.harveynichols.com; 109-125 Knightsbridge SW1; 10am-8pm or 9pm Mon-Sat, 11.30am-6pm Sun; Knightsbridge)

Rippon Cheese Stores

FOOD

27 Map p136, H5

A potently inviting aroma greets you as you approach this cheesemonger: there are 500 varieties of English and European cheeses on offer. The list is sensational, from Black Bomber to Idiazabal, Isle of Mull Truckle and way beyond, all ripened on site (you can taste before you buy). (7931 0628; www.ripponcheese.com; 26 Upper Tachbrook St SW1; 8am-5.30pm Mon-Fri, 8.30am-5pm Sat; Victoria or Pimlico)

Lulu Guinness

FASHION

28 Map p136, F4

Quirky, whimsical and eye-catching British designs (the Japanese love them), from small evening bags resembling bright lips to fun umbrellas and cosmetic bags. (www.luluguinness.com; 3 Ellis St SW1; 10am-6pm Mon-Fri, from 11am Sat; Sloane Sq)

Butler & Wilson

ACCESSORIES

29 Map p136, D5

Bejewelled skulls, blingtastic bracelets, knockout necklaces and a dazzling spectacle of multicolour earrings, brooches, rings, glinting iPhone covers and more. (www.butlerandwilson.co.uk; 189 Fulham Rd; 10am-6pm Mon, Tue & Thu-Sat, 10am-7pm Wed, noon-6pm Sun; South Kensington)

Peter Jones

DEPARTMENT STORE

30 Map p136, E5

This iconic 1960s Chelsea department store has been stylishly modernised – come for fashions, cosmetics and electricals in a funky, futuristic space. (www.peterjones.co.uk; Sloane Sq; 9.30am-7pm Mon-Sat, to 8pm Wed, 11am-5pm Sun; Sloane Sq)

Local Life
A Saturday in Notting Hill

Getting There

Underground Notting Hill Gate station is on the Circle, District and Central Lines.

Underground Ladbroke Grove station on the Hammersmith & City and Circle Lines is also useful.

A Saturday in Notting Hill sees the neighbourhood at its busiest and best. Portobello Market is full of vibrant colour and the area is stuffed with excellent restaurants, pubs, shops and cinemas, making the entire day an event embracing market browsing, the culinary, the grain and grape and, last but not least, a chance to catch a film in a classic picture house setting.

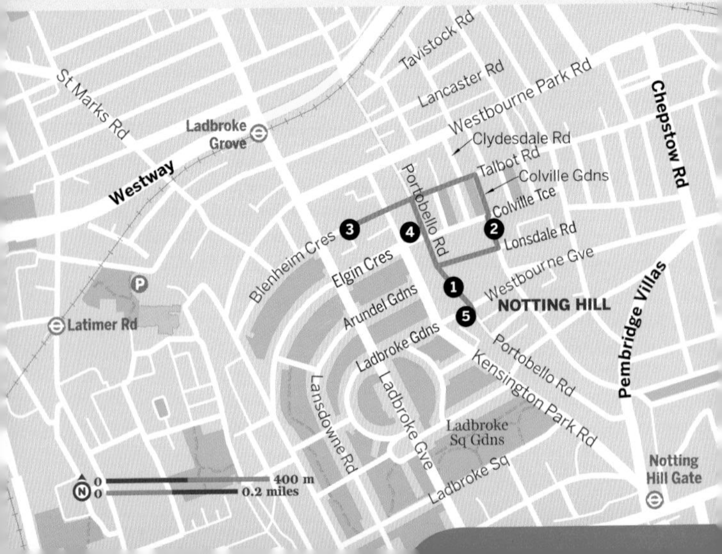

❶ Browse the Market

A 10-minute walk from Notting Hill Gate tube station, iconic **Portobello Road Market** (www.portobelloroad.co.uk; Portobello Rd W10; ⌚8am-6pm Mon-Wed, 9am-1pm Thu, 7am-7pm Fri & Sat, 9am-4pm Sun; ⊖Notting Hill Gate or Ladbroke Grove) mixes street food with fruit and veg, antiques, colourful fashion and trinkets.

❷ Explore a Museum

The unexpected **Museum of Brands, Packaging & Advertising** (www.museumofbrands.com; 2 Colville Mews, Lonsdale Rd W11; adult/child £6.50/2.25; ⌚10am-6pm Tue-Sat, 11am-5pm Sun; ⊖Notting Hill Gate) is fairly low-tech, but eye-catching with sponsored displays at the end of the gallery and exhibits showing the evolution of packaging of well-known products, such as Johnson's Baby Powder and Guinness.

❸ Dine at Mediterraneo

For authentic Italian food, it hardly gets better than **Mediterraneo** (www.mediterraneo-restaurant.co.uk; 37 Kensington Park Rd W11; mains £13-22; ⊖Ladbroke Grove). The pasta is homemade and there is plenty of veal on the menu (a meat that's almost unheard of in English cooking).

❹ Catch a Film

Over 100 years old, the one-of-a-kind **Electric Cinema** (www.electriccinema.co.uk; 191 Portobello Rd W1; ⊖Ladbroke Grove or Notting Hill Gate) is the UK's oldest cinema, updated with luxurious leather armchairs, footstools, tables for food and drink in the auditorium, and the upmarket Electric Brasserie next door. Check out what's on the program; there's mainstream, art house, classics and epic all-nighters.

❺ Drinks at the Earl of Lonsdale

The **Earl of Lonsdale** (277-281 Westbourne Grove W11; ⊖Notting Hill Gate or Westbourne Park) is peaceful during the day, with a mixture of old biddies and young hipsters inhabiting its charming snugs. There are Samuel Smith's ales, and a fantastic backroom with sofas, banquettes and open fires, as well as a fine beer garden shaded by a towering tree of whopping girth.

Notting Hill Carnival

Launched in 1964 by the local Afro-Caribbean community keen to celebrate its culture and traditions, **Notting Hill Carnival** (www.nottinghill-carnival.co.uk, ⌚last weekend of Aug) has become Europe's largest street festival (up to one million people). Musical processions finish around 9pm, although parties in bars, restaurants and seemingly every house in the neighbourhood go on late into the night. There are dozens of Caribbean food stands and celebrity chefs such as Levi Roots often make an appearance, too.

Explore

Regent's Park & Camden

Regent's Park, Camden Market and Hampstead Heath should top your list for excursions into North London. Camden is a major sight with an intoxicating energy, while Hampstead Heath offers you a glorious day out and an insight into how North Londoners spend their weekend. The nightlife is excellent wherever you go, from first-rate pubs in Hampstead to great live music in Camden.

The Sights in a Day

Start your exploration with a morning trip to **Regent's Park** (p152) and outstanding **London Zoo** (p152). For a leisurely and picturesque 15 to 20 minute stroll to Camden, walk alongside **Regent's Canal** (p155) on the north side of Regent's Park, taking in **Primrose Hill** (p152) and its gorgeous park en route. In Camden Town, lunch at **Market** (p153) for top-notch Modern British food or nibble your way around an eclectic variety of snacks at **Camden Market** (p154).

Further explore **Camden Market** (p159) before rewarding yourself with a delectable ice cream from **Marine Ices** (p154) or sitting down in the beer garden of the **Edinboro Castle** (p155) for an afternoon drink prior to hopping on a tour of **Lord's Cricket Ground** (p152) – hallowed turf for London cricket aficionados.

For dinner, Camden has it sorted, simply select from one of the neighbourhood's many winning international restaurants. The rest of the night is easily sewn up: Camden has some tremendous **pubs** (p155) and a glut of **live music options** (p157) embracing most musical persuasions, so night owls will find little reason to leave.

Best of London

Pubs
Edinboro Castle (p155)
Lock Tavern (p155)

Eating
Market (p153)

Live Rock
Proud Camden (p157)
Barfly (p157)

Parks
Regent's Park (p152)

For Kids
London Zoo (p152)

Hidden London Walks
Walking along Regent's Canal (p155)

Getting There

Underground For Regent's Park, Baker St (on the Jubilee, Metropolitan, Circle, Hammersmith & City and Bakerloo lines) is most useful.

Underground Useful stations for Camden are Camden Town and Chalk Farm on the Northern Line. Hampstead is on the Northern Line.

KENTISH TOWN
CAMDEN TOWN
CAMDEN
PRIMROSE HILL
BELSIZE PARK
Kentish Town Rd
Kentish Town West
Camden Rd
Camden St
Camden Market
Camden Town
Chalk Farm Rd
Chalk Farm
St Pancras Way
Bayham St
Parkway
Delancey St
Camden High St
Regent's Canal
Prince Albert Rd
Regent's Park Rd
Gloucester Ave
Haverstock Hill
Adelaide Rd
King Henry's Rd
Primrose Hill
Belsize Park
Gaisford St
Patshull Rd
Lawford Rd
Bartholomew Rd
Rochester Rd
Rochester Pl
Wilmot Pl
Lyme St
Pratt St
Greenland Rd
Arlington
Albert
Holmes Rd
Angler's La
Castle Rd
Lewis St
Hawley Rd
Hartland Rd
Hadley St
Harmood St
Ferdinand St
Jamestown Rd
Inverness St
Oval Rd
Spring Pl
Grafton Rd
Athlone St
Wilkin St
Rhyl St
Marsden St
Prince of Wales Rd
Crogsland Rd
Malden Rd
Queen's Cres
Maitland Park
Maitland Park Villas Rd
Eton College Rd
Eton Villas
Eton Rd
Chalcot Rd
Fitzroy Rd
Ainger Rd
Antrim Rd
England's La
Primose Gardens
Belsize Gve
Belsize Park Gardens
Lambolle Pl
Lambolle Rd
Eton Ave
Lancaster Gve
Fellows Rd
Merton Rise
Huson Cl
Briary Cl
Elsworthy Rise
Elsworthy Rd
Wadham Gdns
Belsize Ave
Ave Rd
Townshen
Edmund's Tce
A
B
C
D
E
1
2
3
4
3
6
7
8
10
11
12
13
14
15
16
17
18
19
20
22
23
24
25
26
27

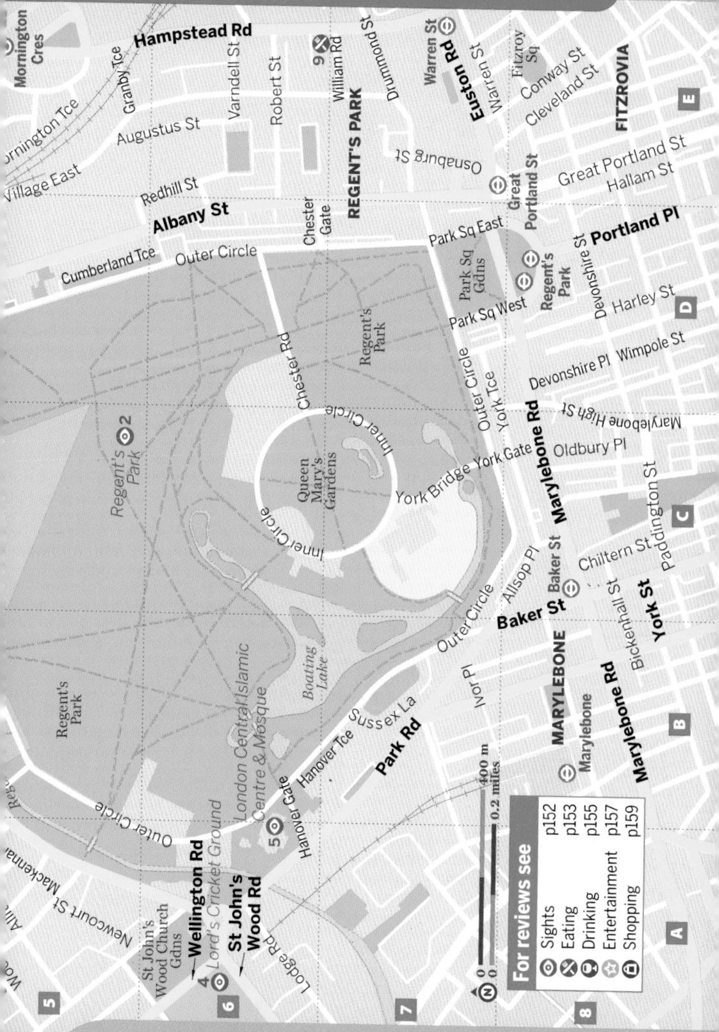
Mornington Cres
Hampstead Rd
Granby Tce
Mornington Tce
Village East
Augustus St
Varndell St
Robert St
William Rd
Drummond St
Warren St
Euston Rd
Warren St
Fitzroy Sq
Conway St
Cleveland St
FITZROVIA
REGENT'S PARK
Osnaburg St
Redhill St
Albany St
Chester Gate
Great Portland St
Great Portland St
Hallam St
Cumberland Tce
Outer Circle
Park Sq East
Park Sq Gdns
Regent's Park
Portland Pl
Devonshire St
Park Sq West
Harley St
Chester Rd
Regent's Park
Outer Circle
York Tce
Devonshire Pl
Wimpole St
Marylebone High St
Inner Circle
Queen Mary's Gardens
York Bridge
York Gate
Marylebone Rd
Oldbury Pl
Regent's Park
2
Paddington St
Inner Circle
Allsop Pl
Baker St
Chiltern St
Baker St
Outer Circle
York St
Bickenhall St
MARYLEBONE
Ivor Pl
Boating Lake
London Central Islamic Centre & Mosque
Regent's Park
Sussex La
Park Rd
Hanover Tce
Marylebone
Marylebone Rd
Hanover Gate
5
Outer Circle
Wellington Rd
Lord's Cricket Ground
St John's Wood Rd
4
St John's Wood Church Gdns
Newcourt St
Mackennal St
Lodge Rd
0 400 m
0 0.2 miles
For reviews see
Sights p152
Eating p153
Drinking p155
Entertainment p157
Shopping p159
A
B
C
D
E
5
6
7
8

Sights

London Zoo

ZOO

1 Map p150, C5

These famous zoological gardens are among the world's oldest but the emphasis today is on conservation, education and breeding. The latest development is Penguin Beach, a beautifully landscaped enclosure featuring a pool with cool underwater viewing areas. Other highlights include Gorilla Kingdom; the lovely Clore Rainforest Lookout and Nightzone; and Butterfly Paradise. Feeding sessions or talks take place throughout the day. (www.zsl.org/london-zoo; Outer Circle, Regent's Park NW1; adult/child £19/15; 10am-4pm Nov-Mar, to 5.30pm Apr–mid-Jul, Sep & Oct, to 6pm mid-Jul & Aug Regent's Park or Camden Town)

Regent's Park

PARK

2 Map p150, C5

The most elaborate and ordered of London's many parks, Regent's Park was created around 1820 by John Nash. Once employed as a royal hunting ground, Regent's Park's current attractions include London Zoo, Regent's Canal along its northern side, an ornamental lake, an open-air theatre in Queen Mary's Gardens, ponds and colourful flowerbeds, rose gardens, as well as sports pitches. (5am-dusk; Baker St or Regent's Park)

Understand

Zoo News

London Zoo is constantly redeveloping enclosures or building new ones. Its next big project is a tiger enclosure that will recreate the Sumatran jungle. Planned for Easter 2013, the new tiger enclosure will be five times as big as the current one.

Primrose Hill

NEIGHBOURHOOD

3 Map p150, C3

Wedged between well-heeled Regent's Park and edgy Camden, the little neighbourhood of Primrose Hill is a supremely desirable part of town. With its independent boutiques (from interior design to bookshops, children's clothes to pet accessories), lovely restaurants and good pubs, it has a rare village feel. The proximity of the gorgeous, eponymous park, with enticing views of London, is another draw.

Lord's Cricket Ground

CRICKET GROUND

4 Map p150, A6

The 'home of cricket' is a must for any devotee of this peculiarly English game: book early for the test matches here, but it's also worth taking the absorbing and anecdotal 90-minute tour of the ground and facilities. Tours take in the famous Long Room and a museum featuring evocative memorabilia. For the London Olympic Games in 2012, Lord's will host the archery event. (www.lords.org; St John's Wood Rd NW8; tours adult/child £15/9; tours when no play 10am, noon & 2pm Apr-Sep; ⊖St John's Wood)

London Central Islamic Centre & Mosque

MOSQUE

5 Map p150, A6

On the western side of Regent's Park is this impressive Islamic Centre & Mosque, a huge white edifice with a glistening dome. Provided you take your shoes off and dress modestly you are welcome to go inside, but the interior is less impressive than the exterior. (www.iccuk.org; 146 Park Rd NW8; daily; ⊖Marylebone)

Eating

Market

MODERN BRITISH ££

6 Map p150, D4

An ode to great, simple British food with a hint of Europe thrown in, this fabulous restaurant is a light and airy space with bare brick walls, steel tables and basic wooden chairs. The menu concocts unforgettable classic delights, such as roast poussin with baby spring vegetables, and whole plaice with caper butter and chips. (www.marketrestaurant.co.uk; 43 Parkway NW1; mains £10-14; closed dinner Sun; ⊖Camden Town)

York & Albany

BRASSERIE ££

7 Map p150, D4

Part of chef Gordon Ramsay's culinary empire, this chic brasserie serves classics with a Mediterranean twist and bakes divine pizzas in its wood-fired oven. The food is pitch-perfect and the setting informal; eat at the bar, in the lounge or the more formal dining room. (www.gordonramsay.com/yorkandalbany; 127-129 Parkway NW1; mains £13-19; breakfast, lunch & dinner; ⊖Camden Town)

MARKET ©

Market restaurant

Manna

VEGETARIAN ££

8 Map p150, B3

Tucked away on a side street in Primrose Hill, this little place does a brisk trade in inventive vegetarian cooking. The menu features such mouth-watering dishes as green korma, wild garlic and pea risotto cake and superb desserts. There are excellent vegan options too and everything arrives beautifully presented, from

Top Tip

Camden Market Snacks

There are dozens of food stalls at the **Lock Market** and the **Stables Market** – virtually every type of cuisine is offered, from French to Argentinian, Japanese and Caribbean. Quality varies but is generally pretty good and affordable, and you can eat on the big communal tables or by the canal.

fan-shaped salads to pyramidal mains. Reservations are usually essential. (7722 8082; www.mannav.com; 4 Erskine Rd NW3; mains £11-14; lunch Sat & Sun, dinner Tue-Sun; ; Chalk Farm)

Bar Gansa

SPANISH ££

Howlingly popular and decked out in loud yellow and red, Bar Gansa near Bar Vinyl (see **16** Map p150; D3) is a focal point of the Camden scene. The menu is mostly tapas, making it very popular with small groups of friends. Live flamenco kicks off on Monday evenings. It stays open late (12.30am or 1.30am) and so doubles up as a bar. (7267 8909; www.bargansa.co.uk; 2 Inverness St NW1; tapas £5; 10am-12.30am Sun-Wed, to 1.30am Thu-Sat; Camden Town)

Mestizo

MEXICAN ££

9 Map p150, E6

If your idea of Mexican food is tacos and gluggy refried beans, think again. This large and very attractive restaurant and tequila bar has everything from *quesadillas* (cheese-filled pasties) to filled corn enchiladas, but go for the specials: *pozole* (a thick fresh corn soup with meat) and several different preparations of *mole* (chicken or pork cooked in a rich chocolate sauce). (www.mestizomx.com; 103 Hampstead Rd NW1; mains £10-20; lunch & dinner; Warren St)

Mango Room

CARIBBEAN ££

10 Map p150, E3

With delightful pastel decor and genteel service, Mango Room is a kind of decaf Caribbean experience, although there's no holding back with the food: grilled sea bass with coconut milk and sweet pepper sauce, salt fish with *ackee* (a yellow-skinned Jamaican fruit), and curried goat with hot pepper and spices. Sounds come from 50s ska music and old reggae tunes. (www.mangoroom.co.uk; 10-12 Kentish Town Rd NW1; mains £10-13; lunch & dinner; Camden Town)

Marine Ices

ITALIAN £

11 Map p150, C2

This Chalk Farm institution started out as a Sicilian *gelateria,* but these days it does some savoury dishes as well, including pizzas and hearty pasta dishes. The ice cream (Caribbean coconut and maple walnut come highly recommended) is excellent; the parlour is particularly popular at weekends when a long line snakes down Haverstock Hill. (www.marineices.co.uk; 8 Haverstock Hill NW3; mains £7-15; lunch & dinner Tue-Sun; Chalk Farm)

Belgo Noord

BELGIAN ££

12 Map p150, C2

This branch of the Belgian restaurant chain does a mean *moules frites* (mussels and chips), which you can wash down with one of the many Belgian beers on offer. (www.belgo-restaurants.co.uk; 72 Chalk Farm Rd NW1; mains £9-16; noon-11pm; Chalk Farm)

Drinking

Edinboro Castle

PUB

13 Map p150, D4

A reliable Camden boozer, the large and relaxed Edinboro has a refined Primrose Hill atmosphere. It boasts a full menu, gorgeous furniture designed for slumping in and a fine bar. Where the pub excels however, is in its huge beer garden, complete with BBQ and table football and adorned with fairy lights for long summer evenings. (www.edinborocastlepub.co.uk; 57 Mornington Tce NW1; daily; Camden Town)

Proud Camden

BAR

Once a Horse Hospital in Stables Market (see **24** Map p150, D3) that tended horses injured pulling barges on the Grand Union Canal, this is now one of Camden's most brilliant bars. The stables have been converted into individual booths where you drink, play table football or pool or watch sports on the large screens. Sounds come from live bands and DJs; it's fantastic in summer, when the terrace is open. (www.proudcamden.com; The Horse Hospital, Stables Market, Chalk Farm Rd NW1; to 1.30am Mon-Wed, to 2.30am Thu-Sat, to 12.30am Sun; Camden Town or Chalk Farm)

Lock Tavern

PUB

14 Map p150, D2

A Camden institution, the black-clad Lock Tavern rocks in all the right places: it's cosy inside, has an ace roof terrace from where you can watch the market throngs, the food is good, the beer plentiful and a roll-call of guest bands and DJs at the weekend spices things up. (www.lock-tavern.co.uk; 35 Chalk Farm Rd NW1; to 1am Fri & Sat; Chalk Farm or Camden Town)

Local Life

Walking along Regent's Canal

The canals that were once a trade lifeline for the capital have now become a favourite escape for Londoners, providing a quiet walk away from traffic and crowds. You can walk from Little Venice to Camden in under an hour; on the way, you'll pass Regent's Park, London Zoo, Primrose Hill, beautiful villas designed by architect John Nash as well as redevelopments of old industrial buildings into trendy blocks of flats. Allow 15 to 20 minutes between Camden and Regent's Park, and 25 to 30 minutes between Regent's Park and Little Venice. There are plenty of exits along the way and signposts all along.

Local Life

North London Sounds

North London is the home of indie rock and many a famous band started playing in the area's grungy bars. Bands and singers that played in Camden bars during their early years include Stereophonics, Coldplay, Amy Winehouse and Feeder. Doors generally open around 7.30pm but bands may not come on until 9pm, sometimes later. Closing time is normally around 2am, although this can vary depending on the event.

Crown & Goose

PUB

15 Map p150, E4

One of our favourite London pubs, this square room features a central wooden bar surrounded by British-racing-green walls studded with gilt-framed mirrors and illuminated by big shuttered windows. More importantly, a friendly, quietly cool crowd, easy conviviality and great food combine with a good range of inexpensive beers. (www.crownandgoose.co.uk; 100 Arlington Rd NW1; to 2am Fri & Sat; Camden Town)

Bar Vinyl

DJ BAR

16 Map p150, D3

Bar Vinyl is the epicentre for Camden's young and urban crowd, with cool kids behind the decks, a record shop downstairs and graffiti whirling along narrow walls. But it's super-friendly at the same time. Weekends are packed and buzzing, midweek nights are quieter, and the music is always good. Happy hour is every night of the week between 5pm and 9pm. (www.barvinyl.com; 6 Inverness St NW1; to 1am Thu-Sat; Camden Town)

Black Cap

GAY

17 Map p150, E4

Camden's premier gay venue, this friendly, sprawling place attracts people from all over North London. Licensed since 1751, there's a great outdoor terrace, the pleasantly pub-like upstairs Shufflewick bar and the downstairs club, for hilarious camp cabaret and decent dance music. (www.faucetinn.com/blackcap; 171 Camden High St NW1; noon-2am Mon-Thu, to 3am Fri & Sat, to 1am Sun; Camden Town)

Queen's

PUB

18 Map p150, B3

Perhaps because this is Primrose Hill, the interior is more cafe than pub. Still, it's a good one, with a nice wine list, ales and lagers and, more importantly, plenty of people-watching to go with your pint; many of Primrose Hill's fashionistas come here for a tipple. (www.thequeensprimrosehill.co.uk; 49 Regent's Park Rd NW1; 11am-11pm; Camden Town or Chalk Farm)

Entertainment

Proud Camden
LIVE MUSIC

It's very trendy indeed at Proud (see 24 Map p150, D3) in Stables Market, with gorgeous Camdenites heading to the sunset-watching terrace for outdoor gigs in summer or indoor booths in winter. It's a great venue in North London that combines live music and exhibitions, and things peak in summer, when the terrace is open. (www.proudcamden.com; The Horse Hospital, Stables Market, Chalk Farm Rd NW1; to 1.30am Mon-Wed, to 2.30am Thu-Sat, to 12.30am Sun; Camden Town or Chalk Farm)

Barfly
LIVE MUSIC

19 Map p150, D2

This typically grungy, indie-rock Camden venue is well known for hosting small-time artists looking for their big break. The focus is on rock from the US and UK, with alternative-music radio station Xfm hosting regular nights. The venue is small, so you'll feel like the band is just playing for you and your mates. (www.barflyclub.com; Monarch, 49 Chalk Farm Rd NW1; daily; Chalk Farm or Camden Town)

Edinboro Castle (p155)

The Horrors performing at Electric Ballroom

Electric Ballroom

LIVE MUSIC

20 Map p150, E3

One of Camden's historic venues, the Electric Ballroom has been entertaining North Londoners since 1938. Many great bands and musicians have played here, from Blur to Paul McCartney, The Clash and U2. There are club nights on Fridays (Sin City: metal music) and Saturdays (Shake: a crowd pleaser of dance anthems from the '70s, '80s and '90s). (www.electricballroom.co.uk; 184 Camden High St NW1; daily; Camden Town)

KOKO

CONCERT VENUE

21 Map p150, E5

Once the legendary Camden Palace, where Charlie Chaplin, the Goons and the Sex Pistols have all performed, Koko remains one of London's better gig venues – Madonna and the Red Hot Chilli Peppers have played here. The theatre has a dance floor and decadent balconies, attracting an indie crowd with Club NME on Friday. Live bands play almost every night of the week. (www.koko.uk.com; 1a Camden High St NW1; 7-11pm Sun-Thu, to 4am Fri & Sat; Mornington Cres)

Roundhouse

PERFORMING ARTS

22 Map p150, C2

Once home to 1960s avant-garde theatre, then a rock venue, the Roundhouse afterwards fell into oblivion before reopening a few years back. It holds great gigs and a smattering of brilliant performances, from circus to stand-up comedy, poetry slam and improvisation sessions. The building's round shape is unique and generally well used in the staging. (www.roundhouse.org.uk; Chalk Farm Rd NW1; daily; Chalk Farm)

Jazz Café

LIVE MUSIC

23 Map p150, E4

Though you may think jazz is this club's main staple, its real speciality is the crossover of jazz into the mainstream. It's a trendy industrial-style restaurant with jazz gigs around once a week, while the rest of the month is Afro, funk, hip hop, R&B and soul styles with big-name acts and a loyal bohemian Camden crowd. (www.jazzcafe.co.uk; 5 Parkway NW1; Camden Town)

Understand

Camden Market

Although – or perhaps because – it stopped being cutting-edge several thousand cheap leather jackets ago, Camden Market gets a whopping 10 million visitors annually. Expect clothes (of variable quality), bags, jewellery, arts and crafts, candles, incense and decorative titbits. Camden Market comprises four distinct market areas: Stables Market, Lock Market, Canal Market and Buck Street Market.

Shopping

Stables Market

MARKET

24 Map p150, D3

Just beyond the railway arches, opposite Hartland Rd, the Stables is the best part of Camden Market, with antiques, Asian artefacts, rugs and carpets, pine furniture and vintage clothing. (www.stablesmarket.com; Chalk Farm Rd NW1; 10am-6pm; Chalk Farm)

Camden Lock Market

MARKET

25 Map p150, D3

Right next to the canal lock, this area of Camden Market has diverse food, ceramics, furniture, oriental rugs, musical instruments and designer clothes. (www.camdenlockmarket.com; Camden Lock Pl NW1; 10am-6pm; Camden Town)

Canal Market

MARKET

26 Map p150, D3

Just over the canal bridge, Canal Market has bric-a-brac from around the world. This is the part of the market that burnt down in 2008 when a liquid petroleum gas heater, which had been left on, started the devastating conflagration that caused £30 million worth of damage. The market was later rebuilt; we love the scooter seats by the canal. (cnr Chalk Farm Rd & Castlehaven Rd NW1; 10am-6pm Thu-Sun; Chalk Farm or Camden Town)

Buck Street Market

MARKET

27 Map p150, E3

This covered market houses stalls for fashion, clothing, jewellery and tourist tat. It's the closest to the station but the least interesting. (cnr Camden High & Buck Sts NW1; 9am-5.30pm Thu-Sun; Camden Town)

Local Life
A Stroll Around Hampstead Heath

Getting There

⊖ Underground For Highgate Cemetery: Archway station (Northern Line).

⊖ Underground Hampstead Heath and Gospel Oak (both Overground), Hampstead (Northern Line).

Sprawling Hampstead Heath, with its rolling woodlands and meadows, feels a million miles away – despite being approximately four – from the City of London. Covering 320 hectares, most of it woods, hills and meadows, it's home to about 180 bird species, 23 species of butterflies, grass snakes, bats, a rich array of flora and expansive views from the top of Parliament Hill.

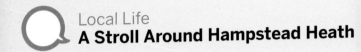

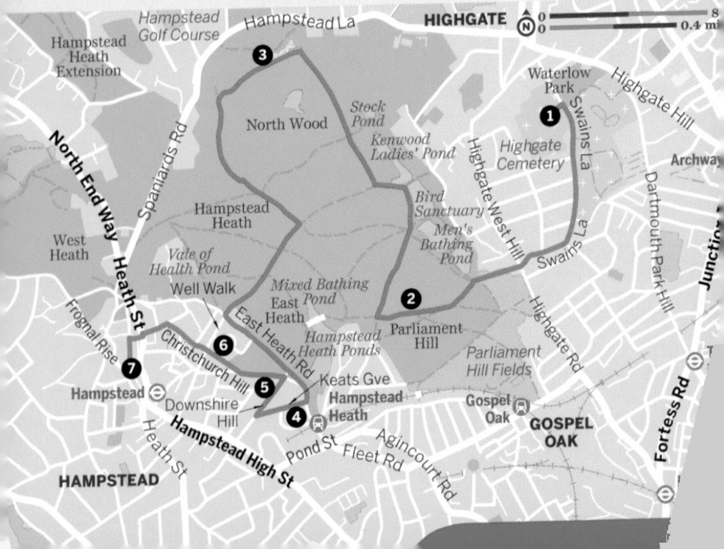

❶ Explore the Local Cemetery

The final resting place of Karl Marx, George Eliot and other notables, **Highgate Cemetery** (www.highgate-cemetery.org; Swain's Lane N6; adult/child £3/free; 10am-5pm Mon-Fri, 11am-5pm Sat & Sun Apr-Oct, closes 4pm daily Nov-Mar Archway) is divided into East and West. To visit the atmospheric West Cemetery, you must take a tour.

❷ Views from Parliament Hill

From the cemetery head down Swain's Lane to the roundabout with Highgate West Hill, and climb up to **Parliament Hill** for some all-inclusive views south over town. Londoners adore coming here for a picnic – so choose your spot, tuck into some sandwiches and feast on the superb vistas. Afterwards, dip a toe in the Men's Bathing Pond or Kenwood Ladies' Pond (open all year round, lifeguard-supervised).

❸ Visit Kenwood House

Traverse the heath to the magnificent neoclassical 18th century **Kenwood House** (Hampstead Lane NW3; admission free; 11.30am-4pm, tours 2.30pm) in a glorious sweep of perfectly landscaped gardens leading down to a picturesque lake, the setting for summer concerts. The house contains a magnificent collection of art including paintings by Rembrandt, Constable, Turner and others.

❹ Call on Keats

Cross the heath to the elegant **Keats House** (www.keatshouse.org.uk; Wentworth Pl, Keats Grove NW3; adult/child £5/free; 1-5pm Tue-Sun May-Oct, Fri-Sun Nov-Apr; Hampstead/ Hampstead Heath), once home to the golden boy of the Romantic poets. Keats wrote *Ode to a Nightingale* while sitting under a plum tree (now-vanished but new tree planted) in the garden in 1819.

❺ Weigh up No 2 Willow Road

Modern architecture fans will want to swing past **No 2 Willow Road** (2 Willow Rd NW3; adult/child £6/3; noon-5pm Wed-Sat Mar-Oct, guided tours 11am, noon, 1pm & 2pm; Hampstead/ Hampstead Heath), the central house in a block of three, designed by the Ernö Goldfinger in 1939. Entry is by guided tour until 3pm (after which nonguided viewing is allowed).

❻ Dinner at Wells Tavern

The popular **Wells Tavern** (7794 3785; www.thewellshampstead.co.uk; 30 Well Walk NW3; mains £10-16; lunch & dinner; Hampstead) serves proper posh English pub grub – Cumberland sausages, mash and onion gravy, or just a full roast with all the trimmings. At weekends you'll need to book.

❼ Evening Drinks at Holly Bush

The beautiful **Holly Bush** (22 Holly Mount NW3; 11am-11pm; Hampstead) is a fitting conclusion to your journey, with an antique Victorian interior, a secluded hilltop location, open fires in winter and a knack for making you stay longer than you had intended. Set above Heath St, it's reached via the Holly Bush Steps.

Explore

The Royal Observatory & Greenwich

Quaint Greenwich (*gren*-itch) by the Thames in South London is packed with grand architecture, while some gorgeous parks and standout sights draw fleets of eager visitors. With the fascinating Royal Observatory and the fabulous National Maritime Museum, Greenwich should be one of the highlights of any visit to London, so allow a day to do it justice.

The Sights in a Day

Arrive early for a morning stroll around **Greenwich Park** (p167) and climb uphill for the delicious views of Greenwich and London from the statue of General Wolfe. Explore the **Royal Observatory** (p167) before heading downhill to gaze up the gorgeous Tulip Staircase of **Queen's House** (p167) and admiring the dazzling artwork in the Painted Hall in the **Old Royal Naval College** (p168).

Restore some calories with oodles of noodles at **Tai Won Mein** (p170) before plunging into the newly expanded **National Maritime Museum** (p167) the world's largest of its kind, and riveting for both adults and children. **Ranger's House** (p167) is well worth exploring for its stunning art collection but save some time for the unique and intriguing **Fan Museum** (p168). If you have any time left, pop into **Discover Greenwich** (p169) to immerse yourself in the royal history of this lovely neighbourhood.

Dine at **Inside** (p169) or the **Old Brewery** (p169) and walk off your meal with a sojourn to the **Greenwich Union** (p170) or a twilight walk along the Thames to the **Cutty Sark Tavern** (p170) for drinks and riverine views.

For a local's day in Greenwich, see p164.

Local Life

A Taste of Greenwich (p164)

Best of London

Stately Architecture

Queen's House (p167)

Old Royal Naval College (p168)

Museums

National Maritime Museum (p167)

Views

Greenwich Park (p167)

All-Round Pubs

Greenwich Union (p170)

Historic Pubs

Cutty Sark Tavern (p170)

Trafalgar Tavern (p164)

Getting There

Train The quickest way from central London is via one of the mainline trains from Charing Cross or London Bridge to Greenwich railway station.

Docklands Light Railway (DLR) Most sights in Greenwich can be easily reached from the Cutty Sark DLR station.

Boat Thames Clipper boats run to Greenwich and Woolwich Arsenal from London Eye Millennium Pier.

Local Life
A Taste of Greenwich

This genteel and charming South London neighbourhood, magnificently placed by a bend in the Thames as it loops around the Isle of Dogs, has heaps to offer beyond its drawcard sights. Linking together more discreet attractions tucked away from the main drag, this itinerary charts an appealing journey through the neighbourhood to conclude with a riverside walk.

❶ Sample Some Sausages at Nevada Street Deli

Pop into this charming wedge-shaped **deli** (☎0208 293 9199; 8 Nevada St, SE10; sandwiches £3.75-4; ⏲daily; DLR Cutty Sark/Greenwich, 🚉Greenwich) on Nevada St, a popular Greenwich spot for sandwiches, mushrooms or gravadlax on toast, a plate of scrumptious handmade sausages in a wealth of varieties (smoked salmon, spinach and fetta cheese) or merely a restorative cup of coffee.

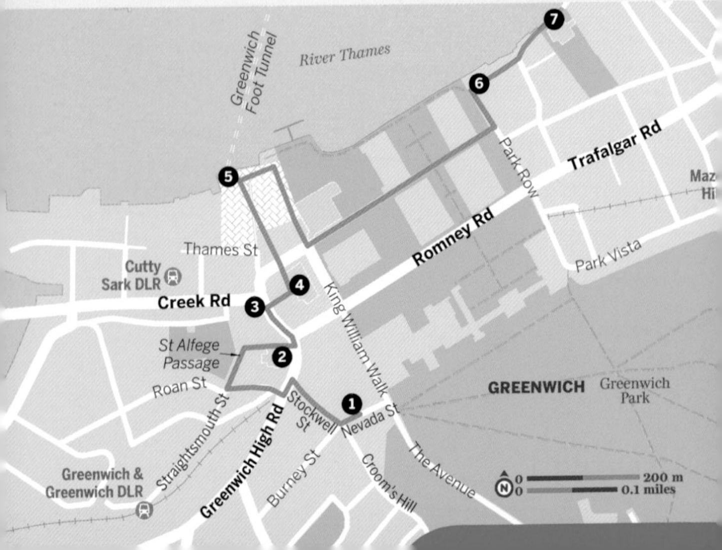

❷ Drop by St Alfege Church

Designed by Nicholas Hawksmoor in 1714, this glorious parish **church** (www.st-alfege.org; Church St SE10; admission free; ⏱10am-4pm Mon-Sat, 1-4pm Sun; Greenwich or DLR Cutty Sark) is a charmer. Pop into lovely St Alfege Passage behind the church for a stunning little stone-paved alley running past the churchyard.

❸ Browse Beehive

Join the Greenwich vinyl junkies at this funky meeting ground of old records (Bowie, Rolling Stones, vintage soul) and retro togs (frocks, blouses, leather jackets and overcoats). **Beehive** (320-322 Creek Rd, SE10; ⏱10.30am-6pm Tue-Sun, 10.30am-6.30pm Sat & Sun; DLR Cutty Sark) is a fab shop to browse. Pop in for a glance and leave with a mod-print dress, vintage Bakelite telephone and a copy of *Hunky Dory*.

❹ Snack at Greenwich Market

Perfect for snacking your way through a world atlas of food while browsing the other market stalls, come to this **market** (www.greenwichmarket.net; Greenwich Market, SE10; ⏱10am-5.30pm Wed, Sat & Sun; DLR Cutty Sark) on Wednesdays, Saturdays and Sundays for delicious food-to go, from Spanish tapas to Thai curries, sushi, French crêpes, Brazilian *churros* and more.

❺ Walk under the Thames

Completed in 1902, the sub-river 370m-long **Greenwich Foot Tunnel** runs under the Thames from the Isle of Dogs and is fun to explore. The lifts down to the tunnel run between 7am and 7pm Monday to Saturday and 10am and 5.30pm on Sunday. Otherwise it's between 88 and 100 steps down and – shudder – up (open 24 hours).

❻ A Drink at the Trafalgar Tavern

Lapped by the brown waters of the Thames, this cavernous **pub** (www.trafalgartavern.co.uk; 6 Park Row SE10; ⏱noon-11pm Mon-Thu, to midnight Fri & Sat, to 10.30pm Sun; DLR Cutty Sark or Maze Hill) with big windows onto the river is steeped in history. Dickens drank here (using it as the setting for the wedding breakfast scene in *Our Mutual Friend*) and prime ministers Gladstone and Disraeli dined on the pub's celebrated whitebait.

❼ Walking by the River

A short walk east along the Thames puts Greenwich's riverside character into clear definition. This section of the Thames Path is most attractive closer to Greenwich, with fantastic views of Canary Wharf and the river. Do what locals do and have an evening drink at the **Cutty Sark Tavern** (p170).

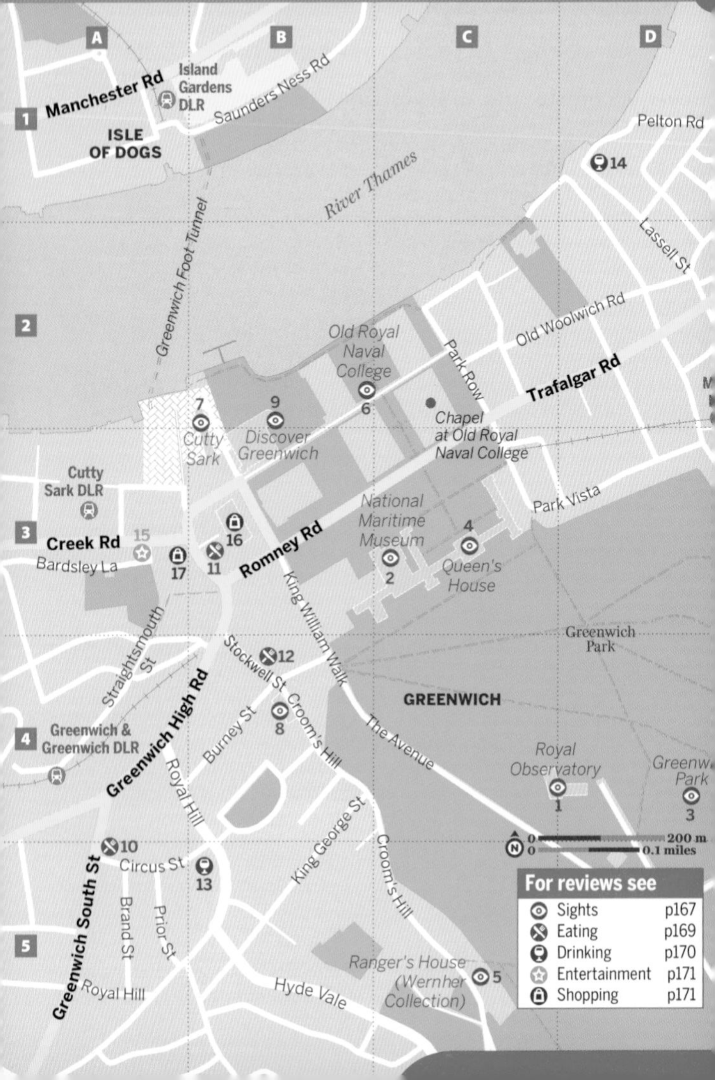
A
B
C
D
1
2
3
4
5
Manchester Rd
Island Gardens DLR
Saunders Ness Rd
ISLE OF DOGS
Pelton Rd
14
River Thames
Lassell St
Greenwich Foot Tunnel
Old Woolwich Rd
Old Royal Naval College
6
Park Row
Trafalgar Rd
7
Cutty Sark
9
Discover Greenwich
Chapel at Old Royal Naval College
Cutty Sark DLR
Creek Rd
15
Bardsley La
17
11
16
Romney Rd
National Maritime Museum
2
4
Queen's House
Park Vista
King William Walk
Straightsmouth St
Stockwell St
12
Greenwich Park
GREENWICH
Greenwich & Greenwich DLR
Greenwich High Rd
Burney St
8
Croom's Hill
The Avenue
Royal Observatory
1
Greenwich Park
3
Royal Hill
King George St
0 200 m
0 0.1 miles
10
Circus St
13
Greenwich South St
Brand St
Prior St
Croom's Hill
Ranger's House (Wernher Collection)
5
Royal Hill
Hyde Vale
For reviews see
Sights p167
Eating p169
Drinking p170
Entertainment p171
Shopping p171

Sights

Royal Observatory LANDMARK

1 ⊙ Map p166, C4

Following an ambitious £15-million renovation, the excellent Royal Observatory is divided into two sections. You now have to pay to access Flamsteed House & Meridian Courtyard (where visitors can delightfully straddle both hemispheres) in the northern portion. The southern half contains the highly informative and free Astronomy Centre and the state-of-the-art **Peter Harrison Planetarium** (adult/child £6.50/4.50; ⊙hourly shows 12.45-3.45pm Mon-Fri, 11am-4.15pm Sat & Sun), London's sole planetarium. (www.nmm.ac.uk/places/royal-observatory;Greenwich Park, Blackheath Ave SE10; adult/child £10/free, astronomy centre free; ⊙10am-5pm; ☒Greenwich or DLR Cutty Sark)

National Maritime Museum MUSEUM

2 ⊙ Map p166, C3

The world's largest maritime museum narrates the dramatic history of Britain as a seafaring nation. Arranged thematically, exhibits include the 19m-long golden state barge built in 1732 for Frederick, Prince of Wales, and the huge ship's propeller on level 1. Museum space increased with the Sammy Ofer Wing, which opened in late 2011. Museum tours run at noon, 1pm and 3pm. (www.nmm.ac.uk; Romney Rd SE10; admission free; ⊙10am-5pm; ☒Greenwich or DLR Cutty Sark)

Take a Break Tai Won Mein (p170) is an excellent noodle restaurant serving big portions.

Greenwich Park PARK

3 ⊙ Map p166, D4

Handsome venue of the 2012 Games equestrian events, this park is one of London's largest and loveliest expanses of green, with a grand avenue, a rose garden, picturesque walks and astonishing views from the crown of the hill near the **statue of General Wolfe**, opposite the Royal Observatory. (⊙dawn-dusk, cars from 7am; ☒Greenwich or Maze Hill, DLR Cutty Sark)

Queen's House HISTORIC BUILDING

4 ⊙ Map p166, C3

The first Palladian building by architect Inigo Jones after his return from Italy was completed in 1638, when it became the home of Charles I and Henrietta Maria. The ceremonial Great Hall is the principal room, with an elaborately tiled floor dating to 1637. The helix-shaped **Tulip Staircase** leads to a gallery on level 2. (www.nmm.ac.uk/places/queens-house; Romney Rd SE10; admission free; ⊙10am-5pm; ☒Greenwich or DLR Cutty Sark)

Ranger's House (Wernher Collection) HISTORIC BUILDING

5 ⊙ Map p166, C5

Built in 1723, this elegant Georgian villa in the southwest corner of Greenwich Park now contains a collection of 700 works of art (medieval and Renaissance paintings, porcelain, silverware, tapestries etc) amassed by one Julius Wernher (1850–1912). The Spanish Renaissance jewellery collection is the best in Europe, and the rose garden fronting the house defies description. (Greenwich Park, Chesterfield Walk SE10; adult/child £7/4; tours 11.30am & 2.30pm Mon-Wed, 11am-5pm Sun early Apr-Sep; Greenwich or DLR Cutty Sark)

Old Royal Naval College

HISTORIC BUILDING

6 Map p166, B2

Now used mainly by the University of Greenwich, the former Naval College is another grand undertaking from Sir Christopher Wren. The highlights here are the magnificent chapel – decorated in a highly elaborate rococo style – and the Painted Hall, with its stunning Baroque murals by Sir James Thornhill. (www.oldroyalnavalcollege.org; King William Walk; admission free; 10am-5pm Mon-Sat, grounds only 8am-6pm Sun; ; DLR Cutty Sark)

Understand

Architectural Style

Greenwich is home to an extraordinary interrelated cluster of classical buildings. All the great architects of the Enlightenment made their mark here, largely due to royal patronage. In the early 17th century, Inigo Jones built one of England's first classical Renaissance homes, the Queen's House, which still stands today. Charles II was particularly fond of the area and had Sir Christopher Wren build both the Royal Observatory and part of the Royal Naval College, which John Vanbrugh then completed in the early 17th century.

Cutty Sark

SHIP

7 Map p166, B2

This Greenwich landmark, the last of the great clipper ships to sail between China and England in the 19th century, was due to reopen in spring 2012 after serious fire damage. Luckily half of the ship's furnishings and equipment, including the mast, had been removed for conservation at the time of the conflagration. (www.cuttysark.org.uk; Cutty Sark Gardens SE10; Greenwich or DLR Cutty Sark)

Fan Museum

MUSEUM

8 Map p166, B4

The world's sole museum entirely devoted to fans has a wonderful collection of ivory, tortoiseshell, peacock-feather and other glorious fans. Set in an 18th-century Georgian town house, there's a Japanese-style garden plus Orangery, with lovely *trompe l'œil* murals and twice-weekly afternoon tea. (www.fan-museum.org; 12 Crooms Hill SE10; adult/child £4/3; 11am-5pm Tue-Sat, noon-5pm Sun; ; Greenwich or DLR Cutty Sark)

Discover Greenwich
MUSEUM

9 Map p166, B2

This new exhibition is the place to come and delve into the history of Greenwich with models and hands-on displays, many aimed at children. The Greenwich Tourist Information Centre is also here.

Take A Break If you need a drink or a meal, drop by the Old Brewery next door.

Eating

Inside
MODERN EUROPEAN ££

10 Map p166, A5

With white walls, modern art and linen tablecloths, Inside is a relaxed kind of place and one of Greenwich's best restaurant offerings. Enter the understated dining room and enjoy superior modern European cooking, with lots of seafood and meat sourced from small local suppliers. (www.insiderestaurant.co.uk; 19 Greenwich South St; mains £12.50-18, 2-/3- course set menu lunch £13/18, set menu early dinner £18/23; closed dinner Sun & all day Mon; DLR/Greenwich)

JANE SWEENEY/LONELY PLANET IMAGES ©

Queen's House (p167)

Top Tip
Greenwich Recital

If possible come to the Old Royal Naval College chapel on the first Sunday of the month, when there's a free 50-minute organ recital at 3pm, or time your visit for sung Eucharist at 11am on Sunday.

Old Brewery
MODERN BRITISH ££

A working brewery with splendidly burnished 1000-litre copper vats at one end and a high ceiling lit with natural sunlight, the Old Brewery is perfectly located after a stagger around Greenwich's top sights. Right by Discover Greenwich (see 9 Map p166, B2) it's a cafe by day, transforming into a restaurant in the evening, serving dishes featuring the best seasonal ingredients. (www.oldbrewerygreenwich.com; Pepys Bldg, Old Royal Naval College, SE10; mains £11.50-26; cafe 10am-5pm Mon-Sun, restaurant 6-11pm Mon-Sat & 6-10.30pm Sun; DLR Cutty Sark)

Tai Won Mein

CHINESE £

11 Map p166, B3

The staff may be a bit jaded but this great snack spot – the Cantonese moniker just means 'Big Bowl of Noodles' – serves epic portions. Flavours are simple, but fresh, and the namesake *tai won mein* seafood noodles – with all manner of creatures from the deep bobbing about in your broth – may have you applauding (but put your chopsticks down first). (39 Greenwich Church St, SE10; 11.30am-11.30pm; mains from £5; DLR Cutty Sark)

Spread Eagle

FRENCH ££

12 Map p166, B4

This smart, French-inspired restaurant and former coaching inn opposite the Greenwich Theatre and near Nevada Street Deli is both a charming and relaxing spot for a meal. (8853 2333; www.spreadeaglerestaurant.co.uk; 1-2 Stockwell St SE10; set menu Sat & Sun 2-/3-course £13/16, lunch/early supper menu Mon-Fri 2-/3-course £16.50/19.50; DLR Cutty Sark or Greenwich)

Drinking

Greenwich Union

PUB

13 Map p166, B5

The award-winning Union plies six or seven Meantime Brewery beers, including raspberry and wheat varieties, and a strong list of ales, plus a great choice of bottled international brews. It's a handsome place, with beaten-up leather armchairs and a welcoming long, narrow aspect out to the conservatory and beer garden at the rear. (www.greenwichunion.com; 56 Royal Hill SE10; daily; DLR Greenwich or Greenwich)

> Understand
>
> **GMT**
>
> The Greenwich Meridian was selected as the global Prime Meridian at the International Meridian Conference in Washington DC in 1884. Greenwich therefore became the world's common zero for longitude and standard for time calculations, replacing the multiple meridians that had previously existed. Greenwich was assisted in its bid by the earlier US adoption of Greenwich Mean Time (GMT) for its own national time zones. Furthermore, the majority of world trade already used sea charts that identified Greenwich as the Prime Meridian.

Cutty Sark Tavern

PUB

14 Map p166, D1

Housed in a delightful bow-windowed, wood-beamed Georgian building directly on the Thames, the Cutty Sark is one of the few independent pubs left in Greenwich. Half a dozen cask-conditioned ales on tap line the bar, with an inviting riverside sitting-out area opposite. It's a 15-minute walk from the Cutty Sark DLR station or hop on a bus along Trafalgar Rd and walk north. (www.cuttysarktavern.co.uk; 4-6 Ballast Quay SE10; daily; DLR Cutty Sark, 177 or 180)

Old Brewery

BAR

Handily situated near Discover Greenwich (see 9 Map p166, B2), the brickwork bar at the Old Brewery is run by the Meantime Brewery, selling its own brew draught Imperial Pale Ale (brewed on site) as well as over 50 beers, from Belgian Trappist ales to fruity and flavoured brews, smoked beers and much more, with tables outside in the courtyard. (www.oldbrewerygreenwich.com; Pepys Bldg, Old Royal Naval College, SE10; 11am-11pm Mon-Sat, noon-10.30pm Sun; DLR Cutty Sark)

Entertainment

Up the Creek

COMEDY

15 Map p166, A3

Bizarrely enough, the hecklers can be funnier than the acts at this great club. Up the Creek was established and is still living in the spirit of the legendary Malcolm Hardee. Mischief, rowdiness and excellent comedy are the norm with open mic nights on Thursdays (£4) and Sunday specials (£6; www.sundayspecial.co.uk). (8858 4581; www.up-the-creek.com; 302 Creek Rd SE10; Fri & Sat; Greenwich or DLR Cutty Sark)

Local Life

Greenwich Comedy Festival

Early September sees Greenwich split its sides playing host to London's largest comedy festival, the **Greenwich Comedy Festival** (www.greenwichcomedyfestival.co.uk) set in the grounds of Old Royal Naval College.

Shopping

Compendia

GIFTS & SOUVENIRS

16 Map p166, B3

Compendia's owners are madly enthusiastic about games – board or any other kind. The shop is excellent for gifts you can enjoy with your mates – backgammon, chess, Scrabble, solitaire and more fringe interests. Look out for the Escher jigsaws and if you're Greenwich Park–bound, pick up a Frisbee, a kite, some juggling balls or even a diabolo. (www.compendia.co.uk; 10 Greenwich Market; 11am-5.30pm; DLR Cutty Sark)

Emporium

FASHION

17 Map p166, A3

Each piece is individual at this lovely vintage shop (unisex), where glass cabinets are crammed with costume jewellery, old perfume bottles and straw hats, while gorgeous jackets and blazers intermingle on the clothes racks. (330-332 Creek Rd SE10; 10.30am-6pm Wed-Sun; DLR Cutty Sark)

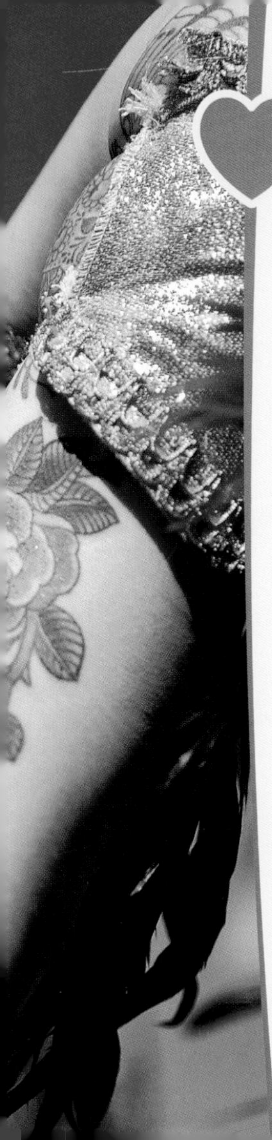

The Best of London

London's Best Walks

London's Best...

Woman in costume, Notting Hill Carnival (p147)
JANE SWEENEY/LONELY PLANET IMAGES ©

Best Walks
Tower of London to the Tate Modern

The Walk

Commencing at one of London's most historic sights, this walk crosses the Thames across magnificent Tower Bridge, before heading west alongside the river, scooping up some excellent views, passing some breathtaking modern architecture, history and Shakespeare's Globe on the way before coming to a halt amid the renowned modern art of the Tate Modern.

Start Tower of London; ⊖ Tower Hill

Finish Tate Modern; ⊖ Southwark or London Bridge

Length 3km; 90 minutes

Take a Break

Head east along Tooley St from the Shard to Magdalen (p114) for scrumptious British fare in a stylish setting, snack your way around Borough Market (p118) or get an elevated perspective on the market from Roast (p115, entrance and lift within Borough Market).

Borough Market (p118)

❶ Tower of London

Rising commandingly over the Thames, the ancient **Tower of London** (p86) enjoys a dramatic location. Be dazzled by the vast Koh-i-Noor diamond, explore the impressive White Tower and tag along with a Yeoman Warder on an enlightening tour.

❷ Tower Bridge

Cross ornate 19th-century **Tower Bridge** (p92) – traversed by over 40,000 people daily – to the south side of the Thames. For information on the bridge (and brilliant views), enter the Tower Bridge Exhibition.

❸ HMS Belfast

Walk west along Queen's Walk past **City Hall** (p113), called the 'Leaning tower of Pizzas' by some. Moored a bit further ahead, **HMS Belfast** (p111), a light cruiser that served in WWII and later conflicts, is a floating museum.

❹ Shard

Pop through the shopping complex of **Hay's Galleria** to Tooley St to see the **Shard**, designed by Italian architect Renzo Piano. The tallest building in the European Union when finally completed in 2012, it will house a five-star hotel, restaurants and London's highest public viewing gallery.

❺ Borough Market

Keep walking west along Tooley St, dip down Borough High St to head up Stoney St to **Borough Market** (p118), overflowing with tasty produce from Thursday to Saturday. If you fancy a beer, keep walking along Stoney St to the **Rake** (p116) on Winchester Walk.

❻ Southwark Cathedral

Southwark Cathedral (p110) is both fascinating and relaxing. Parts of the church date to medieval times – a treasured haul of artefacts include a lovely Elizabethan sideboard and an icon of Jesus.

❼ Shakespeare's Globe

Wander west along Clink St – and past the remains of Winchester Palace – to Bankside and on to **Shakespeare's Globe** (p117). Join one of the tours if you have time.

❽ Tate Modern

Not far west of Shakespeare's Globe is the **Millennium Bridge** (p111) and London's standout modern and contemporary art gallery, the **Tate Modern** (p104). The most dramatic entrance to the Tate Modern is off Holland St in the west, where you access the **Turbine Hall** (p105) down the ramp.

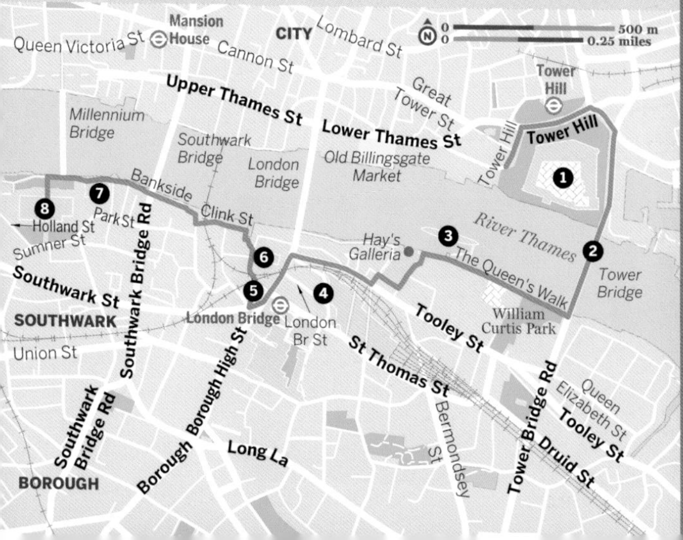

Best Walks
Royal London

The Walk

Lassoing in the cream of London's top royal and stately sights, this attraction-packed walk ticks off some of the city's truly must-do experiences on one comprehensive route. Don't forget to pack your camera – you'll be passing by some of London's most famous buildings and historic sites, so photo opportunities abound. The walk conveniently returns you in a loop almost to your starting point for easy access to other parts of London.

Start Westminster Abbey; ⊖Westminster or St James's Park

Finish Banqueting House; ⊖Westminster

Length 3.5km; two hours

Take a Break

Pack a picnic to eat in lovely St James's Park (p34) if it's a sunny day. Alternatively, Inn the Park (p37) along the route is a finely located choice for a meal, drink and excellent views.

DAVID COPEMAN / ALAMY ©

Banqueting House (p35)

❶ Westminster Abbey

Start by exploring mighty **Westminster Abbey** (p24), preferably getting here early (before the crowds). The much smaller, yet delightful **St Margaret's Church** north alongside the abbey is known as the 'parish church of the House of Commons.'

❷ Cabinet War Rooms & Churchill Museum

Walk around Parliament Sq, past the **UK Supreme Court** (free to sit in courtrooms during hearings) on the west side of the square, to the **Cabinet War Rooms & Churchill Museum** (p34) on King Charles St to discover how Churchill coordinated the Allied war against Hitler.

❸ Buckingham Palace

Walking to the end of Birdcage Walk brings you to majestic **Buckingham Palace** (p28) where the state rooms are accessible to ticket-holders from August to September; alternatively pay a visit to the **Royal Mews** (p29) and the **Queen's Gallery** (p29), both nearby.

❹ St James's Park

Amble along The Mall and enter **St James's Park** (p34) – one of London's most attractive royal parks. Walk alongside **St James's Park Lake** for its plentiful ducks, geese, swans and other water fowl.

❺ Trafalgar Square

Return to The Mall and pass through Admiralty Arch to **Trafalgar Square** (p50) for regal views down Whitehall to the Houses of Parliament.

❻ Horse Guards Parade

Walk down Whitehall to the entrance to **Horse Guards Parade** (p35), where the dashing mounted sentries of the Queen's Household Cavalry are on duty daily from 10am to 4pm, when the dismounted guards are changed.

❼ Banqueting House

On the far side of Whitehall, magnificent **Banqueting House** (p35) is the last surviving remnant of Whitehall Palace, which once stretched most of the way down Whitehall but vanished in a late 17th century fire. Further down Whitehall is the entrance to **No 10 Downing Street** (p36) and beyond that, Parliament Sq and the **Houses of Parliament** (p30).

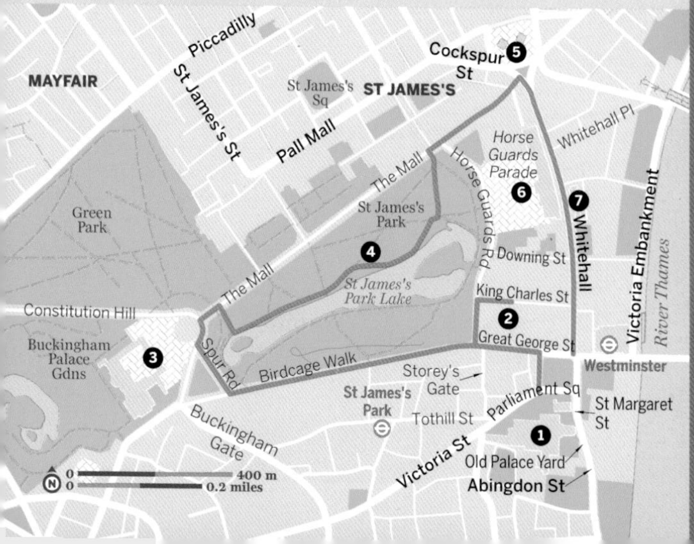

Best Walks
South Bank to the Houses of Parliament

The Walk

Packing some supreme views, this easily manageable walk along the Thames kicks off at London's signature cultural hub – the Southbank Centre – before gravitating naturally towards one of the city's most distinctive architectural gems: the Houses of Parliament. Along the way you will pass the iconic London Eye, elegant Westminster Bridge and some of the most superlative vistas the city can muster.

Start Southbank Centre; ⊖Waterloo or Embankment

Finish Jewel Tower; ⊖Westminster

Length 1.5km; one hour

Take a Break

Pack a picnic to eat in Jubilee Gardens next to the London Eye (p110) or feast on the excellent cuisine at stylish Skylon (p113) at Royal Festival Hall.

London Eye (p110) and County Hall

❶ Southbank Centre

London's leading cultural landmark and the world's largest single-run arts centre, the **Southbank Centre** (p118) is anchored by the 1950s outline of the refurbished **Royal Festival Hall**. Bibliophiles may find themselves drawn to the **South Bank Book Market** (p119) beneath the arches of Waterloo Bridge.

❷ London Eye

If you want to ride the **London Eye** (p110) – the huge Ferris wheel twirling above the Thames – you may need a fast-track ticket to get ahead of the queues. Alternatively, relax on the grass of **Jubilee Gardens** if the sun is shining; the gardens are a welcoming green space earmarked for ambitious prettification in 2012.

❸ County Hall

Begun in 1909 but not completed until 1922, **County Hall** is an impressive building faced in Portland stone with first-rate views across the Thames to the Houses of Parliament. For many years, County Hall was the home of local government for London; today it houses the **Sea Life London Aquarium** (p112), a film museum and hotels.

❹ Westminster Bridge

Completed in 1862, seven-arched Westminster Bridge is a later Gothic construction to the 15-arch bridge of Portland stone upon which William Wordsworth penned his sonnet *Composed upon Westminster Bridge, September 3, 1802*. Today's bridge features in the early scenes of horror film *28 Days Later*.

❺ Houses of Parliament

At the end of Westminster Bridge rises the elaborate Gothic stonework of the **Houses of Parliament** (p30), also called the Palace of Westminster. The three imposing towers of the Houses of Parliament are the Clock Tower (colloquially called 'Big Ben'), Victoria Tower at the southwestern corner and Central Tower between the two.

❻ Jewel Tower

With a history of over 700 years, the **Jewel Tower** stands on the far side of Abingdon St from Victoria Tower. The tower was one of two buildings (the other was Westminster Hall) which survived the 1834 fire that destroyed the Palace of Westminster. One of London's oldest surviving structures, the tower contains an exhibition on parliamentary history.

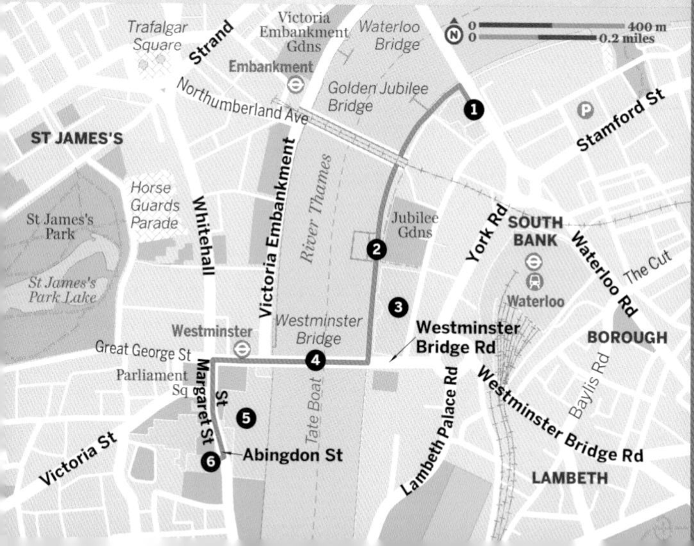

Best Eating

Once the laughing stock of the cooking world, London has got its culinary act together over the past two decades and is now an undisputed dining destination. There are plenty of fine, Michelin-starred restaurants, but it is the sheer variety on offer that is extraordinary: an A-Z of world cooking and a culinary expression of the city's cultural diversity.

World Food

One of the joys of eating out in London is the sheer profusion of choice. For historical reasons Indian cuisine is widely available (curry has been labelled a national dish), but Asian cuisines in general are very popular: Chinese, Thai, Japanese and Korean restaurants are all abundant, as well as elaborate fusion establishments blending flavours from different parts of Asia.

Food from continental Europe – French, Italian, Spanish, Greek, Scandinavian – is another favourite, with many classy Modern European establishments. Restaurants serving other types of cuisines tend to congregate where their home community is based.

Gastropubs

While not so long ago the pub was where you went for a drink, with maybe a packet of potato crisps to soak up the alcohol, the birth of the gastropub in the 1990s means that today, just about every pub offers full meals. The quality varies widely, however, from defrosted on the premises to Michelin-star worthy.

TRICIA DE COURCY LING/ALAMY ©

☑ Top Tips

- Make reservations at weekends, particularly if you're in a group of more than four people.
- Top-end restaurants offer great value set lunch menus; à la carte prices are sometimes cheaper for lunch too.
- Many West End restaurants offer good-value pre- or post-theatre menus.

Best British

Dinner by Heston Blumenthal (p141) Winning celebration of British cuisine with both traditional and modern accents.

Laughing Gravy (p113) Tremendous British menu and relaxing setting.

Skylon (p113)

Market (p153) Calming combination of bare brick walls and a classic, wholesome British menu.

Magdalen (p114) Stylish and delightful restaurant with excellent cooking and attentive staff.

Best European

Vincent Rooms (p36) Impressive culinary skills from the apprentice chefs at Westminster Kingsway College.

Bocca di Lupo (p53) Sophisticated Italian cuisine in Soho.

Launceston Place (p140) Fantastic looks, outstanding food.

Best Asian

Yauatcha (p53) Top-drawer dim sum in a stylish, contemporary dining environment.

Mooli's (p53) For succulent, flavour-packed and addictive Indian rotis.

Cinnamon Club (p37) Sure-fire Indian cuisine served within the elegant Old Westminster Library.

Rasoi Vineet Bhatia (p141) Serene Indian dining, elegantly tucked away off the King's Rd.

Best for Views

Skylon (p113) Stunning Thames vistas, fine international menu.

Oxo Tower Restaurant & Brasserie (p114) To-die-for views matched by excellent fusion menu.

Min Jiang (p142) Peking duck and panoramas of Kensington Gardens.

Worth a Trip

The fantastic **Providores & Tapa Room** (☎7935 6175; www.theprovidores.co.uk; 109 Marylebone High St W1; mains £18-26; ⏰lunch & dinner; ⊖Baker St or Bond St) is split over two levels: tempting tapas (£2.80 to £15) on the ground floor (no bookings); and outstanding fusion cuisine in the elegant dining room above. There's a fantastic brunch on Saturdays and Sundays.

Best Drinking & Nightlife

There's little Londoners like to do more than party. From Hogarth's 18th-century Gin Lane prints to Mayor Boris Johnson's decision to ban all alcohol on public transport in 2008, the capital's obsession with drink and its effects shows absolutely no sign of waning. Some parts of London only come alive in the evening and surge through the early hours.

Pubs

At the heart of London social life, the pub (public house) is one of the capital's great social levellers.

You can order almost anything you like, but beer is the staple. Some pubs specialise, offering drinks from local microbreweries, fruit beers, organic ciders and other rarer beverages; others proffer strong wine lists, especially gastropubs. Some pubs have delightful gardens – crucial in summer.

Unless otherwise stated, all pubs and bars reviewed in this book open at 11am and close at 11pm from Monday to Saturday and at 10.30pm on Sunday. Some pubs and bars stay open longer; most close around 2am or 3am at the latest.

Bars

Generally open later than pubs, but closing earlier than clubs, bars tempt those keen to skip bedtime at 11pm but not up for clubbing. They may have DJs and a small dance floor, door charges after 11pm, a more modern decor and fancier (and pricier) drinks, including cocktails.

JACK CAREY/ALAMY ©

Top Tips

- Check the listings in Time Out (www.timeout.com) or the Evening Standard (www.thisislondon.co.uk).
- Dress to impress (no jeans or trainers) in posh clubs in areas like Kensington; further east, it's laid-back and edgy.

Best All-Round Pubs

Edinboro Castle (p155) Cultured Primrose Hill boozer with beer garden.

Lock Tavern (p155) Top Camden pub with roof terrace and live music.

Greenwich Union (p170) Inviting Greenwich pub with strong menu of beers.

Lock Tavern (p155)

Black Friar (p98) Fine pub with distinctive, much-loved interior and bags of character.

Best Historic Pubs

George Inn (p116) History and age-old charm in spades.

Cutty Sark Tavern (p170) Sup on a great range of ales down by the river.

Queen's Larder (p77) Classic Bloomsbury pub with royal connections and a cosy disposition.

Trafalgar Tavern (p165) With a distinguished pub pedigree, this is perfect for a riverside pint.

Best Bars

Experimental Cocktail Club (p55) Cocktails for the adventurous in divine surrounds.

Academy (p55) Cocktails for the connoisseur.

Vertigo 42 (p98) Room with a view, classic cocktails.

Galvin at Windows (p142) Twilight views, through a raised cocktail.

French House (p47) Bohemian Soho bolt-hole with bundles of history.

Best Clubs

Cargo (p101) Creative music menu and trendy Shoreditch locale.

Catch (p101) Guaranteed good night out in Shoreditch.

Madame Jo Jo's (p56) The place for kitsch, cabaret and burlesque in a subterranean setting.

Worth a Trip

Bob Dylan and John Lennon have performed at cafe-bar **Troubadour** (www.troubadour.co.uk; 265 Old Brompton Rd SW5; 9am-midnight; Earl's Court), still a relaxed boho hangout decades later. There's live music (folk, blues) most nights and a large, pleasant garden open in summer. You'll be spoilt for choice when it comes to imbibing – Troubadour runs a wine club and has a wine shop next door.

Best Entertainment

Whatever soothes your soul, flicks your switch or floats your boat, from inspiring theatre to dazzling musicals, comedy venues, dance, opera or live music, London has an energetic and innovative answer. In fact, you could spend several lifetimes in London and still only sample a fraction of the astonishing range of entertainment on offer.

Theatre

A night out at the theatre in London is a must-do experience. London's Theatreland in the dazzling West End has a concentration of English-speaking theatres (over 40 in number) rivalled only by New York's Broadway. With the longest history, London theatre is also the world's most diverse, from Shakespeare's classics to boundary-pushing productions, raise-the-roof musicals that run and run, or productions from tiny theatres stuffed away above pubs.

Classical Music

Music lovers will be spoiled for choice with London's four world-class symphony orchestras, two opera companies, various smaller ensembles and fantastic venues (and reasonable ticket prices). The Southbank Centre, Barbican and Royal Albert Hall all maintain an alluring program of performances, with traditional crowd-pleasers as well as innovative compositions and sounds. The Proms (p144) is the largest event on the festival calendar.

London Sounds

London has long generated edgy and creative sounds. There's live music – rock, blues, jazz, folk, whatever – going on every night of the week, from steaming clubs to crowded pubs or ear-splitting concert arenas.

☑ Top Tips

- Cut-price standby tickets are sometimes available at several theatrical venues, including the National Theatre, the Barbican and the Southbank Centre.
- Most mainstream and art-house cinemas offer discounts all day Monday and most weekday afternoon screenings.

Best Theatre

Shakespeare's Globe (p117) For the authentic open-air Elizabethan effect.

National Theatre (p117) Cutting-edge productions in a choice of three theatres.

BBC Proms concert, Royal Albert Hall (p144)

Royal Court Theatre (p144) Constantly innovative and inspirationally driven Sloane Sq theatre.

Best for Classical Music & Opera

Royal Albert Hall (p144) Splendid red-brick Victorian concert hall south of Kensington Gardens.

Royal Festival Hall (p118) London's leading concert venue, on the South Bank.

Royal Opera House (p57) The venue of choice for classical ballet and opera buffs.

Best for Live Jazz

Ronnie Scott's (p58) Legendary Frith St jazz club in the heart of the West End.

Pizza Express Jazz Club (p58) Big jazz names, pizazz and pizzas.

Best Live Rock

12 Bar (p57) Rocking West End venue: small but packing a big punch.

Proud Camden (p157) Fantastic and much-loved North London live music venue.

Barfly (p157) Undersized but ambitious club with an ear for up-and-coming names.

Worth a Trip

Wigmore Hall (www.wigmore-hall.org.uk; 36 Wigmore St W1; ⊖Bond St) is one of the best concert venues in town for its fantastic acoustics, beautiful art nouveau hall, great variety of concerts and recitals and sheer standard of performances. Built in 1901 as the recital hall for Bechstein Pianos, it has remained one of the top places in the world for chamber music.

Best Gay & Lesbian

The city of Oscar Wilde, Quentin Crisp and Elton John does not disappoint its gay visitors, proffering a fantastic mix of brash, camp, loud and edgy parties, bars, clubs and events year-round. A world capital of gaydom on par with New York and San Francisco, London's gay and lesbian communities have turned good times into an art form.

Gay & Lesbian by Neighbourhood

Fashionable Shoreditch (p100) is home to London's more alternative gay scene, often very well mixed in with local straight people. The long-established gay village of Soho has lost some ground to the edgy East End.

Worth a Trip

Vauxhall in South London is now home to London's mainstream muscle boys. Areas with thriving lesbian communities include Stoke Newington and Hackney in northeast London.

Sealing Vauxhall's reputation as the new gay nightlife centre of London, **Fire** (www.fireclub.co.uk; South Lambeth Rd SW8; 10pm-4am; Vauxhall) is an expansive, smart space under the railway arches, hosting A:M on Friday, Later on Sunday afternoons, followed by the Sunday all-nighter, Orange.

Best Events

Lesbian & Gay Film Festival (www.bfi.org.uk/llgff) Hosted by the BFI Southbank (p118) in early April.

Gay Pride (www.pridelondon.org) In late June/early July, one of the world's largest gay prides.

Best Bars & Clubs

Edge (p56) London's largest gay bar and seven-nights-a-week crowd pleaser.

LEBRECHT MUSIC AND ARTS PHOTO LIBRARY/ALAMY ©

Top Tip

▶ Check out www.gingerbeer.co.uk for the full low-down on lesbian events, club nights and bars.

Candy Bar (p57) One of Lesbian London's most enduringly popular bars.

Heaven (p57) Long-standing club and still a Saturday night magnet on the gay scene.

Best Markets

The capital's famed markets are a treasure trove of small designers, unique jewellery pieces, original framed photographs and posters, colourful vintage pieces, priceless vinyls and countless bric-a-brac. The antidote to impersonal, carbon-copy high-street shopping, most markets are outdoors, but they are always busy – rain or shine.

London Life

Shopping at London's markets isn't just about picking up bargains and rummaging through mounds of knick-knacks and earthly odds-and-ends – although they give you plenty of opportunity to do that. It's also about taking in the character of this vibrant city: Londoners love to trawl through markets – browsing, chatting and socialising.

Worth a Trip

A heady, cosmopolitan blend of silks, wigs, knock-off fashion, Halal butchers and the occasional Christian preacher on Electric Ave, **Brixton Market** (www.brixtonmarket.net; Reliance Arcade, Market Row, Electric Lane & Electric Ave SW9; 8am-6pm Mon-Sat, 8am-3pm Wed; Brixton) is worth a trip, especially for nearby **Brixton Village** (10.30am-6pm Mon-Wed, to 10pm Thu-Sat, 10.30am-5pm Sun; Brixton), an indoor market that has recently enjoyed a riveting renaissance.

Best Markets

Borough Market (p118) Bustling cornucopia of gastronomic delights, south of the river.

Portobello Market (p147) London's best known market in ever hip Notting Hill.

KIMBERLEY COOLE/LONELY PLANET IMAGES ©

Top Tip

▶ Look out for plentiful freebie snack samples at Borough Market.

Smithfield Market (p99) Steeped in history (and gore) and one of London's classic markets.

Greenwich Market (p165) Fascinating for gift ideas or for highly moreish snacking on the go.

Camden Market (p159) One of North London's must-see markets.

Best Shops

From charity-shop finds to designer 'it bags', there are thousands of ways to spend your hard-earned cash in London. Many of the big-name shopping attractions, such as Harrods, Hamleys and Portobello Market have become must-sees in their own right, but chances are that with so many temptations, you'll give your wallet a full workout.

High Street Chains

Many shoppers bemoan chains taking over the high street, leaving independent shops struggling. But since the shops are cheap, fashionable and always conveniently located, Londoners keep going back for more. As well as familiar overseas retailers, such as Gap, H&M, Urban Outfitters and Zara, you'll find a number of home-grown chains, including French Connection UK (www.frenchconnection.com), Jigsaw (www.jigsaw-online.com), Karen Millen (www.karenmillen.com), Marks & Spencer (www.marksandspencer.co.uk), Miss Selfridge (www.missselfridge.com) and TopShop (www.topshop.com).

Opening Hours

London shops generally open from 9am or 10am to 6pm or 7pm Monday to Saturday. The majority of West End shops (Oxford St, Soho and Covent Garden), Chelsea, Knightsbridge, Kensington, Greenwich and Hampstead also open on Sunday, typically from noon to 6pm but sometimes 10am to 4pm. Shops in the West End open late (to 9pm) on Thursday; those in Chelsea, Knightsbridge and Kensington open late on Wednesday. If a major market is in swing on a certain day, neighbouring stores will probably also fling open their doors.

MATTHEW CHATTLE/ALAMY ©

☑ Top Tip

▶ In shops displaying a 'tax free' sign, visitors from non-EU countries are entitled to claim back the 20% value-added tax (VAT) they have paid on purchased goods.

Best Shopping Areas

West End (p59) Grand confluence of big names for the well-heeled and well-dressed.

Knightsbridge (p134) Harrods and other top names servicing London's incurable shopaholics.

Best Department Stores

Harvey Nichols (p145) Packed with sleek brand-name fashions,

Harrods (p135)

expensive fragrances, jewellery and more.

Harrods (p135) Garish, stylish and just this side of kitsch, yet perennially popular.

Liberty (p60) An irresistible blend of contemporary styles in an old-fashioned mock-Tudor atmosphere.

Fortnum & Mason (p38) London's oldest grocery store with staff still dressed in old-fashioned tailcoats.

Best for Books

John Sandoe Books (p135) A charmingly old-fashioned bookshop much-loved by customers.

Stanfords (p60) Should be your first port of call for travel books.

Foyles (p47) Sprawling bookshop with a vast range of reading (and listening) material.

Waterstone's Books (p60) Largest bookshop in Europe, with knowledgeable staff and regular author readings and signings.

Best for Gifts

Penhaligon's (p38) Beautiful range of perfumes and home fragrances, overseen by very helpful staff.

Compendia (p171) Comprehensive collection of games, puzzles and toys – many obscure.

Shepherds (p39) Top quality stationery, fine paper, first-rate photograph albums and diaries.

Worth a Trip

The shops working out of the incredibly secure, subterranean **Silver Vaults** (www.thesilvervaults.com; 53-64 Chancery Lane WC2; 9am-5.30pm Mon-Fri, to 1pm Sat; Chancery Lane) constitute the world's largest collection of silver under one roof. The different businesses tend to specialise in particular types of silverware – from cutlery sets to picture frames and much jewellery. Quality is guaranteed.

Best
Museums & Galleries

London's museums and galleries top the list of the city's must-see attractions and not just for rainy days that frequently send locals scurrying for cover. Some of London's museums and galleries display incomparable collections that make them acknowledged leaders in their field.

Museums at Night

Nights are an excellent time to visit museums as there are far fewer visitors. Many museums open late once or twice a week, but several museums organise special nocturnal events to extend their range of activities and to present the collection in a different mood. Hop onto museum websites to see what's in store. (Some museums only arrange night events once a year, in May.)

Admission & Access

National museum collections (eg British Museum, National Gallery, Victoria & Albert Museum) are free, except for temporary exhibitions. Private galleries are usually free (or have a small admission fee), while smaller museums will charge an entrance fee, typically around £5 (book online at some museums for discounted tickets). National collections are generally open 10am to around 6pm, with one or two late nights a week.

Specialist Museums

Whether you've a penchant for fans, London transport or ancient surgical techniques, you'll discover museums throughout the city with their own niche collections. Even for non-specialists these museums can be fascinating to browse and to share the enthusiasm the curators instil in their collections.

☑ Top Tip

▶ Many of the top museums also have fantastic restaurants, worthy of a visit in their own right.

Best (Free) Collections

British Museum (p64) Supreme collection of rare artefacts.

Victoria & Albert Museum (p126) Unique array of decorative arts and design in an awe-inspiring setting.

National Gallery (p44) Tremendous gathering of largely pre-modern masters.

Tate Modern (p104) A feast of modern and contemporary art, wonderfully housed.

Main entrance hall, Tate Modern (p104)

Natural History Museum (p130) Major hit with kids and adults alike.

Best Small Museums

London Transport Museum (p52) An absorbing exploration of London's transport history.

Old Operating Theatre Museum & Herb Garret (p112) Unique, eye-opening foray into old-fashioned techniques of surgery.

Best Museum Architecture

Victoria & Albert Museum (p126) A building as beautiful as its diverse collection.

Natural History Museum (p130) Architectural lines straight from a Gothic fairy tale.

Tate Modern (p104) Disused power station transformed into iconic gallery.

Tate Britain (p34) Grandiose sibling of the Tate Modern.

National Maritime Museum (p167) Standout museum collection housed within wonderful architecture.

Worth a Trip

The **Horniman Museum** (www.horniman.ac.uk; 100 London Rd SE23; admission free; 10.30am-5.30pm; Forest Hill) is a treasure-trove of discoveries, from a huge stuffed walrus to slowly undulating jellyfish, a fierce papier mâché statue of Kali and a knock-out music exhibition. The Music Gallery, the aquarium and conservatory are all highlights, as are the 6.5 hectares of magnificent hillside gardens.

Best
Parks & Gardens

Glance at a colour map of town and be struck by how much is olive green – over a quarter of London is parks and gardens. Some of the world's most superb urban parkland is here: most of it well-tended, accessible and delightful in any season.

OLIVER STREWE/LONELY PLANET IMAGES ©

Access & Activities

Usually always free to access, London's royal and municipal parks are typically open from dawn till dusk. Larger parks, such as Regent's Park (p152), may have football pitches and tennis courts. Or you might find options for playing golf, such as at Richmond Park and Greenwich Park (p167). Many have popular jogging routes or cycle tracks and larger, wilder expanses (such as Richmond Park) are ideal for cross-country running or orienteering.

If you have young kids, parks are also ideal as most have playgrounds. Many parks are also the venue for open-air concerts, sporting competitions and other fun outdoor events and activities, including horse riding (Hyde Park p138; and Richmond Park), kite-flying and Frisbee-throwing.

An abundance of wildlife thrives in London parkland, especially in the larger parks with woodland or those with lakes (such as St James's Park, p34), while gardens (such as Kew Gardens, p40) boasts an astonishing range of plant life.

Heaths & Commons

Less formal or well-tended public spaces that can also be freely accessed are called commons or heaths. Wilder and more given over to nature than parks, the best-known heath is magnificent Hampstead Heath (p160) in North London.

Best Parks

Hyde Park (p138) Gorgeous, and massive, green paradise at the heart of Kensington.

St James's Park (p34) Enthralling views, splendid location and a divine allotment.

Greenwich Park (p167) Fine royal park graced with one of London's most superb viewpoints.

Regent's Park (p152) The most formal of London's royal parks, great for sports.

Boaters on the Serpentine, Hyde Park (p138)

Best Gardens

Kew Gardens (p40) Astonishing range of botanical specimens and delightful views.

Kensington Gardens (p138) Highly desirable and good-looking appendage to Hyde Park.

Wildlife Garden (p133) Pastoral pocket of greenery and wildlife in the heart of Kensington.

Best Park & Garden Architecture

Kew Gardens (p40) Gorgeous Victorian glasshouse architecture, a palace, pagoda, Japanese gate and more.

Kensington Gardens (p138) One of London's best-loved palaces, a lavish Victorian memorial and famous art gallery.

Greenwich Park (p167) The Royal Observatory, Ranger's House and delicious views over Greenwich's stately buildings.

Worth a Trip

Covering almost 10 sq km, **Richmond Park** (admission free; 7am-dusk Mar-Sep, from 7.30am Oct-Feb; ⊖/Richmond, then 65 or 371) is the largest urban parkland in Europe, offering everything from formal gardens and ancient oaks to unsurpassed views of central London 12 miles away. Herds of more than 600 red and fallow deer basking under the trees add their own magic.

Best Architecture

London is sprinkled with architectural refrains from every period of its long history. This is a city for explorers: keep your eyes peeled and you'll spot part of a Roman wall enclosed in the lobby of a postmodern building near St Paul's, say, or a galleried coaching inn dating from the Restoration tucked away in a courtyard off a high street in Borough.

London Style

Unlike other world-class cities, London was never methodically planned, despite being largely burned to the ground in 1666. The city has instead developed in an organic (read: haphazard) fashion, so although you can easily lose track of its historical narrative, a multitude of stories is going on concurrently, creating a handsome patchwork ranging across the centuries.

The Shard and South Bank

Beyond the architectural renaissance reshaping the Lea Valley with the Olympic Park (p196), parts of South London and the City are undergoing a transformation. The centrepiece of the London Bridge Quarter (www.londonbridgequarter.com) – a costly commercial, business and transport regeneration scheme in Borough – is the Shard (p174). Approaching completion at the time of writing, the spike-like Shard will poke dramatically into Borough skies from 2012, its sharp form visible from across London. The new Tate Modern Project extension will add a dramatically modern and inspirational add-on to the southern facet of the Tate Modern when it opens in 2016.

☑ Top Tip

▶ Celebrating buildings with a range of events, walks, talks, tours and debates, the biennial London Festival of Architecture (www.lfa2012.org) will next be staged from 23 June to 8 July 2012.

Best Modern Architecture

30 St Mary Axe (p95) The bullet-shaped, iconic tower of the City.

Lloyd's of London (p94) Richard Roger's innovative 'Inside-Out' building.

The Shard (p174) Set to rise triumphantly over London Bridge in 2012.

Tate Modern (p104) Former power station,

Hampton Court Palace (p120)

now powerhouse of modern art.

Millennium Bridge (p111) Elegant and sleek span across the Thames.

City Hall (p113) 'Glass gonad' or 'Darth Vader's Helmet'? Your call.

Best Early Architecture

Westminster Abbey (p24) Titanic milestone in London's ecclesiastical architectural history.

Westminster Hall (p31) Magnificently ancient relic at the heart of Westminster Palace.

Tower of London (p86) Legend, myth and blood-stained history converge in London's supreme bastion.

All Hallows-by-the-Tower (p93) Fragments from Roman times in one of London's oldest churches.

Best Stately Architecture

Buckingham Palace (p28) The Queen's pied-à-terre.

Houses of Parliament (p30) Extraordinary Victorian monument and seat of British parliamentary democracy.

Queen's House (p167) Beautiful Inigo Jones Palladian creation in charming Greenwich.

Old Royal Naval College (p168) Admire the stunning Painted Hall and breathtaking Chapel.

Hampton Court Palace (p120) Get lost in the famous maze or ghost-hunt along Tudor hallways.

Best Monuments

Monument (p93) Spiral your way to the top for panoramic views.

Albert Memorial (p139) Convoluted and admirably excessive chunk of Victoriana.

Wellington Arch (p139) Topped by Europe's largest bronze sculpture.

Nelson's Column (p50) Kids will give their eyeteeth to climb on the four lions.

Best Sports & Activities

London bristles with cutting-edge sports facilities and the choice of activities is enormous. And with the Olympic Games towel-flicking sedentary locals into action, every other Londoner seems to be training for a half-marathon or triathlon, cycling to work, dusting off their football boots or pumping iron.

Tickets

Getting tickets for Premier League football matches during the August to mid-May season in London is tricky, as seats are snapped up by season ticket holders. Tickets for all other enclosed sporting events need to be booked well in advance. The entertainment weekly **Time Out** (www.timeout.com) has the best information on fixtures, times, venues and ticket prices.

Worth a Trip

The main focus of the **Olympic Park** (www.london2012.com/olympic-park; ⊖Stratford or Hackney Wick) is the Olympic Stadium and the striking Aquatics Centre. The award-winning Velodrome (aka the 'Pringle') has been much praised for its fine lines, sustainable credentials and functional appeal. The 114m, spiralling red structure is Anish Kapoor's ArcelorMittal Orbit, or the 'Hubble Bubble Pipe', offering a vast panorama from its viewing platform.

Top Tips

- Barclays Cycle Hire Scheme (p214) is excellent for short hops.
- For cricket matches, the English Cricket Board (☎0870 533 8833; www.ecb.co.uk) has full details of match schedules and tickets.

Best Parks for Sports & Activities

Regent's Park (p152) Football, tennis, cricket, rugby, athletics, boating.

Hampstead Heath (p160) Football, swimming, running, kite-flying, tennis.

Richmond Park (p193) Horse-riding, fishing, golf, cycling.

Best For Free

London may be one of the world's most expensive cities, but it won't always cost the earth. Many sights and experiences are free or won't cost you a penny (or very little). Become a London freeloader for the day and cash in on some tip-top freebies.

Worth a Trip

Arguably London's finest small gallery, the **Wallace Collection** (www.wallacecollection.org; Hertford House, Manchester Sq W1; admission free; 10am-5pm; Bond St) is an enthralling glimpse into 18th-century aristocratic life. The sumptuously restored Italianate mansion houses paintings by Rembrandt, Titian, Rubens, Poussin, Velázquez and Gainsborough, a spectacular array of medieval and Renaissance armour, stunning chandeliers and a sweeping staircase reckoned to be one of the best examples of French interior architecture in existence.

Best Free Museums

National Gallery (p44) Magnificent art collection, entirely on the house.

Victoria & Albert Museum (p126) The spectacular V & A easily consumes a day of totally gratis exploration.

Natural History Museum (p130) The architecture, stunning galleries, animatronic T. *rex*: all free.

Tate Modern (p104) The art here may cost the earth, but it's still free to view.

Best Free Sights

Houses of Parliament (p30) When parliament is in session, it's free to watch UK democracy in action.

Changing of the Guard (p34) London's most famous open air freebie.

JOHN HAY/LONELY PLANET IMAGES ©

Top Tips

- All state-funded museums and galleries are free (if you avoid the temporary exhibitions).
- Under-16s travel free on buses, under-11s travel free on the tube, under-5s go free on the trains.
- For one weekend in September, London Open House (www.londonopenhouse.org) opens the front doors to over 700 private buildings for free.

Best For Kids

London is a fantastic place for children. The city's museums will fascinate all ages, and you'll find theatre, dance and music performances perfect for older kids and teens. Playgrounds and outdoor spaces, such as parks, city farms and nature reserves are perfect for either toddler energy-busting or relaxation.

Museum Activities

London's museums are anything if not child friendly. You'll find storytelling at the National Gallery (p44), arts and crafts workshops at the Victoria & Albert Museum (p126), train making workshops at the London Transport Museum (p52) plus tons of finger painting opportunities at Tate Modern (p104) and Tate Britain (p34). Also check museum websites for details on popular sleepovers at the British Museum, the Natural History Museum, the Science Museum and other museums.

Eating with Kids

Most of London's restaurants and cafes are child-friendly and offer baby changing facilities and high chairs. Pick your places with some awareness – avoid high-end and more quiet, small restaurants and cafes if you have toddlers or babies, and go for noisier/more relaxed places and you'll find that you'll be welcomed.

London is a great opportunity for your kids to taste all the world's cuisines in close proximity to each other, so pick from good-quality (and MSG-free) Chinese, to Italian, French, Mexican, Japanese and Indian restaurants. Many places have kids' menus, but ask for smaller portions of adult dishes if your children have a more adventurous palate; you'll find that most places will be keen to oblige.

☑ Top Tips

- Under-16s travel free on buses, under-11s travel free on the tube and under-5s go free on the trains.
- In winter months (November to January), ice rinks appear at the Natural History Museum, Kew Gardens, Somerset House, the Tower of London and Hampton Court Palace.

Science Museum (p138)

Best Sights for Kids

London Zoo (p152) Close to 750 species of animals, and an excellent Penguin Beach.

Sea Life London Aquarium (p112) Magnificent menagerie of aquatic creatures right by the Thames.

London Eye (p110) Survey London from altitude and tick off the big sights.

London Bridge Experience & London Tombs (p112) Squeamish fun, gruesome gore and chilling thrills.

Best Museums for Kids

Science Museum (p138) Bursting with imaginative distractions for technical tykes, plus a fun-filled basement for little ones.

Imperial War Museum (p110) Packed with exciting displays, war planes and military what-not.

British Museum (p64) Meet the mummies at London's best museum.

Natural History Museum (p130) Gawp at the animatronics T. *rex* and the thrilling Dinosaur Gallery.

Best Views

Getting the right angle on something can be critical. London has an excellent collection of hills and elevated positions to bring the city into glorious perspective.

Best Hill Views

Greenwich Park (p167) Clamber up to the Royal Observatory for sweeping views.

Parliament Hill (p161) Choice panoramas over London from the north of town.

Richmond Hill, near Richmond Park (p193) Only view in the country protected by an act of Parliament.

Best Views from Structures

London Eye (p110) The perfect perspective on town.

Monument (p93) Wraparound, 360° views await your ascent to the top.

St Paul's Cathedral (p82) Clamber up into the dome for some of London's finest views.

Rhizotron and Xstrata Treetop Walkway (p41) Staggering views over the Victorian glasshouses and into Kew Gardens.

ArcelorMittal Orbit (p196) Best view of Olympic Park from the tallest sculpture in the UK.

Westminster Cathedral (p140) Impressive views over London from the tower of this fascinating cathedral.

Best Restaurant Views

Oxo Tower Restaurant & Brasserie (p114) Grab a front row seat for top views across the Thames.

Skylon (p113) Tuck into some of the best river views from a restaurant in town.

Portrait (p55) Like the restaurant, the views are a picture.

Best Bar Views

Vertigo 42 (p98) Hope for clear skies and settle down for the bravura performance of sunset.

Galvin at Windows (p142) The Hyde Park perspective and high altitude combine to work wonders.

Cutty Sark Tavern (p170) Historic Greenwich pub with an eye-catching riverside position.

Best Tours

Best Boat Tours

Thames River Boats (7930 2062; www.wpsa.co.uk; Westminster Pier, Victoria Embankment SW1; Kew adult/child one way £12/6, return £18/9, Hampton Court adult/child one way £15/7.50, return £22.50/11.25; 10.30am, 11.30am, noon & 2pm Apr-Oct; Westminster) Boats upriver from Westminster Pier to the Royal Botanic Gardens at Kew (1½ hours) and on to Hampton Court Palace (another 1½ hours, noon boat only).

Thames River Services (7930 4097; www.westminsterpier.co.uk; Westminster Pier, Victoria Embankment SW1; adult/child one way £8.40/4.20, return £11/5.50; tours every 30min 10am-4pm, to 5pm Apr-Oct; Westminster) Cruise boats leaving Westminster Pier for Greenwich, stopping at the Tower of London.

Best Bus Tours

Big Bus Tours (0207 233 9533 www.bigbustours.com; adult/child £27/12; every 15 min 8.30am-6pm) Informative commentaries in eight languages; ticket includes a free river cruise and four thematic walking tours.

Original Tour (www.theoriginaltour.com; adult/child £26/13; every 20 min 8.30am-5.30pm) Open top hop-on, hop-off bus tour.

Best Walking Tours

Association of Professional Tourist Guides (APTG; 7611 2545; www.touristguides.org.uk; half-/full-day £127/200; Holborn) Hire a prestigious Blue Badge Guide (know-it-all guides).

London Walks (7624 3978; www.walks.com; adult/child £8/free) A huge array of walks, including Jack the Ripper tours, Beatles tours and a Sherlock Holmes tour.

London Mystery Walks (0795 738 8280; www.tourguides.org.uk; adult/child £10/9; Aldgate) Tour Jack the Ripper's old haunts. You must book in advance.

PAUL CARSTAIRS/ALAMY ©

Best Specialist Tours

London Duck Tours (www.londonducktours.co.uk; adult/child from £21/14; Waterloo) Amphibious craft based on D-Day landing vehicles depart from behind the London Eye and cruise the streets of central London before making a dramatic descent into the Thames at Vauxhall.

Open City (www.open-city.org.uk; prices vary; 10am Sat) This charity organises architectural tours to one of four different areas (Square Mile, South London, the West End or Docklands) weekly.

Best
Hidden Sights

London sightseeing may seem to be all about ticking off the big ticket sights, but the city is full of attractions tucked away from the crowds. Tracking them down is an opportunity to get off the beaten trail to unearth the bizarre, concealed or simply unexpected.

SECRET CINEMA ©

Secret London

London's hidden sights may be just steps away from a drawcard sight, or entirely worthy of an expedition in themselves. From specialist museums to an early 19th-century windmill in Brixton, a Chinese pagoda, canal-side walks and gothic tombstones, London's unexpected treasures range across the genres.

Admission

Some of London's unexpected treats are entirely free to explore, while others – especially the tours – will carry a fee and may need to be booked in advance, or as part of a group.

☑ Top Tips

- Secret Cinema (www.secretcinema.org) arranges films and locations that are secret till disclosed on the day of screening (could be a cemetery, a park, a warehouse, wherever), creating a sense of mystery and adventure.

Best Unusual Sights

Fan Museum (p168) Absorbing specialist collection of this 3000-year old device.

Monument (p93) Memorial to the Great Fire of London, topped with wrap-around views.

Wildlife Garden (p133) Bucolic slice of countryside in the heart of town.

Old Operating Theatre Museum & Herb Garret (p112) Get to grips with surgical techniques of yesteryear.

Wellcome Collection (p72) Captivating and intriguingly eclectic collection of miscellanea.

Greenwich Foot Tunnel (p165) Wander under the Thames from Greenwich to the Isle of Dogs.

Best Hidden London Gems

Michelin House (p140) Beautiful Art Nouveau treasure buried along Fulham Rd.

Chinese Pagoda (p40) Stunning 250-year old Oriental addition to the famous gardens at Kew.

Westminster Cathedral (p140) An often overlooked interior dappled

Highgate Cemetery (p161)

with moments of dazzling beauty.

Bedford Square (p68) Soak up the charms of London's best-preserved Georgian square.

Cafe in the Crypt (p52) Enjoy a coffee in the highly atmospheric crypt of St-Martin-in-the-Fields.

Electric Cinema (p146) London's oldest cinema is as classic as much of its repertoire.

Best Behind-the-Scenes Tours

Highgate Cemetery (p161) Explore the sublimely overgrown western part of the cemetery.

British Library (p72) Don't judge a book by its cover, hop on an eye-opening tour.

St Paul's Tours (p82) Snatch a look at the marvellous Geometric Staircase and the Quire.

Albert Memorial (p139) Hop over the barrier for closer scrutiny of the Frieze of Parnassus.

All Hallows-by-the-Tower (p93) Free 20-minute tours of the church, six months a year.

Best Hidden London Walks

Walking along Regent's Canal (p155) Sample London's canal-side charms from Camden to Little Venice.

Literary Bloomsbury (p68) Follow in the footsteps of the literati around good-looking Bloomsbury.

Worth a Trip

Built for one John Ashby in 1816, **Brixton Windmill** (www.brixtonwindmill.org; Blenheim Gardens SW2; ⊖Brixton) is the closest windmill to central London still in existence. It was later powered by gas and milled as recently as 1934. It's been refitted with sails and machinery for a wind-driven mill and is occasionally open for tours (check website for details), or you can simply admire it from the outside.

Best
Royal Sights

Nobody does royal pageantry quite like the British and there's nowhere in the UK that puts on such a prodigious royal display as London. All of the UK's royal highlights are in town and many of them are accessible, from the Changing of the Guard at Buckingham Palace to Hampton Court Palace and the Crown Jewels in the Tower of London.

Royal London

London's top royal sight is Buckingham Palace (p28). But the city's palaces are dotted around the city, from the Tower of London (for the Crown Jewels) to magnificent Hampton Court Palace (p120) in the southwest of London, and the delicious royal sights of Greenwich (p162).

Royal Engagements

Keep up to date with the activities of the Royal Family on www.royal.gov.uk, the official website of the UK monarchy, or on Facebook (www.facebook.com/TheBritishMonarchy), both of which have copies of the Court Circular, detailing royal engagements. The Queen's Diamond Jubilee arrives in 2012, so expect a right royal year.

Best Palaces & Properties

Buckingham Palace (p28) The magnificent state rooms fling open their doors between August and September.

Hampton Court Palace (p120) Marvellously well-preserved Tudor gem by the Thames: a superb day out.

Kensington Palace (p138) Recently restored palace in Kensington Gardens.

Queen's House (p167) Delightful 17th century building embracing a gorgeous Tulip Staircase.

Kew Palace (p41) London's smallest royal palace.

St James's Palace (p36) The official abode of English monarchs for over three centuries.

Best Royal Events

Changing of the Guard (p34) Showpiece performance in the forecourt of Buckingham Palace.

Changing of the Guard at Horse Guards Parade (p35) More accessible than the display at Buckingham Palace.

Trooping the Colour (p208) Splendour and pageantry every June in honour of the Queen's official birthday.

Ceiling in the Painted Hall, Old Royal Naval College (p168)

Best Royal Parks

St James's Park (p34) Delightful park right at the heart of royal London.

Hyde Park (p138) London's largest and perhaps best known royal park.

Greenwich Park (p167) Fabulous views and delightful location in one of London's most scenic neighbourhoods.

Kensington Gardens (p138) Fabulously expansive adjunct to Hyde Park, dotted with signature sights.

Green Park (p35) Adorable tract of natural beauty in the West End.

Best Royal Sights

Crown Jewels (p87) Glittering opulence and a diamond almost as big as The Ritz.

Westminster Abbey (p24) Warrants a visit for the elegant Henry VII Lady Chapel alone.

Banqueting House (p35) Last surviving remnant of the magnificent Tudor Whitehall Palace.

Buckingham Palace (p28) The Queen's stately London abode.

Royal Mews (p29) For a peek at the Queen's opulent transport options and resplendent horses.

Old Royal Naval College (p168) Admire the gorgeous chapel and the exquisite Painted Hall.

Worth a Trip

The only Crown Cemetery, **Brompton Cemetery** (Old Brompton Rd SW5; 8am-dusk daily, free tours 2pm Sunday; West Brompton or Fulham Broadway) was the inspiration for many of Beatrix Potter's make-believe characters. A local resident in her youth, Potter seems to have adopted names of the deceased, including Mr Nutkin, Mr McGregor, Jeremiah Fisher, Tommy Brock – even a Peter Rabbett.

Best Churches

London's churches vault the centuries from ancient times to the modern day in a greater concentration than anywhere else in the UK. Ranging across the denominations, London's houses of worship constitute some of the best examples of rare historic architecture in town, from the Saxon remnants of All Hallows-by-the-Tower to the mighty stonework of St Paul's Cathedral and Westminster Abbey.

Loss and Survival

Hundreds of London churches have vanished through the centuries – especially during the Great Fire of London (p96) and the Blitz of WWII – but great numbers also survived. Some churches, such as St Paul's Cathedral (p82) were badly damaged but then rebuilt in an entirely different, and then more modern, style. Others – such as St James's Piccadilly – were badly damaged during WWII and then gradually restored. A large number of London's churches, such as Southwark Cathedral (p110), embrace architectural fragments of vastly different eras that trace the history of London in their stonework, from the middle ages to the modern day.

Best Large Churches

St Paul's Cathedral (p82) London's most famous and enduring ecclesiastical icon.

Westminster Abbey (p24) Hallowed site of coronation for England's sovereigns since William the Conqueror.

Westminster Cathedral (p140) Byzantine mosaics glitter within its sombre, unfinished interior.

Top Tip

▶ Churches can be excellent venues for free music recitals.

Southwark Cathedral (p110) Spanning the centuries from the Normans to the Victorian era and beyond.

Best Historic Churches

All Hallows-by-the-Tower (p93) City church with a Saxon crypt and intriguing fragments from the Roman era.

St Bartholomew-the-Great (p93) Authentic Norman remains and an age-old sense of tranquillity.

Southwark Cathedral (p110)

St Stephen Walbrook (p94) Seventeenth century Wren masterpiece in the City.

St Mary Woolnoth (p93) Hawksmoor's twin-towered 18th century City gem.

St Mary-le-Bow (p93) Another elegant ecclesiastical triumph from Sir Christopher Wren.

Best Churches for Free Recitals

St Martin-in-the-Fields (p52) Hosts free lunchtime concerts at 1pm on Monday, Tuesday and Friday.

St James's Piccadilly (p52) Free lunchtime recitals (suggested donation) on Monday, Wednesday and Friday at 1.10pm.

St George's Bloomsbury (p74) Check website for details of the church's program of concerts, some free.

Best Church Cafes & Restaurants

Restaurant At St Paul's (p95) Fine Modern British fare in a classic setting.

Café Below (p95) Cafe with oodles of atmosphere in the crypt of St Mary-le-Bow.

Café in the Crypt (p52) Excellent cafe with tombstone flooring in this historic church.

Worth a Trip

Magnificent **Temple Church** (www.templechurch.com; Temple EC4; admission £3; 2-4pm Wed-Sun; Temple or Chancery Lane) was built by the Knights Templar. The church has a distinctive design: the Round (consecrated in 1185 and designed to recall the Church of the Holy Sepulchre in Jerusalem) adjoins the Chancel (built in 1240), the heart of the modern church (both severely damaged by a bomb in 1941 and lovingly reconstructed).

Best Festivals & Events

London is a vibrant city all year round, celebrating both traditional and modern festivals and events with energy and gusto. From Europe's largest outdoor carnival to the floral blooms of the Chelsea Flower Show and the pomp and ceremony of Trooping the Colour, London has entertaining occasions for all tastes.

Worth a Trip

Held in May at the Royal Hospital in Chelsea, the **Chelsea Flower Show** (www.rhs.org.uk; Royal Hospital Chelsea, Royal Hospital Rd SW3) is the world's most renowned horticultural show, attracting the cream of West London society, and the flower-mad.

Best Festivals

Notting Hill Carnival (p147) London's most vibrant outdoor carnival is a celebration of Caribbean London; August.

Chinese New Year in Chinatown (p46) Chinatown fizzes in this colourful street festival; late January or February.

The Proms Two months of classical concerts around the Royal Albert Hall (p144); July to September.

London Film Festival Premier film event held at the BFI Southbank (p118) and other venues; October.

Best Events

Changing of the Guard (p34) Daily draw on the forecourt of Buckingham Palace, pulling huge crowds.

Trooping the Colour The Queen's official birthday in June sees parades and pageantry; Horse Guards Parade (p35).

New Year's Celebration On 31 December the famous countdown to midnight in Trafalgar Square (p50) is met with terrific fireworks.

Top Tip

▶ For a list of events in and around London, check www.visitlondon.com or www.timeout.com/london.

Survival Guide

Survival Guide

Before You Go

When to Go

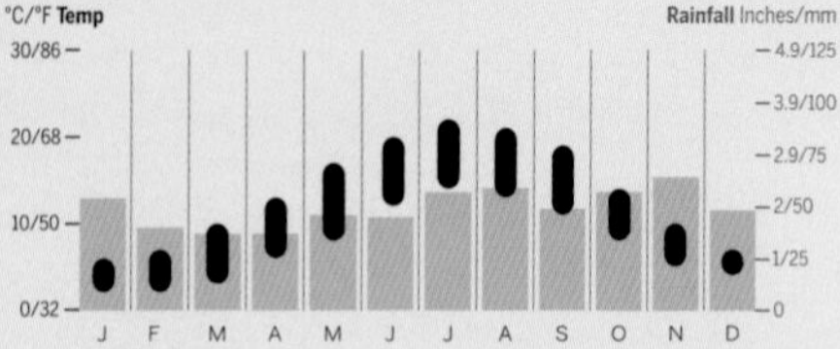

➡ **Winter (Nov-Feb)** Cold, short days with much rain and occasional snow. Museums and attractions quieter and prices lower.

➡ **Spring (Mar-May)** Mild, wet, trees in blossom. Major sights begin to get busy; parks starting to look lovely.

➡ **Summer (Jun-Aug)** Warm to hot, sunny with long days. Main tourist and holiday season. Sights can be crowded but parks are lovely.

➡ **Autumn (Sep-Nov)** Mild, generally sunny, good-looking season, kids back at school, London quietens down after summer.

Book Your Stay

➡ Great neighbourhoods to stay in are around the National Gallery & Cover Garden, Kensington, St Paul's & the City and the South Bank.

➡ Be aware that room prices will skyrocket during the 2012 Olympic Games.

➡ Bed and breakfasts come in a tier below hotels, but often have boutique-style charm, a lovely old building setting and a personal level of service.

➡ There are some fantas hotels in London, whatev the price tag, but deman can often outstrip supply - especially at the bottom end of the market – so book ahead, particularly during holiday periods ar in summer.

➡ Under £100 and you're at the more serviceable, budget end of the market Look out, though, for weekend deals that can t a better class of hotel :hin reach.

f you're in London for veek or more, a short-'m or serviced apart-ent can be economical d gives you more sense living in the city.

seful Websites

nely Planet (www.hotels.elyplanet.com) Bookings.

IA central reserva-ns system (☎0800) 1700; www.yha.org.uk) ostel room bookings.

sit London (www.visit don.com) London tourist ganisation's website th a wide range of commodation options d special deals.

ndonTown (☎7437 70; www.londontown.com) otel bookings and deals.

st Budget

ink261 (www.clinkhostels.m) Thoroughly refur-shed and top-notch stel in King's Cross.

nurch Street Hotel ww.churchstreethotel.com) cellent value, vibrantly esigned boutique hotel Camberwell.

IA Earl's Court (www.a.org.uk) Cheerful, endly, central.

YHA Oxford St (www.yha.org.uk) Highly central, intimate and attractive.

Best Midrange

Dean Street Townhouse (www.deanstreettownhouse.com) Gem at the heart of Soho with a wonderful boudoir atmosphere.

Rough Luxe (www.roughluxe.co.uk) Rough and the smooth, stylishly done, in King's Cross.

Kennington B&B (www.kenningtonbandb.com) Lovely B&B in an 18th-century South London house.

40 Winks (www.40winks.org) Seriously charming two-room boutique guesthouse in Stepney Green.

Best Top-End

No 10 Manchester Street (www.tenmanchesterstreethotel.com) Impeccable service, wonderful Edwardian townhouse boutique hotel in Marylebone.

One Aldwych (www.onealdwych.co.uk) Upbeat luxury hotel with spacious and stylish rooms in Aldwych.

Rookery (www.rookeryhotel.com) Absolute charmer fitted out with antique furniture in Clerkenwell.

Zetter Hotel & Townhouse (www.thezetter.com) Two very different properties, both exemplary, in Clerkenwell.

Arriving in London

☑ **Top Tip** For the best way to get to your accommodation, see p16.

Heathrow Airport

Some 15 miles west of central London, **Heathrow** (LHR; www.heathrowairport.com) is the world's busiest international airport, with five terminals (Terminal 2 closed for refurbishment until 2014). Each terminal has currency-exchange facilities, information counters and accommodation desks.

➡ **Underground** (www.tfl.gov.uk) Underground trains (single £5, from central London one hour) run from just after 5/5.45am from/to the airport (5.50/7am Sunday) to 11.45pm/12.30am

(11.30pm Sunday in both directions).

➡ **Heathrow Express** (www.heathrowexpress.com) This train (one way/return £16.50/32, 15 mins, every 15 mins) runs from Heathrow Central station to Paddington station. Trains run from approximately just after 5am in both directions between 11.45pm (from Paddington) and just after midnight (from the airport).

➡ **Heathrow Connect** (www.heathrowconnect.com) Travelling between Heathrow and Paddington station, this train service (one way £8.50, 25 mins, every 30 mins) makes five stops en route. First trains leave Heathrow at about 5.20am (6am Sunday); last service is around midnight. From Paddington, services leave between approximately 4.30am (6am Sunday) and 11pm.

➡ **Taxi** A metered black cab trip to/from central London costs between £45 and £65 (£55 from Oxford St), 45-60 mins.

➡ **National Express** (www.nationalexpress.com) Coaches (one way/return from £5/9, 45 mins to 90 mins, every 30 minutes to one hour) regularly link the Heathrow Central Bus Station with **Victoria coach station** (Map p136, G5; 164 Buckingham Palace Rd SW1; ⊖Victoria). The first bus from Heathrow Central Bus station (at Terminals 1, 2 and 3) is at 5.25am, the last at 9.40pm. The first bus leaves Victoria at 7.15am, the last at 11.30pm.

➡ **Night Bus** N9 bus (£1.30, 1¼ hr, every 20 mins) connects Heathrow with central London.

Gatwick Airport

Some thirty miles south of central London, **Gatwick** (LGW; www.gatwickairport.com) is smaller than Heathrow. The North and South Terminals are linked by a 24-hr shuttle train (approx three minute journey between terminals).

➡ **National Rail** (www.nationalrail.co.uk) Regular train services to/from London Bridge (30 mins, every 15 to 30 mins), King's Cross (45 mins, every 15 to 30 mins) and London Victoria (30 mins, every 10 to 15 mins). Fares vary, allow £7 to £10 for a single.

➡ **Gatwick Express** (www.gatwickexpress.com) Train service (one way/return £18/31, 30 mins, every 15 mins) from station near South Terminal to Victoria station. From Gatwick, services run between about 4.30am and 1.35am. From Victoria, they leave between 3.30am and 12.30am.

➡ **National Express** (www.nationalexpress.com) Coaches (one way/return £7.50/15, 65 to 90 mins) run from Gatwick to Victoria coach station at least once an hour between 6am and 9.45pm, operating hourly on the hour from Victoria between 7am and 7pm (fewer services till 11.30pm).

➡ **easyBus** (www.easybus.co.uk) Nineteen-seater budget minibuses (one way £10, from £2 online 70 mins, every 20 mins) from Earl's Court/West Brompton to Gatwick, 3am to 11.30pm daily. Departures from Gatwick between 4.30am and 1am. Tickets can be purchased from the driver (also ticket outlets at the airport in both the North and South Terminals).

➡ **Taxi** A metered trip to/from central London costs about £90 (takes just over an hour).

t Pancras nternational tation

urostar (www.eurostar.
om) The high-speed assenger rail service nks St Pancras International station with iare du Nord in Paris two hours) or Bruxlles Midi in Brussels two and a half hours), vith up to two dozen aily departures. Fares ary enormously, from ,69 for the cheapest eturn to more than ,300 for a fully flexible eturn at busy periods. 'here are services to vignon in the south of 'rance (seven hours) n summer and to the 'rench Alps in winter eight to 10 hours). (ing's Cross St Pancras s on the Victoria, Piccadilly, Northern, Hamnersmith & City, Circle nd Metropolitan lines f the Underground.

Getting Around

'ublic transport in ondon is excellent, f pricey. Managed by **Transport for London** (www.tfl.gov.uk), it has an excellent, multilingual website with live updates on traffic, a journey planner, maps and detailed information on all modes of transport. The cheapest way to travel across the network is with an Oyster Card (p214), a smart card.

Underground, DLR & Overground

☑ **Best for**...getting around quickly, easily and cheaply.

➡ There are several networks: London Underground ('the tube', 11 colour-coded lines), Docklands Light Railway (DLR, a driverless train operating in the eastern part of the city) and Overground network.

➡ First trains operate around 5.30am Monday to Saturday and 7am Sunday. The last trains leave around 12.30am Monday to Saturday and 11.30pm Sunday.

➡ London is divided in nine concentric fare zones.

➡ It's always cheaper to travel with an Oyster card than a paper ticket.

➡ Children under the age of 10 travel free.

➡ Some stations, most famously Leicester Sq and Covent Garden, are far closer in real life than they appear on the map.

Bus

☑ **Best for**...London views and for going where the Underground doesn't run.

➡ Bus services normally operate from 5am to 11.30pm.

➡ Oyster cards are valid on all bus services, including night buses, and are cheaper than cash fares. If you only travel by bus, the daily cap is £4. Bus journeys cost a flat fare (non-Oyster/Oyster £2.20/1.30) regardless of how far you go.

➡ At bus stops with a yellow background, if you don't have an Oyster card, you must buy your ticket before boarding the bus at the stop's ticket machine (you will need the exact amount in coins).

➡ Children under 11 travel free; those aged 11 to 18 years do as well but require an Oyster photocard.

Travel Passes & Tickets

Oyster cards are chargeable smart cards valid across the entire London public transport network. Fares for Oyster-users are lower than standard tickets. If you are making many journeys during the day, you never pay more than the appropriate Travelcard fare (peak or off peak) once the daily 'price cap' is reached. Paper single and return tickets still exist but are substantially more expensive compared to using Oyster. Visitor Oyster cards are pre-loaded with credit and ready to use.

➡ Touch your card on a reader upon entry and then touch again on your way out. Credits are deducted accordingly. For bus journeys, just touch once upon boarding.

➡ Oyster cards are purchasable (£5 refundable deposit) and topped up at any Underground station, travel info centre or shop displaying the Oyster logo.

➡ Simply return your Oyster card at a ticket booth to get your deposit back, as well as any remaining credit.

➡ Day Travelcards are no cheaper than Oyster cards on the Underground, DLR, Overground and buses, but (unlike Oyster cards) can also be used on National Rail lines.

➡ Excellent 'bus spider maps' at every bus stop detail every route and destination available from that particular area.

➡ For interactive online bus maps, click on www.tfl.gov.uk.

➡ Over 50 night bus routes (prefixed with the letter 'N') run from midnight to 4.30am.

➡ Another 60 bus routes run 24-hours; the frequency decreases between 11pm and 5am.

Bicycle

☑ **Best for**...short distances, although traffic can be intimidating.

➡ The new Barclays Cycle Hire Scheme (www.tfl.gov.uk) is straightforward and particularly useful for visitors.

➡ Pick up a bike from one of the 400 docking stations dotted around the capital. Drop it off at another docking station.

➡ The access fee costs £1/5 for 24 hours/a week Insert your debit or credit card in the docking station to pay your access fee.

➡ The first 30 minutes is free, then it's £1 for the first hour, £4 up to two hours, £15 for three hours or £50 for 24 hours (the pricing structure encourages short journeys).

➡ Take as many bikes as you like during your access period (24 hrs/one week), leaving five minutes between each trip.

➡ Return the bike at any free dock; wait for the green light to make sure the bike is locked.

➡ If the docking station is full, consult the terminal to find available docking points nearby.

➡ You must be 18 to buy access and at least 14 to ride a bike.

'edicabs

- Three-wheeled cycle ickshaws, seating two or hree passengers have ong been a regular part f the Soho scene.
- They're less a mode f transport than a gimnick for tourists and the ccasional drunk on a aturday night.
- Expect to pay about £5 or a trip across Soho. For nore information visit www.londonpedicabs.com.

Taxi

☑ **Best for**...late nights nd groups to share the ost.

- Fully-licensed **London lack Cabs** (www.ondonblackcabs.co.uk) are vailable for hire when he yellow sign above he windscreen is lit; just tick your arm out to ignal one.
- Fares are metered, with he flag-fall charge of 2.20 (covering the first 36m during a weekday), ising by increments of 0p for each subsequent 68m.
- Fares are more expenive in the evenings and vernight.
- You can tip taxi drivers up to 10% but few ondoners do, simply rounding up to the nearest pound.
- **Zingo Taxi** (☎0870 070 0700) uses GPS to connect your mobile phone to that of the nearest free black-cab driver. This service costs £2 and the cost of the cab to reach you (maximum £3.80).
- Minicabs must be hired by phone or directly from one of the minicab offices (every high street has at least one and most clubs work with a minicab firm to send revellers home safely).
- Women travelling alone at night can choose **Lady Mini Cabs** (☎7272 3300; www.ladyminicabs.co.uk), which has female drivers.

Boat

☑ **Best for**...views

- **Thames Clippers** (www.thamesclippers.com) boats are fast and you're always guaranteed a seat and a view.
- Boats run from 6am to just after 10pm, every 20 to 30 mins, running from London Eye Millennium Pier to Woolwich Arsenal Piers and points in between. Fares cost £3.50 to £5.50 for adults, £1.70 to £2.80 for children; discounts for Oyster card holders and travel card holders.
- See p201 for details on sightseeing boat tours on the Thames, including boats to Hampton Court Palace and Kew Gardens.

Car & Motorcycle

☑ **Best for**... independence.

- London was the world's first major city to introduce a congestion charge to reduce the flow of traffic into its centre. For full details log on to www.tfl.gov.uk/roadusers/congestioncharging.
- The following agencies have several branches across the capital: **easyCar** (www.easycar.com), **Avis** (www.avis.com), **Hertz** (www.hertz.com). Book in advance for the best fares, especially at weekends.
- If you need a car for just a couple of hours or half a day, try the self-service pay-as-you-go scheme, **Streetcar** (☎0845 644 8475; www.streetcar.co.uk).
- Cars drive on the left in the UK.
- All drivers and passengers must wear seatbelts and motorcyclists must wear a helmet.

➡ Expensive parking charges, traffic jams, high petrol prices, efficient traffic wardens and wheel clampers make car hire unattractive for most visitors.

Essential Information

Business Hours

➡ Reviews in this book won't list opening hours unless they significantly differ from these standards.

Information	9am-5pm Mon-Fri
Sights	10am-6pm
Banks	9am-5pm Mon-Fri
Shops	9am-7pm Mon-Sat, 11am-5pm Sun
Restaurants	Noon-2.30pm & 6-11pm
Pubs & bars	11am-11pm

Discount Cards

➡ **London Pass** (www.londonpass.com) offers free entry and queue-jumping to major attractions; check the website for details.

➡ Passes start at £15.83 per day (for six days), but can be altered to include use of the Underground and buses.

Electricity

230V/50Hz

Emergency

➡ Dial ☎999 to call the police, fire brigade or ambulance in an emergency.

Money

☑ **Top Tip** Some large stores also take euros.

➡ The unit of currency of the UK is the pound sterling (£).

➡ One pound sterling consists of 100 pence (called 'p', colloquially).

➡ Notes come in denominations of £5, £10, £20 and £50; coins are 1p, 2p, 5p, 10p, 20p, 50p, £1 and £2.

➡ Unless otherwise noted all prices in this book are in pounds sterling.

ATMs

➡ Ubiquitous ATMs generally accept Visa, MasterCard, Cirrus or Maestro cards and more obscure ones.

➡ There is usually a transaction surcharge for cash withdrawals with foreign cards.

➡ Nonbank-run ATMs that charge £1.50 to £2 per transaction are usually found inside shops (particularly expensive for foreign bank card holders).

Changing Money

➡ The best place to change money is in any local post office branch, where no commission is charged.

➡ You can also change money in most high-street banks and some travel-agent chains, as well as at the numerous bureaux de change across London.

Compare rates and atch for the commission small print.

redit & Debit Cards

Credit and debit cards e accepted almost niversally in London, om restaurants and ars to shops and even me taxis.

American Express and ner's Club are less dely used than Visa and asterCard.

ipping

Many restaurants add discretionary' service arge to your bill; it's le- l but should be clearly dvertised. In places that n't, you are expected leave a 10% to 15% (unless service was nsatisfactory).

You can tip taxi drivers to 10% but most eople round up to the earest pound.

ublic Holidays

Top Tip On New Year's e, travel is free between .45pm and 4.30am on ses, the tube, trams d DLR services. London verground services are so free from 11.45pm to e last train.

ew Year's Day January

Good Friday Late March/April

Easter Monday Late March/April

May Day Holiday First Monday in May

Spring Bank Holiday Last Monday in May

Summer Bank Holiday Last Monday in August

Christmas Day 25 December

Boxing Day 26 December

Safe Travel

☑ **Top Tip** Keep your passport, money and credit cards separate.

➡ London's a fairly safe city considering its size, so exercising common sense should keep you safe.

Telephone

➡ Some public phones still accept coins, but most take phonecards (available from retailers, including most post offices and some newsagents) or credit cards.

Useful phone numbers (charged calls):

Directory enquiries, international (☎118 661/118 505)

Directory enquiries, local & national (☎118 118/118 500)

Operator, international (☎155)

Operator, local & national (☎100)

Reverse charge/collect calls (☎155)

Phone codes worth knowing:

International dialling code (☎00)

Local call rate applies (☎08457)

National call rate applies (☎0870/0871)

Premium rate applies (☎09) From 60p per minute.

Toll-free (☎0800)

Calling London

➡ London's area code is ☎020, followed by an eight-digit number beginning with 7 (central London), 8 (Greater London) and 3 (non-geographic).

Money-Saving Tips

Visit free museums and sights (p197)

Buy an Oyster Card (p214)

- You need dial the 020 only when calling London from elsewhere in the UK or from a mobile.
- If calling London from abroad, dial your country's international access code, then 44 (the UK's country code), then 20 (dropping the initial 0), followed by the eight-digit phone number.

Do's and Don'ts

Do

- Stand on the right on escalators and ascend or descend on the left.
- Let others off the tube first.
- Drive on the left.
- Expect traffic to stop at zebra crossings.
- Look right first when crossing the road.

Don't

- Forget your umbrella.
- Forget to queue for virtually everything.
- Forget to open doors for others.

International Calls & Rates

- International direct dialling (IDD) calls to almost anywhere can be made from most public telephones.
- Many private firms offer cheaper international calls than British Telecom (BT). In such shops you phone from a metered booth.
- Some cybercafes and internet shops also offer cheap rates for international calls.
- PIN-activated international calling cards, available at most corner shops, are usually the cheapest way to call abroad.
- Skype can be restricted in hostels and internet cafes due to noise and/or bandwidth issues.

Local & National Call Rates

- Local calls are charged by time alone; regional and national calls are charged by both time and distance.
- Daytime rates apply from 6am to 6pm Monday to Friday.
- The cheap rate applies from 6pm to 6am Monday to Friday; weekend rates apply from 6pm Friday to 6am Monday.

Mobile Phones

- The UK uses the GSM 900 network, covering Europe, Australia and New Zealand, but is not compatible with the North American GSM 1900 or Japanese mobil[e] technology.
- If you have a GSM phone, check with your service provider and enquire about roaming charges.
- It's usually better to buy a local SIM card fro[m] any mobile phone shop (ensure your handset is unlocked first).

Tourist Information

Britain Visitor Centre (Map p32, C1; www.visitbritain.com; 1 Regent St SW1; 9.30am-6pm Mon, 9am-6pm Tue-Fri, 9am-4pm Sat, 10am-4pm Sun & bank holidays Sep-May, to 5pm Sa[t] Jun-Sep; Piccadilly Circus) London's main tourist office.

Visit London (0870 15[6] 6366; www.visitlondon.com).

Visa Requirements

COUNTRY	TOURISM	WORK	STUDY
European Economic Area (except Romania & Bulgaria)	x	x	x
Australia, Canada, New Zealand, South Africa, USA	x (up to 6 mths)	√	√
Other nationalities	√	√	√

ravellers with isabilities

New hotels and modern urist attractions are gally required to be ccessible to people in heelchairs, but many storic buildings, B&Bs nd guesthouses are in der buildings, which are hard (if not impossible) to adapt.

- Transport is improving its access. Only 62 of London's tube stations have step-free access; the rest have escalators or stairs.
- The DLR is entirely accessible for wheelchair users.
- All buses are low-floor vehicles and wheelchair users travel free.
- Transport for London publishes the *Getting Around London* guide, which contains the latest information on accessibility for passengers with disabilities. Download it from www.tfl.gov.uk.

Visas

The table above indicates who will need a visa for what, but make sure you check www.ukvisas.gov.uk or with your local British embassy for the most up-to-date information.

Behind the Scenes

Send Us Your Feedback

We love to hear from travellers – your comments help make our books better. We read every word, and we guarantee that your feedback goes straight to the authors. Visit **lonelyplanet.com/contact** to submit your updates and suggestions.

Note: We may edit, reproduce and incorporate your comments in Lonely Planet products such as guidebooks, websites and digital products, so let us know if you don't want your comments reproduced or your name acknowledged. For a copy of our privacy policy visit lonelyplanet.com/privacy.

Our Readers

Many thanks to the travellers who wrote to us with useful advice and anecdotes:

Craig, Stefan Carlsson, William Cookson, Ken Drake, Jos Jennekens, Jennifer Nickless, Denise Pulis.

Damian's Thanks

Damian Harper would like to thank Daisy Harper, Bill Moran, Daniel Hands, Matthew Scudamore and George Whitman, plus Jo Cooke and all the staff at Lonely Planet. Thanks of course to Timothy and Emma for being so incredible.

Acknowledgments

Cover photograph: London Eye and Palace of Westminster at dusk/Richard l'Anson. Many of the images in this guide are available for licensing from Lonely Planet Images: www.lonelyplanetimages.com.

This Book

This 3rd edition of Lonely Planet's Pocket London guidebook was researched and written by Damian Harper. The previous two editions were written by Joe Bindloss and Sarah Johnstone. This guidebook was commissioned in Lonely Planet's London office, and produced by the following:

Commissioning Editor Joanna Cooke **Coordinating Editor** Karyn Noble **Coordinating Cartographer** James Leversha **Coordinating Layout Designer** Lauren Egan **Managing Editors** Barbara Delissen, Bruce Evans, Martine Power **Managing Cartographers** Shahara Ahmed, Diana Von Holdt, Amanda Sierp **Managing Layout Designer** Chris Girdler **Assisting Editor** Carly Hall **Cover Research** Naomi Parker **Internal Image Research** Aude Vauconsant **Thanks to** Laura Crawford, Janine Eberle, Ryan Evans, Liz Heynes, Laura Jane, Jennifer Johnston, David Kemp, Trent Paton, Piers Pickard, Lachlan Ross, Michael Ruff, Julie Sheridan, Laura Stansfeld, John Taufa, Gerard Walker, Clifton Wilkinson

Index

See also separate subindexes for:

Eating p229
Drinking p230
Entertainment p230
Shopping p231

Eating

Sights p000
Map Pages **p000**

Shopping

Our Writers

Damian Harper

Born off the Strand within earshot of Bow Bells (favourabl wind permitting), Damian grew up in Notting Hill way before it was discovered by Hollywood. A Wykehamist, forme Shakespeare and Company bookseller and linguist with tw degrees, Damian has been authoring guidebooks for Lonel Planet since the late 1990s. Damian currently lives in Sout London with his Chinese-born wife and two kids.

Contributing Writers

Emilie Filou contributed to Westminster Abbey & Westminster, National Gallery & Covent Garden, British Museur & Bloomsbury, A Saturday in Notting Hill, A Stroll Around Hampstead Heath, Regent's Park & Camden, The Best of London, Survival Guide.

Vesna Maric contributed to The Best of London.

Sally Schafer contributed to A Night out in Shoreditch, St Paul's & the City.

Published by Lonely Planet Publications Pty Ltd
ABN 36 005 607 983
3rd edition – May 2012
ISBN 978 1 74179 713 8

10 9 8 7 6 5 4 3 2 1
Printed in China